Cambridge History of Medicine

EDITORS: CHARLES WEBSTER AND CHARLES ROSENBERG

Plague and the poor in Renaissance Florence

Plague and the poor in Renaissance Florence

Ann G. Carmichael

Department of History
Department of History and Philosophy of Science
Indiana University

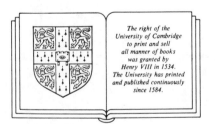

The right of the
University of Cambridge
to print and sell
all manner of books
was granted by
Henry VIII in 1534.
The University has printed
and published continuously
since 1584.

CAMBRIDGE UNIVERSITY PRESS

CAMBRIDGE

LONDON   NEW YORK   NEW ROCHELLE

MELBOURNE   SYDNEY

Published by the Press Syndicate of the University of Cambridge
The Pitt Building, Trumpington Street, Cambridge CB2 1RP
32 East 57th Street, New York, NY 10022, USA
10 Stamford Road, Oakleigh, Melbourne 3166, Australia

First published 1986

Printed in the United States of America

Library of Congress Cataloging in Publication Data
Carmichael, Ann G.
Plague and the poor in Renaissance Florence.
(Cambridge history of medicine)
Bibliography: p.
1. Plague – Italy – Florence – History.
2. Florence (Italy) – History – To 1421.   I. Title.
II. Series.
RC172.C37   1986   614.4'245'51   85-17451

British Library Cataloguing in Publication Data
Carmichael, Ann G.
Plague and the poor in Renaissance
Florence. – (Cambridge history of medicine)
1. Plague – Italy – Florence – History
I. Title
614.5'732'0094551   RC178.182F5/
ISBN 0 521 26833 8

For Gibson

Contents

List of graphs, maps, and tables   *page* ix
Preface   xiii

Introduction   I

1 Recurrent epidemic diseases: plague and the other
   plagues   10
   Periodic epidemicity   *10*
   A plague was many plagues   *14*
   Plague misdiagnosed   *18*

2 Florentine deaths in the first plague century   27
   Florence's Books of the Dead   *28*
   Causes of death in the Books of the Dead   *35*
   Normal years and plague years   *54*
   A general picture of Florentine health and disease   *57*

3 Plague in Florence   59
   Demographic background   *60*
   Mortality rates of major and minor plagues   *61*
   Seasonal characteristics of minor plagues   *62*
   Geographical distribution of plague   *67*
   Individual diagnoses of plague   *78*
   Contagion and the minor plagues   *85*
   Were the minor plagues true plague?   *87*

4 The social effects of plague in Florence   90
   Demographic significance of minor plagues   *90*
   Legislative significance of minor plagues   *96*
   Social significance of emerging plague legislation   *103*

5 Plague controls become social controls   108
   Plague controls in 1348   *108*
   Plague controls after 1348   *110*

The evolution of true plague controls   116
Plague legislation for the poor   121

Conclusion   127

Appendixes
I   Limitations of the Books of the Dead and the means
    for estimating numbers of children   133
II Deaths by quarter in Florence (parts 1–6)   136

Notes   143
Bibliographical essay   166
Index   177

List of graphs, maps, and tables

Graphs

2-1 Deaths from Bachi by Year, 1424–1457: Adults and Children Compared *page* 42

2-2 Seasonal Incidence of Deaths from Bachi, 1424–1457 43

2-3 Deaths from Pondi by Year, 1425–1456: Adult and Child Deaths Compared 47

2-4 Deaths from Pondi by Month, 1425, 1430, 1444, and 1450 48

2-5 Seasonal Incidence of Deaths from Mal Maestro, 1424 to 1457 51

3-1 Florentine Deaths Reported in the Grascia Morti 63

3-2 Registered Deaths per Day, 1399–1400 66

3-2 a Registered Deaths per Day during the Plague, 1400: Daily Count Recorded by the *Grascia* Scribe 66

3-3 Deaths per Day in Non-epidemic and Plague Years by Season, 1424–1458 67

3-4 Minor Plague, 1424–1425: Total Deaths per Day Compared to Plague Deaths per Day 68

3-5 Minor Plague, 1429–1430: Total Deaths per Day Compared to Plague Deaths per Day 68

3-6 Minor Plague, 1448–1450: Total Deaths per Day Compared to Plague Deaths per Day 69

3-7 Minor Plague, 1456–1457: Total Deaths per Day Compared to Plague Deaths per Day 70

4-1 Deaths from Plague by Year: Male and Female Deaths Compared 93

4-2 Causes of Child Deaths, 1439 95

Maps

3-1a Location of Deaths in the Quarter of Santo
      Spirito, 1–15 June 1430   74
3-1b Location of Deaths in the Quarter of Santo
      Spirito, 15–30 June 1430   74
3-1c Location of Deaths in the Quarter of Santo
      Spirito, 1–15 July 1430   75
3-1d Location of Deaths in the Quarter of Santo
      Spirito, 15–31 July 1430   75
3-2   Western Half of the Quarter of Santo
      Spirito   76
3-3   Plague-affected Districts in Florence,
      1456   82

Tables

1-1   References to undifferentiated "pestilence"
      compared to references to bubonic plague in
      literary accounts, 1350–95, 1405–50, 1451–95,
      throughout Italy   15
1-2   Chronicle descriptions of plague,
      1475–9   16
2-1   Reporting deaths from plague in Florence:
      percentages of *P* diagnoses compared to all
      reported diagnoses by year, 1424–58   34
2-2   Seasonal incidence of pondi during major pondi
      years   35
2-3   Major "causes" of death reported in the *Grascia
      morti* and *Libri dei Morti,* by year   36
2-4   Deaths from old age, by year, comparing death
      totals to percentage of female victims of old
      age   38
2-5   Cases of smothering in the *Grascia Morti*   54
2-6   Seasonal deaths per day during nonepidemic
      years, 1424–58   55
2-7   Seasonal deaths per day during epidemic years,
      1427, 1444, 1446   56
3-1   Burials in Santa Maria Novella, fourteenth-
      century epidemic years, by half-month   64
3-2   Deaths in the quarter of San Giovanni, among
      total Florentine deaths   72
3-3   Death totals in 1400: percentage totals in the
      quarters of San Giovanni and Santo Spirito   72
3-4   Death totals in 1430: percentage totals in the
      quarter of Santo Spirito   73

3-5   Deaths in Borgo Tegolaia, summer 1430,
        showing the clustering of deaths geographically
        and in households   78
3-6   All plague deaths reported in Florence, July–
        August 1456: the clustering of deaths within
        parishes and households   81
3-7   Cases of plague in two families, 1456   83
3-8   Deaths in the family of Barla di Stagio
        degli Strozzi, 1430   84
4-1   Child victims among total deaths, epidemic years,
        1424–58   92
4-2   Child victims among all deaths during a
        major plague year, May through October,
        1400   94
5-1   The decision to build a lazaretto: northern Italian
        cities in the mid-fifteenth century   120
5-2   Timing of the creation of temporary (crisis) and
        permanent health boards: northern Italian
        communes in the fifteenth century   122
A-I   Sex ratio of deaths in nonplague years,
        1400 excepted   135
A-II   Deaths by quarter in Florence
        Part 1: January–15 March   136
        Part 2: 16 March–30 April   137
        Part 3: 1 May–15 June   138
        Part 4: 16 June–31 August   139
        Part 5: September–October   140
        Part 6: November–December   141

Preface

It has become very popular to assume that changes in the natural world, especially the influence of disease-causing microorganisms, have repeatedly altered the course of human history. Buffeted by forces outside human control, past societies could only bear weak and helpless testimony to disaster. Such has been the usual tone of the history of plagues and epidemic disease: a saga of human efforts to cope with social and demographic catastrophe, spawned by unforeseen and unassailable microenemies.

It is true that fourteenth- and fifteenth-century observers could not have imagined the currently known explanations for recurrent bubonic plagues, nor could they have done more than guess at a germ theory of disease. Nevertheless they responded to epidemics in ways that shaped their perceptions of the causes of plague mortality and that altered the patterns of their deaths. It is the purpose of this book to analyze the evidence for, and causes of, mortality in Florence in the first century after the Black Death of 1348, and to show how changes in infectious diseases and changes in legislation and human behavior interacted.

Thus in the much larger historical picture, it is the purpose of this book to offer weight to the argument that conscious decisions influence patterns of mortality. Not all of the daily tragedies of disease and death are inadvertent. Above all, many such losses are well tolerated and augmented, a legacy that Westerners are often too quick to disown with more comfortable sagas of the terrible dominance of killer microbes felled later by the scientific triumph of humans over nature.

A theme this grand, could a historian ever prove it, is the work of a lifetime of research, not the testimony of one preliminary monograph. This book is but a limited analysis of records from Florence, 1300 to 1500, enhanced slightly with evidence drawn from other northern Italian cities of that period. It results from my quest, for almost a decade, to articulate some historical meaning to the list of over 11,000 names of those who died in Florence in 1400, names I encountered when I first opened the second oldest Book of the Dead in the Florentine State Archives. Fifteen years ago I would never have imagined myself counting and recounting deaths recorded in fifteenth-century Florence, and I certainly could not have envisioned the many people I would want to thank for that experience.

Foremost among those who helped and guided me is Ronald G. Witt, who introduced me to the economic and demographic history of medieval and early modern Europe, and led me to Florentine studies. Ron Witt has given his support, wisdom, and encouragement to every phase of this book, answering the earliest naive question I posed, directing the dissertation on which the book is based, and guiding me through every doubt and query that subsequently emerged.

Supported for six years at the outset of my graduate career by the generous funding of the Josiah Macy, Jr., Foundation, I was able to pursue the M.D. and Ph.D. degrees simultaneously, without the need to abandon scholarship for the marketplace. As director of the medical history training program at Duke University, Gert H. Brieger, so patient a teacher, wide-ranging in his knowledge of the history of medicine, allowed me the freedom to wander from the usual paths of medical history. Thereafter my early explorations in the Florentine State Archives would have been fruitless without the substantial help and guidance of David Herlihy, whose encouragement has sustained me ever since. My use of the Florentine Archivio di Stato was improved greatly with a summer fellowship from the Renaissance Society of America, under the direction of Anthony Molho. In extending the boundaries of this study beyond Florence, I am most grateful to the Gladys Krieble Delmas Foundation for supporting a summer research trip to Venice and to Indiana University for supporting my research in the Mantuan State Archives. All my research was facilitated by the generous help of the staffs and directors of Italian municipal and state archives and libraries. An early précis of my dissertation appeared in the form of an article I wrote, entitled "Plague Legislation in the Italian Renaissance," which was published by *The Bulletin of the History of Medicine* 57 (1983):508–25. I am grateful for permission to republish some of these materials.

In rethinking and rewriting the dissertation, and in incorporating the materials collected since then, I would especially like to express my gratitude to my friend and colleague, Helen Nader, and to Edward Muir, both of whom offered extensive commentary and suggestions on revising the entire manuscript. I feel likewise fortunate to have had a brilliant series editor, Charles Rosenberg, who extended valuable criticism.

I also wish to give a special word of thanks to my colleagues M. Jeann Peterson, for her wise and witty comments on various parts of the manuscript, and George C. Alter, for his incredibly patient help as I wrestled with primitive statistical and demographic concepts. Dr. Stephen Ell graciously read and commented on early versions of the more medical chapters; Professors John Norris and Guido Ruggiero saved me from making several embarrassing overstatements. Although I can acknowledge much assistance from others, undoubtedly flaws and errors may remain in the text, and these are my responsibility.

Close friends and family have warmly supported and encouraged me over the years. In Florence Franca Toraldo di Francia's good humor nursed me through the frustrations of both research and learning to speak Italian, while her son and daughter-in-law, Cristiano Toraldo and Frances Lansing Toraldo, gave me the existential support for the career choices I made. My own immediate family, however, suffered longest with the drafts and revisions, but in turn made it all worth doing. Especially my son Gibson, and to him I dedicate the book.

Introduction

During the fifteenth century plagues assaulted cities in northern Italy more frequently than during the late fourteenth century. In the earlier century, pestilences that were described as bubonic plague visited major cities once in every fifteen to twenty years. In the 1400s plagues hit some cities, for example, Venice and Florence, at least once a decade. In contrast to the devastating effects of plague on rural areas in the fourteenth century, the countryside was usually spared this scourge during the fifteenth century. Thus the basic experience confronting fourteenth- and fifteenth-century observers on the frequency and extension of plague led them to different conclusions about how plague spread.

There were many other differences between the fourteenth- and fifteenth-century epidemics that reshaped the attitudes of Italian city dwellers toward plague in the fifteenth century. Fourteenth-century plague survivors could not have defended the conclusion that plague was a contagious disease of the poor. Too many prominent citizens died in the outbreaks before the fifteenth century. But wealthy Florentines of the 1430s could be reasonably sure that flight from the city would protect them from plague. When they returned the records would show clearly the heavy mortality in working-class districts of the city and the loss of whole families to plague; at the same time prosperous districts were relatively spared. Florentine secular and religious leaders were certain by the 1450s that all the evidence supported the tenet that this was a contagious disease. By midcentury, Florentine legislators were beginning to consider serious changes in traditional sanitary policy in order to accommodate the general conviction that one must control the contagious spread of disease. The next generation of leaders would articulate clearly the further "experience" that plague and poverty were close companions.

Not only were the Florentines' stated motives for adopting new plague controls similar to those of their northern Italian neighbors, but they also adopted containment measures against plague similar to and nearly simultaneously with legislation in Venice, Mantua, Siena, Perugia, Milan, and other areas from which we possess some record. Novel plague legislation appeared throughout northern Italy during the second half of the fifteenth century. But when new sanitary policies were elaborated, during the middle third of the fifteenth century, professional medical opinion did not concur with the legislators' model of plague spread. In fact most of the serious medical concern with a contagion theory did not surface until the sixteenth century. Nevertheless the absence of a scientifically defended contagion theory did not stop policymakers from outlining strategies for the isolation of plague sufferers and plague "carriers" far beyond the originally passive, defensive quarantine devised in the fourteenth century. By the 1460s northern Italian leaders in many different cities all agreed that plague hospitals were necessary to decrease the spread of a contagious disease.

To be so convinced, the leaders of the mid-fifteenth century must have been persuaded that their experience of plague was unambiguous despite what doctors were saying and that the new policies could be justified on the grounds of plague contagion alone. This book will show that from our twentieth-century perspective the misdiagnosis of plague – attributing to plague many deaths that could have been caused by other infectious diseases spread by human contact – was prevalent during the fifteenth century and effectively supported the legislators' stance. But even without the problem of determining just who died from plague, fifteenth-century legislators found the new measures attractive because the legislation successfully addressed social disruptions created by plagues. The eventual adoption of the contagion principle of plague defense served the need both to solve the problem of recurrent epidemic disease and to confront the growing burden of urban poverty.

My concern with plague will involve two main questions. First, I will tackle the problem of the extent to which true plague (*Yersinia pestis*) epidemics may have occurred by considering what other infectious diseases contributed significantly to outbreaks of "pestilence." Rather than elaborate mechanisms whereby plague could have behaved as the fifteenth-century cases present themselves, I have chosen to explore the historical significance of the probability that other ordinary, nonplague causes of death were common during the plague years. Historical demographers have often acknowledged heavy losses among infants and children during mortality crises. Some scholars even have suggested that epidemic crises due to causes other than plague certainly contributed to the demographic collapse throughout Europe from 1400 to 1450. This study will examine in detail, and with surprisingly good fifteenth-century evidence, the causes of death other than plague. We will not be as concerned here, however, with the number who died and the demographic effects of epidemics as we will with the social and historical significance of different causes of death in the fifteenth century. The records of causes of death do have social significance even if they are not demographically precise. Furthermore differentiating victims of true plague from victims of other diseases during a plague year is more important in historical epidemiology than in historical demography because attention to these details is the only way to pinpoint the changes in the behavior of human infections over time.[1]

Second, I will discuss the historical effects of changes in plagues and in plague controls. Northern Italian city-states led the rest of Europe in adopting measures for dealing with recurrent plague: the quarantine, the lazaretto (pest house), and health boards. Yet these and other means of segregating and isolating the sick, with very few exceptions, were not adopted until fully a century after the Black Death of 1348. Most cities saw ten or eleven plagues before they decided that this was a contagious disease, best interrupted by controlling the sources of contagion. The controls adopted could not have been either rational or successful in dealing with the disease caused by *Y. pestis*. They would have been very effective, however, in controlling other contagious diseases that have escaped historians' attention.

Many questions have been overlooked in the attempts to remember who built the first lazaretto, devised the first quarantine, created the first permanent health boards, and wrote the first medical treatise on contagion. There are few studies of how a diagnosis was made; there are even fewer studies of other diseases besides plague that affected the lives of early Renaissance Italians. Many scholars have asserted that differential mortality – between rich and poor, between young and old, between male and female – was important, but few have actually attempted to analyze such phenomena. Here I will present evidence that all do not die equally before epidemic infections, and I will discuss how differential mortality could be historically important. I believe that differential mortality in plague years justified many of the changes in legislative policy.[2]

In discussing both the biological aspects of past plague and their historical effects, I will focus on a case study of Florentine mortality during the early fifteenth century, made possible by the survival of early urban death registers. The Florentine Grain Office's Books of the Dead allow us to examine the mortality in Florence from 1385 to 1458 in detail not usual with records this early. I selected for analysis a manageable sequence from 1385 to 1458, hand-counting over 60,000 cases. The series originally was little more than a register of all burials performed by communal gravediggers, but by 1424 included diagnoses of causes of death during epidemic years. With deaths alone one could show the decline in absolute mortality from plague during the early fifteenth century. Because burial place, and often residence of the deceased, were registered as well, we can document the pronounced clustering of deaths during fifteenth-century epidemics. But with the inclusion of diagnoses, we can derive a rare glimpse of both ordinary and epidemic mortality that cannot be inferred from good demographic studies. The Florentine registers are unique, as far as I know, in providing this diagnostic information before 1450.[3] But Florentine experience with plague was probably typical of other Italian cities in the early fifteenth century.

Thus this study seeks to show that there is much we do not know about epidemic diseases in the two centuries after plague appeared in Europe. There are two separate histories here, that of *Y. pestis* and other infections that have been mistaken for it, and that of the importance of epidemics in shaping human history, unconnected to the identification and description of diseases familiar in twentieth-century medicine. Plagues changed; and plagues changed medical and social history.

Throughout this book we will be concerned with what is true plague and what merely assumes the label "plague" as a matter of historical convenience. Although the most important issues this study seeks to address concern how and why fifteenth-century Florentines came to revise their procedures for dealing with epidemics, these issues cannot be discussed without an analysis of the actual disease environment that conditioned fifteenth-century perceptions. In other words, I have of necessity undertaken an epidemiological study that depends on twentieth-century models and understanding of infectious diseases.

Some readers will argue that such concerns are present-minded, distorting the fifteenth-century Florentine view of epidemics. Others may find that shifting back and forth between Renaissance usage of the word "plague" and modern meanings of the term is confusing. Thus I offer the following brief summary of my assumptions about how "true" *Y. pestis* plague is caused, and the extent to which I consider this twentieth-century material useful in understanding fifteenth-century "plague."

The ecology of plague is extremely complex. It is not normally a disease of humans; plague cannot become "endemic," no matter how frequently it afflicts human populations. The disease is almost always acquired indirectly by an arthropod vector, or directly from an infected mammal. There are no human carriers of plague like a "Typhoid Mary," continually shedding the bacterium.[4] Thus it is inappropriate to discuss first the signs, symptoms, and effects of human infection with this disease. Human cases of plague are in fact uncommon, a fact fundamental to understanding the biological and historical significance of recurrent plague in Europe.

Yersinia pestis, the microorganism that causes plague, commonly infects the rodents of several large families. The disease can become enzootic, chronically affecting animal communities, and can reach epizootic proportions when susceptible animal hosts have contact with the organism. Most known cases of human plague have resulted from direct or indirect consequences of epizootic plagues; human plague rarely occurs without the presence of plague-infected mammals.[5]

But the black commensal rat, *Rattus rattus*, so popular in historians' descriptions of epizootic plague, is by no means at the beginning of the story; it is only the proximal transmitter of plague to humans. In all the research conducted on plague during the past thirty years, the domestic black rat has played no part in maintaining plague in any area studied. Plague zoologists distinguish "wild plague," sometimes called "sylvatic plague," from "domestic plague." Both "natural" or permanent plague foci and temporary foci can exist, the latter depending on

a wide variety of circumstances primarily involving epizootic hosts (domestic rats or susceptible wild rodents and their constituent fleas). Such temporary infected areas may persist for decades or, under certain circumstances, become plague-free only to be reinfected from permanent foci (via contiguity, long-range transport, etc.).[6]

There are no natural plague foci in Europe today, and even the historical plagues may have depended on the periodic reintroduction of the organism from Middle Eastern or Balkan regions.[7]

Since 1928 plague researchers have suspected that the infection was separately maintained in wild rodents, and since the 1950s that concept has predominated in plague surveillance and control. In wild plague *Y. pestis* displays a periodic pattern of epizootic extension depending on the rodent reservoirs and on the flea vectors, and thus on the seasons favoring these two hosts. Latent infection may occur, though rarely, in hibernating animals, and rodent warrens can preserve live plague bacillus for months, even years, because the microclimate there is favorable to the survival of both insect vector and microorganism. Plague is spread by the movements of rodents, not humans, into affected areas and warrens as well as out of them, and by the transfer of infected fleas. Plague survives in any region because a fairly wide variety of resistant rodents survive with minimal plague infection. Susceptible species, such as *R. rattus,* cannot perpetuate the disease. As a species, *R. rattus* does not become resistant to plague infection.[8]

Plague is thus a disease of field rodents, advancing slowly and regularly "field to field, . . . burrow to burrow, in thin epizootic trails winding across the countryside, infecting village rats in passing."[9] Investigators in Iran, India, Java, Madagascar, and Kenya all found the same complex of resistant rodents and highly susceptible rodents supporting permanent plague in natural foci. Violent epizootics break out among susceptible rodents, and the dispersal of infected animals in turn spreads the plague to new, resistant rodents. Epizootics occasionally lead to human infection.

The bacillus responsible for plague, *Y. pestis,* was renamed in

1971 from the older *Pasturella pestis,* a name still seen occasionally in historical literature. The international committee on biological nomenclature changed the name not only to honor Alexandre Yersin, the student of Pasteur working in Southeast Asia who first isolated the organism, but also because other members of the *Pasturellae* are relatively harmless to humans. Not so *Yersinia* species. Among this genus "enterocolitica" and "pseudotuberculosis" species are human pathogens. Among animals *pestis* is by far the most stable and widespread of the *Yersinia* species.[10]

Yersinia pestis always retains its bacteriological identification as a Gram-negative, bipolar-staining, facultative anaerobic, non-lactose-fermenting, non-spore-forming bacterium. The full microbiolgical details are available elsewhere and need not detain us here.[11] *Y. pestis* can vary in virulence and in infectivity, independently of levels of host nutrition, immunity and host ecodemography, whether that host be human, rodent, other mammal, or flea. Many different antigens are included in the genetically determined makeup of the organism, and variations among these can elaborate antigens more or less effective in first infecting a cell and then reproducing the microorganism in the face of the hosts' normal immunological defenses. Pathogenicity, or the relative lethality of the microorganism may, moreover, vary among different population groups of the same host species, as well as between members of what historian Emmanuel Le Roy Ladurie called the *ménage à quatre,* the complex of bacillus, rodent, flea, and other mammal.[12] Each member population involved in this long chain of transmission could conceivably contribute to separate and dramatic variations in the pathogenicity of *Y. pestis.* Natural selection of one or more specific antigen types in the rat may not enhance the reproduction of the bacillus in the flea.

Adding to the complexity of plague, we could consider the role of the arthropod vector, usually a flea.[13] The insect must feed on an animal with plague septicemia (organisms in the bloodstream), and then successfully transmit that infection to another animal before it dies. Entomologists derive elaborate formulas for determining both "vector efficiency" and "vector capacity" based on flea counts and speciation of all the fleas involved in wild plague, and on the ability of each species to become "blocked" (unable to feed without infecting the host) with the growth of a bolus of plague organisms in the forestomach. Both the transfer of fleas from one species of mammal to another and the blockage of a flea more than temporarily are fairly rare biological events.

In the western United States, for example, plague is enzootic among ground squirrels and meadow voles, but transfer of fleas, infected or not, to rats has not been observed, even where rats are abundant.[14] Massive interspecies transfer of plague may, however, occur during epizootics. This is not well documented, but it appears to be the most likely circumstance for transferring plague to commensal rodents, and ultimately to humans.

This somewhat technical review of plague ecology emphasizes to the historian that biological details can occasionally impede useful analysis of past plagues. One might easily surmise that virtually any event external and exogenous to human societies may explain the disappearance, as well as the many appearances, of plague in Europe. The judicious selection of relevant ecological conditions could defend a retrospective diagnosis of *Y. pestis* for any given outbreak of pestilence. When we consider the variety of clinical forms human plague can assume, as we shall do throughout this book, a diagnosis of plague could be defended for almost any epidemic in early modern Europe. Since anything can be plague, it is difficult to gain a confident sense of the change in the disease over time, or to be sure that true plague behaved differently five hundred years ago than it does today.

In order to escape this logical trap, which potentially undermines any venture in historical epidemiology, the present study will make two assumptions at the outset. First, unless there is very persuasive, unassailable evidence to the contrary we must begin from the position that infectious diseases, including *Y. pestis,* in human communities of the European late Middle Ages are similar in both epidemiological and individual clinical presentation to analogous twentieth-century infections. Second, no study of epidemic crises in early modern Europe should overlook a very simple epidemiological maxim that common things occur commonly. The general level of technological and socioeconomic development in fifteenth-century cities helped determine the causes and circumstances of human illness and death in both normal years and years of high mortality. Many epidemic crises of the late Middle Ages could not possibly have been due to plague alone.

Many researchers have of course acknowledged that different infectious diseases could contribute to mortality during plague years.

This observation is one of common sense. However, many researchers assume that details about all the different individual causes of death in a mortality crisis merely qualify generally valid, population-level phenomena of past human plagues. The supramortality from plague itself is enormous, they argue, and the overall demographic and epidemiological effects of a plague thus give a faithful picture of the behavior of *Y. pestis* at the population level.[15]

Since this book is not devoted to a case study exploring the demographic effects of plague in early modern Europe, it examines the phenomena of nonplague causes of death during plague years, as well as nonplague epidemics, as events having historical significance quite apart from the demographic context in which they are usually discussed. "Accessory" causes of death in an epidemic of plague reveal much about the circumstances in which a diagnosis of plague was made. The original diagnoses of plague, in individual cases and in epidemics, were made by persons who saw plague's significance quite differently than we do. Furthermore the diagnoses made in the past were not necessarily based on unchanging criteria. A fifteenth-century diagnosis of plague had consequences in the fifteenth century that need historical examination, if only because those consequences involved altering the ecological conditions of plague occurrences.

1

Recurrent epidemic diseases: plague and the other plagues

True plagues, the bubonic plagues caused by the microorganism *Y. pestis,* began in late medieval Europe with the extraordinary mortality of 1348. Very little has been written about nonplague epidemics of the fourteenth and fifteenth centuries. Other pestilences seem to have little significance when seen in the chilling light of a scourge that returned at least once every fifteen years and claimed thousands, even millions, of lives. Yet the other plagues significantly shaped both patterns of death and attitudes toward death in Renaissance Italy. Along with plague, epidemics of dysentery, smallpox, and influenza also influenced mortality and morbidity patterns in both plague and nonplague years. They contributed to every observer's notions of who was most likely to die and where, when, and how one might expect death to come. Although the names of the other plagues disappeared from chronicles and diary records once the recurrent threat of bubonic plague became apparent, their symptoms persisted in the records, indiscriminately mingled with those of bubonic plague.

PERIODIC EPIDEMICITY

One of the most important features of epidemics in the early Renaissance is that many of them returned regularly.[1] Someone surviving to the age of twenty-five would almost certainly have witnessed several different epidemics, although plague was the only disease he or she was likely to view as distinctive and recurrent. In the fourteenth century chroniclers were particularly aware of the recurrence of bubonic plague as a discrete disease and often mentioned at least one past outbreak. Five major plagues struck northern Italy in the fourteenth century and all were described as *anguinaia, giandussa,* and *glandulorum,* words that note the prominent inguinal swellings many plague victims show when close to death.

During the fourteenth century chroniclers and diarists were particularly sensitive to the unique clinical features of the new infection. From 1350 to 1400 "pestilence" was usually qualified by reference to specific symptoms its victims suffered.[2] In Tuscany, for example, "plague" meant something quite precise in the later fourteenth century. Matteo Villani wrote of the plague of 1363, "The wondrous mortality of anguinaia began anew this year, similar to that which had its beginning in the years 1348 to 1350." Another chronicler from Lucca noted the specific characteristics of a plague there in 1371: "to die with inguinal or axillary swellings, blisters and buboes." The plague of 1374 was to Marchionne Stefani but the "usual pestilence of inguinal or axillary swellings," and in 1383 he said that it killed "in the same way as the other mortalities, with that sign of great swelling under the arm and over the leg at the groin."

Although contemporaries were less interested in describing other epidemics, during the fourteenth century nonplague plagues returned regularly. But accounts of the spread of disease from 1385 to 1393 show that these lesser epidemics were often masked by the great killer. General infections and hardships were common to the larger region of northern Italy in a period of war and crop failure during these years. Many chroniclers reported pustular eruptions that could have included cases of smallpox. In 1387, all Europe seems to have been afflicted with a severe influenza. Both of these diseases, though their presence is often difficult to detect, were regarded as routine, periodic epidemics.

There are surprisingly few explicit references to smallpox in late medieval Europe, but scattered accounts from northern Italy suggest that the disease returned to major centers in the fourteenth century at least once a generation, or every twenty-five to thirty years. An account from Vicenza in 1387, for example, refers to a pustular infection among the diseases ravaging northern Italy:

[The epidemic began] among children; first it stirred up pustules or measles with vomiting and refusal to eat, then with a great flux of the body. Whence it passed to adults and the elderly. Both fevers and glandular swellings appeared, and people almost without number were annihilated. However, the peasants suffered much more, because of the wars.[3]

In 1388 a Florentine chronicler described an epidemic common to Milan, Venice, Ferrara, and their general districts as *febbri pestilenziose* and *posteme velenose* (pestilential fevers and velenous pustules). It struck in the late summer and everywhere deaths from it were considerable.[4] Perhaps the separately described epidemic in Reggio in Emilia, called *maxima et horribilis* by a chronicler there, was the same disease.[5] The infection appeared in Tuscany in 1389 and 1390 and a Florentine chronicler reported "pestilential pustules" in Pistoia that claimed victims after a two- or three-day illness. In Florence in 1390 there were the same *aposteme pestilenziose*.[6]

One cannot be certain about the nature of these pestilential pustules, since witnesses describe neither the precise character of the pustules nor their location on a victim's body. But we can be sure that any one region would have been likely to suffer some of the same infections as did cities and territories with whom her citizens were in frequent contact. Northern Italian city-states and regions were not epidemiologically isolated from each other.

If smallpox epidemics did return periodically, their immunizing effects would have left most vulnerable that segment of the population born since the last epidemic. The disease itself should have been distinguishable from plague. Smallpox victims do not form buboes, the large swellings in the groin, armpit, or other site of lymphatic tissue that uniquely characterize bubonic plague. Fourteenth-century evidence suggests that smallpox outbreaks occurred, at least in Tuscany, every twenty-five to thirty years.

According to several observers smallpox was mixed with the anguinaia, or bubo-forming plague, in the second plague pandemic.[7] Scattered reports of an outbreak of smallpox distinct from plague occur in central Italy from 1360 to 1363. In 1363, both Sienese and Florentine chroniclers were able to distinguish the two diseases, noting that *vaiuolo* attacked so many children, youths, and even adults that it was "an incredible and wearying thing to behold." Saint Catherine of Siena suffered from smallpox when she was around fourteen years old, in 1363, a plague year as well.[8] Small wonder that this second plague was later called the plague of children. Many historians have mistaken the high mortality among young children as evidence for a long-lasting immunity to plague formed by the survivors of 1348. Plague was in some regions complicated by a second epidemic that preyed upon young children.

Both Naples and Florence had epidemics of *varioli* (the Latin equivalent of vaiuolo), in 1335–6, long before the novel plague infection arrived. Many individuals may have escaped reinfection until the 1360s.[9] If these few references to epidemics of a pustular eruption are true evidence of smallpox, the disease came to Tuscany at regular intervals in the fourteenth century, and the "pestilential pustules" of 1390 may have been encompassed within yet another wave of smallpox. To the north a Bolognese chronicler reported that vaiuoli were claiming lives in 1393.[10]

So also influenza displayed the periodic epidemicity of nonplague plagues, and an influenzal respiratory epidemic swept through northern Italy during the early spring of 1387.[11] Influenza, too, was easy for contemporaries to distinguish from *peste, pestilenzia, morbo,* and *mortalità,* and was of interest to chroniclers before the fifteenth century. It tended to claim lives only among the very old and the very young. Influenza usually had a late winter onset, a month-long stay in urban areas, a high attack rate, and acute respiratory symptoms.

A Florentine chronicler described the episode of "colds and fever" that hit Florence in 1387: The fever "killed many people, both old and young, and many women. But the old died much more [frequently] than did the young." Nearly everyone in Florence was affected. In February, said another chronicler, "everyone" in Lombardy suffered from a disease of "cold and fever" and was acutely ill for around eight days. A second Tuscan chronicler verified the extension of influenza (he attributed it to malign stellar aspects) throughout the province and the supramortality among the aged. Yet another chronicler described the epidemic as a "catarrh." By March a similar affliction was reported in Germany as well. In the fourteenth century influenza had probably been as frequent as smallpox. Pandemics occurred in 1323 and in 1367. In 1404, 1414, and again in 1427, influenza returned.[12] Clearly pandemics of influenza punctuated the lives of urban residents during the Renaissance, although probably not as frequently as they have our own lives during the past century.

Of course the picture is not so simple. Although it is impossible to be certain about the actual demographic or epidemiological effects of any disease to which we attach a modern name, the independent occurrences of both plague and nonplague epidemics can be seen. Infections like smallpox and influenza seemed to be an inescapable fact of life in the cities of Renaissance Italy, just as was the recurrence of plague. Observing this periodic epidemicity is complicated by the many other cases of nonperiodic, infectious diseases that were included in the imprecise Renaissance diagnoses of plague or smallpox or influenza.

The epidemics prevalent from 1385 to 1393 undoubtedly included other infections besides plague, smallpox, and influenza. The Florentine chronicler described well an acute epidemic dysentery in 1390, preceding the pestilential pustules, and numerous chroniclers refer to sheep and cattle epizootics.[13] These latter particularly could have caused many cases of human disease and that would explain cases of pustular eruption or respiratory infections.

For example, one possible cause of the pestilential pustules could have been anthrax. In the Bolognese territory, just north of Florence, epizootic diseases oppressed the countryside. The region had seen at least two different types of cattle and sheep plague. Anthrax (sometimes called malignant pustule, or woolsorters' disease) could explain a pustular epidemic disease. After a mild respiratory onset, this bacillary infection spreads to local lymph nodes, just as does plague. Generalized sepsis (infection) in victims occurs rapidly, within four to six days.[14]

The cutaneous form of anthrax that might account for the pestilential pustules described by chroniclers is usually obtained from an infected animal, particularly the animal's skin or hide. Cutaneous anthrax is quite striking, but it carries a much lower case fatality rate than the respiratory or gastrointestinal forms of the disease that can follow in its wake. The latter two forms of the disease are caused in most cases by the spores from the bacillus, which are highly volatile and extremely resistant to heat or cold. Both respiratory and gastrointestinal anthrax claim fatalities in over 50 percent of the cases. Anthrax might occur in any season since production of the disease is not dependent on the habits of an insect vector. Anthrax epidemics are now rare, but in a large trading town like Florence where wool working was a major industry, pestilential pustules due to anthrax were not an improbable cause of discrete epidemics. Most epidemics would be small, localized, and rural, often preceded by a more widespread sheep or cattle murrain, the common name given to epizootic anthrax.

A PLAGUE WAS MANY PLAGUES

After periodic epidemicity a second prominent feature of epidemics in the Renaissance is that even those epidemics specifically called

Table 1–1. *References to undifferentiated "pestilence" compared to references to bubonic plague in literary accounts, 1350–95, 1405–50, 1451–95, throughout Italy*

	"Pestilence"	Bubonic plague
1350–95	17	162
1405–50	189	41
1451–95	214	130

Source: Alfonso Corradi, *Annali delle epidemie occorse in Italia*, vols. 1, 4, 5.

plague were themselves usually a mixture of infections. Chroniclers and diarists of the fifteenth century were generally less careful witnesses than those of the previous century in noting the symptoms of epidemic diseases, as Table 1–1 reveals.[15]

The very imprecise character of literary references does not allow us to conclude that "pestilence" had any precise meaning. As the table suggests, nonbubonic pestilences were especially frequent in the fifteenth century. Undifferentiated plagues, those described without specific reference to buboes, were often a mixture of epidemic infections, and were frequently less severe in overall mortality.

But plague did not simply displace other infections, even in years of major outbreaks. For example, during the plagues of 1475–80 chroniclers noted a strange battery of symptoms in the disease arsenal, but most still called the affliction plague. Very few describe the presence of buboes on victims (see Table 1–2). Instead, a wide range of other symptoms characterized those suffering and dying during these years. Arguing that Rome had been infected the previous autumn by pilgrims coming for the Jubilee, Giovanni da Itri in 1476 remembered that pestilential fevers with *carbonchi* (which also could be translated pestilential pustules) had appeared among the "usual" autumn maladies. Some were called *antraci e negre pustole:* anthrax-like black pustules. "Worms were seen in many children," he added, "to a much greater extent than is usual, and in many of these we later saw swellings in the groin and similar things." But Giovanni da Itri was a physician, engaged here in public debate about the nature of this plague. It was, he concluded, just a little plague (*pesticula*), not *pestis,* true plague.[16] Even

Table 1–2. *Chronicle descriptions of plague, 1475–9*

City or region	Year(s)	Symptoms	Name
Friuli	1475	None given	Peste
Bologna	1476	None given	Peste
Milan	1476	None given	Peste
Rome	1476	Fevers, tumors, black pustules, worms	None given
Milan	1477–9	Acute fevers, delirium, measles, black & violet spots	None given
Brescia	1477–9	Famine, severe headache	Mal del zucho
Venice	1477–8	Famine, delirium	Mal mazzucco
Dalmatia	1478	None given	Peste
Mantua	1478	Famine	Peste

Source: Corradi, 1, 4, and 5, *ad annum.*

so the outbreaks of 1477–80 were the most lethal of the fifteenth-century series of plagues in northern Italy.

With much less medical expertise, a diarist from Parma described the loss of over 22,000 people in Milan in 1477: "Innumerable people had acute fever, accompanied by madness and delirium, so much so that many hurled themselves out of windows; and in any house that the disease entered, everyone perished; going through the city one saw nothing but crosses and priests."[17] Even more were said to have died in Brescia this same year, 30,000–34,000 by a chronicler's estimate, so many that bodies awaiting burial were often attacked by dogs.[18]

The Brescian chronicler reveals even more about the epidemiological setting of this plague:

The stricken who were conducted to the lazaretto perished miserably because there were so many there the physicians could not look after them. The physicians were few in number, and nearly all succumbed while in service. To the health of the souls, the priests and friars were

more fearful than curing, and refused to aid the sick. In fact, [they en-
couraged] processions, an ill-advised piety, which made the epidemic
worse. The beggars and migrants whom famine had forced into the city
were sealed into a brothel, whereby their very great corruption would
not be spread further.[19]

The gravediggers were accused of committing robberies and other
nefarious acts, including sexually molesting corpses. For over four
months, the chronicler claimed, more than 200 died each day.

Repeatedly during these harsh few years, chronicle, diary, and
legislative accounts relate severe food shortages and famines created by the segregation of poorer people, either deliberately or
because the rich had fled. In Mantua, prisoners were not fed during the crisis and finally they wrote to the marchese, "We are sev-
enty-two prisoners within the cruel walls of this prison, dying of
hunger. The *cittadini* have fled the city, and no alms come in. We
are in great tribulation and abundant misery, beset with bedbugs,
fleas and lice."[20] Famished peasants in the territory of Sondrio
threatened to sack the homes of the rich during the plague,
screaming that they were dying of hunger.[21] The viceroy lamented that he could find no more gravediggers and that corpses
lay unburied several days. The plague raged on, so lethal that
comparatively few suffered at any one time; most of those infected
died within a day of exhibiting symptoms of illness. A chronicler
from Modena said that the 20,000 dead in Venice were mostly
people of little social standing (*tutta bassa zente*).[22]

The Brescian chronicler reported that local physicians and residents had a distinct name for this epidemic – *mal del zucho,* or *del
mazuch.*[23] It came with a "most terrible bewilderment of one's senses" (a delirium), which suddenly seized the victim. The dominant
symptoms, then, in the epidemics from 1477 to 1479 in Italy were
not those of bubonic plague. A physician in Milan, Matteo da
Busti, claimed that a patient he had attended at the end of March
1479 had the same "choleric fever" and many signs of malignity
that were characteristic of the 1477 fever "from which so many
died." Two physicians called in to view a body further described
a body covered with violet and black spots or stains (*morbilli*).

Over 100 years ago Alfonso Corradi argued that this epidemic
was better diagnosed as typhus fever than plague, for the prominent features of it were adult mortality, associated with famine,

with symptoms of petecchiae and delirium.[24] His hypothesis was ignored by Hans Zinsser, who in his famous *Rats, Lice and History*, concluded that the earliest certain accounts of typhus in Europe appeared in 1489 and 1490. Whether the pestilences of the late 1470s in northern Italy included typhus fever or other infections, the symptoms of many deaths are not those classically associated with plague. The example illustrates here that unmixed, pure bubonic plague was an unlikely occurrence.[25]

The example also illustrates the changing social characteristics of fifteenth-century epidemics. Herding poorer people into isolation hospitals was not characteristic of plague provisions in the fourteenth century. Isolation of plague sufferers and their contacts may have had more profound effects on the differential mortality rates of rich and poor than it did on the spread of plague. Truly contact-borne infections, which plague is not, were more likely to spread within the miserable populations of a lazaretto.

PLAGUE MISDIAGNOSED

The pestilences of 1385–93 showed a variety of other infections besides plague that regularly assaulted urban centers, and revealed some evidence for periodic epidemicity of other major infectious diseases, particularly smallpox and influenza. The pestilences of 1475–80 included years of severe famine mixed among those of true plague and, almost certainly, epidemic typhus fever. In both cases attributing the cause of the epidemic to plague involves a historical oversimplification, for contemporaries of the epidemics recognized the presence of nonplague infection.

There is a third major feature of epidemics in the Renaissance that can be illustrated with the detailed letters of Mantuan officials during the plague of 1478: The individual cases of epidemic infections were occasionally misdiagnosed. That is, if we take a viewpoint outside the system of diagnosis by which late medieval physicians understood what plague was, and if we apply twentieth-century medical understanding to the fifteenth-century descriptions of plague victims, there is good reason to mistrust many diagnoses of plague made in the fifteenth century as evidence of *Y. pestis* infection. Although such a point of view is admittedly anachronistic, culturally if not nosologically, it is nonetheless worthwhile to ask if *Y. pestis* infection is the most likely diagnosis of individual plague cases, as well as individual epidemics, in the fifteenth century.

By the middle third of the fifteenth century, vicars and mayors in the Mantuan territory were required to inform the powerful Gonzaga lords of Mantua if plague had broken out in their territory.[26] In some cases their letters were so thorough that they described all the particulars of the cases of suspected plague in surrounding districts, including the appearance of the body after death. Often the examples suggest that officials or local worthies took the responsibility for diagnosing a case of plague, but they occasionally called in experts, that is, physicians and surgeons, to view the corpse. In many cases gravediggers must have been responsible for alerting officials in charge of public health defenses, as the report of one official reveals, 8 December 1463: "I ordered the body of this youth who died this morning examined; the gravedigger had found him *pestilentiato*."[27]

The mayor of Ostiglia, a small fortress town on the Po River toward Ferrara, kept the marchese informed of suspect cases in 1479. One such was the case of a wife of a Mantuan provisionary, who died 22 August with two swollen inguinal glands (*infiata dua cossa*). Suspecting plague, an emissary of the Gonzaga family, Giovanfrancesco, sent for two doctors from Quistello. They decided that this was not a plague case, although the basis for their decision was not made clear in the letters. Gonzaga nevertheless decided to segregate the household, since the woman had had a fever prior to her death. Possibly it was already evident at this time that two other members of the household had become ill.[28]

On 29 August one of the woman's two daughters died, a young woman of around twenty years, and Gonzaga sent four men from the commissary's office to view the body. They found no "marks" and pronounced the body "clean."[29] On 3 September the second daughter died, again without any marks or stains (*macula*) on the body. A third daughter died on 6 September. Apparently she had not been ill on 29 August, since only two daughters were mentioned at that time. On this alarming occasion, eight persons, two of whom were surgeons, were sent to view the corpse. Again they found the body unmarked. "What is the cause of these deaths, one right after the other, I don't know," lamented Giovanfrancesco, "especially since there has been nothing showing on the bodies."

On 7 September an old woman, over sixty years, died in Ostiglia. She had been ill about five days, and the body showed a bubo (*angonaglia*) with inflammation of the surrounding groin area. The swelling was red and much discolored. An arm was mottled. Those in her house claimed that she had been complaining of pain in one leg for some time, but had been feeling a little better than usual prior to her demise. She had gotten up and gone out to fetch grain, but shortly after this trip she had become febrile. She died a few days afterward. Gonzaga expressed real doubt about this case, but wanted to trust the story of her relatives that the woman had only overexerted herself. He nevertheless decided to segregate this household as well.[30]

In these few cases from Ostiglia, several "signs" were either present or sought to alert local officials that plague had appeared. The most obvious was the one that first aroused concern: the bubo, or inguinal swelling. But in both cases where this sign was present on a victim, the evidence was ultimately disregarded. Instead teams of examiners scanned bodies for a second sign of marks of some sort (they used the word *machiato* to say a body was "stained"). Even when physical signs were absent, Gonzaga felt that multiple cases in one household warranted plague precautions. Finally, the presence of any of these signs in conjunction with a fever suggested a suspect case.

At a distance of over 500 years the only "sign" among these that seems to be reliable in the diagnosis of plague is recent or acute inguinal (and/or axillary) lymphatic swelling, the bubo. Although there are other infections that may cause enlargement of a regional lymph node, little else will produce a sudden, grossly visible inflammation. Chroniclers in the early plague epidemics described buboes as large as eggs or oranges or even grapefruit. Patients with a large plague bubo experience a dramatic rise in body temperature, later become disoriented and finally die, usually within two to four days after the appearance of the bubo. We could readily assume that *Y. pestis* infection was responsible for cases in which this sequence of symptoms occurred.[31]

Furthermore, plague is merciless compared to most of the diseases we can discern in the records of fifteenth-century Italy. Sixty percent of all untreated victims die, regardless of their previous state of nutrition. Among bubonic plague sufferers, 60 percent or more of those bitten by a flea will display the bubo in an area readily visible to an examiner, whether or not the victim is among the 60 percent who ultimately die. In the 40 percent of bubonic plague cases without visible buboes either the disease progresses too rapidly for the bubo to form – such cases were referred to as "septicemic" plague in older historical literature – or the lymph nodes involved were those lying close to internal organs and are thus not visible on the exterior of an intact corpse or body. Nevertheless, the occasional presence and recognition of angonaglia as a true sign of plague suggest that bubonic *Y. pestis* was certainly part of the complex of disease in these recurrent fifteenth-century plagues.

The time course of the older woman's inguinal inflammation might make us doubt that she suffered from plague, just as it did Giovanfrancesco de' Gonzaga. But if the bubo was consistently reported as the major sign of plague, we could be assured that most instances of plague diagnosis were correct. Moreover, if the bubo was consistently the sign of plague, many of the atypical, satellite cases could be comfortably ascribed to plague as well. For example, even when the descriptions are not classic for the short course of *Y. pestis,* many cases in the Mantuan territories were probably recurrent plague. These cases give minimal description of the bodies of persons probably dead from plague:

27 May 1478, the physician Maestro Gaspare visited a man in Mantua and found "the whole skin bruised over the shin, and a bubo in the groin, very blackened."

A woman dead in one house in the city, 5 June 1478, with signs "in each groin."[32]

But there are cases where fever alone was cited as the diagnostic feature, making the diagnosis of plague doubtful. Fever alone makes a retrospective diagnosis of plague a difficult one, even though elevated temperatures and eventual delirium are fairly constant symptoms in the later stages of plague infection. Examples of doubtful plague cases include:

29 May 1478 a young man of 22 years died of a continuous fever and his wife died 2 June. No signs on either body, but called "plague."

In the house of Filippo di Aldigeri, a second woman gravely ill, 28 July 1478, with intense fever and pain [not swelling] in the groin.

5 June 1478 the rector of the hospital refused to see a little boy who carried the diagnosis of plague, though the only "signs" the boy had were fever and headache.[33]

Blotches or stains on the bodies are also not very common features of infection with Y. *pestis,* yet these were often a "certain" sign for which many Mantuan investigators searched. Consider the following lengthy case from a vicar in the hill town of San Martino, near Marcaria (on the road toward Brescia). Baldasar Suarda, a Gonzaga emissary, wrote to the marchese 29 July 1478:

Monday morning the vicar of San Martino came here and, not wanting to enter, called me to the bridge. There he reported that the previous night two little children died, both in the same house. The oldest of these two brothers was 14 years old. Because about ten days ago their father died after a rather brief illness, [the vicar was suspicious and decided that] two physicians should view the bodies. They in turn found that one boy had some extremely evident signs; the other was covered by petecchiae [*tutto petechiato*]. Thus the vicar came here carrying the message that your excellency should be advised, especially because many people came to visit the father of these boys before he died, and taking no precautions at all freely conversed with him then.[34]

The vicar reported that now several other children in the village were sick, and two little girls in a second house had died. Here it is slightly unclear whether the petecchiae were considered different from the "evident signs" on one of the bodies, but many cases this year suggest that such bloody patches on the skin were used in the absence of other signs to diagnose plague. The following also occurred in Mantua in 1478:

29 July, a Franciscan friar died "with marks on his back." Maestro Marchesino said it was plague.

The same day the barber Maestro Crescimbeno died after three days of continuous fever. His body was "marked all over by black blotches."[35]

Occasionally a different word, *carbone,* is used to indicate a feature that might have been seen in true plague cases. The word, corresponding to the French *charbon,* is frequently translated as "plague pustule," and is a black, necrotic lesion on the skin at the site where the flea originally injected bacilli. The flea bites a human host only after the preferred rat host is no longer available. If the flea is infected with plague, a bolus or wad of bacteria that blocks the flea's upper digestive tract, proventriculus, is spit into the skin of the victim as the flea desperately attempts to feed. Y. *pestis* then causes local tissue destruction and cell death, leading to the blackened color of the carbone. Many of the bacilli are simultaneously carried through the bloodstream or through lymphatic channels to the local lymph node where the lymph cells attempt to manufacture a successful antibody. Buboes are more frequent in the groin because fleas usually bite the legs of prospective human hosts.

There is nothing to limit numerous fleas from biting a single unfortunate host, so several carbone could be present on a victim at death. But this is not likely to occur in many victims during the same epidemic. More usually descriptions of a body stained all over with black patches would be a reference to non-raised petecchiae or to larger hemorrhagic areas under the skin surface. Here one would suspect an infectious agent that attacks the small blood vessel walls, or profound septicemia impeding normal blood circulation. It could occur with an overwhelming *Yersinia* infection, where a septicemia involving large numbers of organisms circulating through the bloodstream plugs capillaries with the rapidly multiplying bacilli, thus causing extravasation of blood and organisms into the skin, as well as into other tissues. This does not commonly occur with *Y. pestis,* but it is possible.

Two other epidemics would be more likely to produce the complex of acute fever, delirium, and petecchiae that is described in some of these "plague" cases. One is epidemic, louse-borne typhus. The chroniclers' descriptions of the 1477–9 plagues suggested this possibility as well as plague. Typhus (rickettsia) organisms are carried to humans by body lice (in epidemic typhus fever), and by rat fleas (in endemic, murine typhus), and actually attack the walls of blood vessels, causing an infection and inflammation of the small arterioles. These epidemics are more frequently winter and early spring infections, since crowding and multiple layers of poorly cleaned clothing would help support louse infestation.[36]

A second epidemic infection that produces deep hemorrhagic lesions on the skin is meningococcemia. Florid meningococcal meningitis was not described clearly until the early nineteenth century, and the rigid spine and seizures of classic meningitis are not described by any of the fifteenth-century accounts surveyed here. Nevertheless, this generalized infection is a rapidly progressing, highly contagious disease that characteristically produces early symptoms of a slight cold, then progressive fever, disorientation, and severe vasculitis that leads to subcutaneous bleeding. The rash is characterized as "purpuric" and would fit nicely the fifteenth-century observation of purplish-black stains on a corpse.[37]

Epidemics of meningococcemia are not as widespread as those that are transmitted by the flea and louse. But they are reasonably common among persons living in close quarters, and frequently are seen among the very age group represented by the small Mantuan sample: older children and young adults. Meningitis in an epidemic form is rarely seen.in the industrial "First" World, but epidemics in Africa have claimed tens of thousands of lives.[38]

Finally, it is possible that many of the bizarre mixture of symptoms reported during this cycle of epidemics could have included cases of poisoning, particularly by fungal toxins known as "mycotoxicoses." Spoiled grains, and the moldy grain pastes often offered to the starving and to migrants, can easily contain lethal amounts of toxins, and the most prevalent among these, ergot and alimentary toxic aleukia, even in nonlethal doses could be responsible for hemorrhages into the skin, delirium, headache, and a wide variety of psychic and gastrointestinal symptoms.[39] The late 1470s were times of hardship and weather disasters, increasing the likelihood of fungal poisoning. But because in many places, such as Milan, the clinical symptoms were discrete enough to be recognized repeatedly by physicians, it is unlikely that mycotoxins could account for all the mortality and morbidity of these years. Poisoning with grain toxin is not this predictable in the amounts of toxin ingested, or in the specific chemical toxins one would be likely to consume.[40]

One of the most consistent "signs" of plague feared by community leaders in Mantua was the clustering of plague cases in a limited number of households. Multiple deaths in a single dwelling were worrisome even in the absence of any obvious clinical sign. If a local leader wanted to impress the marchese of Mantua, for example, he might claim to err on the side of caution, citing the clustering of deaths:

[27 November 1478] From the tenth [of this month] until now, five persons have fallen ill, all with pleurisy accompanied by acute, pestilential fever. Three are now dead and the other two gravely ill. Accordingly I have been advised on all of this by our physician, who has examined the urine in these cases, and all the other signs, and has concurred with me that I must be extremely attentive to these developments. . . . Until now, no sign of pestilence on the sick or dead has appeared, other than these I have mentioned. Nevertheless I have taken the immediate precautions of [restricting all communication and commerce with this area].[41]

In many of the cases, multiple deaths in one household were reason enough to initiate plague controls, in particular the segregation of the survivors within that house. The residence was either sealed up and provisions for food and water made, or the remaining family members were sent to a lazaretto. On 22 May 1478, the *Collaterale generale* of Mantua, Benedetto Agnello, specially appointed to oversee plague details, informed the marchese of the precautions he was taking on a routine basis. The daily report that day called Gonzaga's attention to the house of a builder, Maestro Pietro de Mozanega, whose daughter had died 10 May, after a brief, three-day illness. On 21 May, Pietro's wife died after only two days' illness, with headaches and acute fever. The following day one son died, ill "some days" and another son was unwell. Signs were never found on any of these bodies. The second son died two days later, and Benedetto decided to segregate the household and area. The collaterale did not stress headaches and fever, nor did he find a physical sign to justify the diagnosis of plague. Instead rapid deaths and multiple household cases seem to have motivated him to make plague provisions.[42]

Like many deaths in one home, death after a very brief illness was cause for alarm in itself. For example, on 29 July 1478, Benedetto segregated a household where a fifteen-year-old girl died after a brief illness. Not only were there no signs, there were no other deaths in the house or even nearby.[43] A more elaborate case reported on 17 November 1463 further illustrates just how important this timing of illness and death could become for those diagnosing plague:

God have mercy on us this day and save us: for a daughter of one Antonio de Corrio is dead at fourteen years of age and has only been sick eight days. The neighbors swear that this young girl was greatly troubled with ear pain a few months ago, and that recently she arose before dawn to wash her hair, but then went back to sleep. She awoke later with a fever which continued until her death. The pain [in her ears?] came back too. The neighbors were adamant that she thus did not die of plague.

Now I am sick and tired of this, so I naturally had the body seen by Maestro Marchesino. Even he said that he found nothing except swelling around one ear.[44]

Nevertheless the entire area, a blind alley that included this house, was segregated and plague provisions were made. Most likely the ear infection involved a substantial mastoiditis (an infection of the honeycomb-like bone behind the ear) and extension of the infection to the brain or meninges. The neighbors and physician were probably right that the illness was not plague. But the official was little concerned with these objections since the terminal illness had been so brief.

These, then, were some of the signs used to diagnose plague: buboes, petecchiae, pustules, rapid illness, fever, and multiple household cases. If all were used in the diagnoses, there would be little reason to suppose that plague was consistently misdiagnosed. If the bubo predominated as a sign, we could still be reasonably comfortable after five centuries that there was not much error in the ascription of a death to plague. But if the person conferring the diagnosis seized upon any one sign instead of the bubo as solely diagnostic, confusion of plague with other infections could easily result.

Nothing seems to illustrate the plurality of infections common in northern Italy during the fourteenth and fifteenth centuries as clearly as does an examination of the process of diagnosing an individual's suffering. The frequent mention of nonplague symptoms in these diagnoses indicates that other epidemics were present in the midst of plague, and may have returned to the cities as regularly as did bubonic plague.

Nevertheless, noting the presence of nonplague pestilences does not really uncover their significance. The central portion of this book will thus be devoted to an in-depth case study examining the incidence and prevalence of many infectious diseases, including plague, in Renaissance Florence. From a survey of the incidence of nonplague pestilences, from the descriptions of misery, of famine, and of the forced isolation of families, and from the reasonable suspicion that dysenteries and other secondary infections accompanied plague epidemics, claiming additional lives, we must conclude that true plague is often difficult to view apart from the other "plagues" of the fifteenth century.

2

Florentine deaths in the first plague century

There are comparatively few accounts of the ordinary causes of death in the Renaissance. Physician-humanists, the medical elite of the fifteenth century, were often preoccupied with medicine's importance in the larger intellectual sphere of natural philosophy, and with serving the needs of wealthy clients.[1] Most of their discussions of illness fit into an intellectual context that bears little resemblance to modern, scientific medicine. Busy practitioners, university trained or not, left no record of their day-to-day practice so it is impossible to know directly their concerns in normal or epidemic years, and difficult to guess what causes of death were regarded as ordinary. Laymen, eyewitnesses to famines and epidemics, were deeply concerned with the magnitude of a disaster, and with the threat it posed to their own survival.[2] Their accounts speak little of ordinary mortality. One of the few Renaissance sources that reveals both normal and epidemic mortality is the series of Florentine Books of the Dead, which were kept by both the Florentine Grain Office and by the physicians' and spicers' guild. The latter records, however, only survive after 1450.

The Books of the Dead kept by the Grain Office offer information about the causes of death that differs in two fundamental respects from other available sources about fifteenth-century epidemics. First, they do not omit normal, noncrisis years. They survive from 1385 and continue until the end of the eighteenth century. Although there are many gaps in the record through the fifteenth century, largely because some books have disappeared, they were a continuous recording of deaths in a major Renaissance city. Second, they were not limited to the perceptions of a single individual or group of individuals living in only one generation. Here we will consider why the records were kept, the content and accuracy of the surviving registers, the kinds of information they contain, and the picture they give of the spectrum of disease in a fifteenth-century city.[3]

FLORENCE'S BOOKS OF THE DEAD

Why they were kept

The Grain Office, or *Grascia*, was a department of Florentine government constructed from at least two older units. First, the *Uffi-ciali dell'Abbondanza* had been solely concerned with the provision and distribution of grain, with ensuring safe passage to market, and with controlling prices during times of crisis. To these were added in 1375 at least some of the duties of the old communal Executor of the Ordinances of Justice, basically a judicial division enforcing the peace between warring factions of landed aristo-crats. The office was then renamed the Grascia. Statutes surviving from 1378–9 give the Grascia authority over "prostitutes, servants and the dead, and many other things as well."[4] A chronicler tells us that in 1383 it was already a custom to keep a count of those who died, but the first surviving register of deaths begins two years later.[5]

Until 1390 the recording scribes say that the books are about "gravediggers and cooks." In addition some of the statutes of the Grascia are recopied there, and an occasional court proceeding against someone who violated one of the sumptuary laws is bound into the record. This may be the important clue to the early use of these death registers: the Grascia had to enforce sumptuary legis-lation. Statutes gave them unspecified powers over agricultural workers, prostitutes, slaves, servants, guards, and wet nurses, whereas their concern with the equally menial cooks and grave-diggers seems to focus on display at celebrations. The cooks re-port what they served at weddings and banquets, the names of those who hired them, and how many guests attended. The gravediggers provide much more detail about the deaths of wealthier Florentine males. Presumably the interest here was in excessive funeral display, just as it had been for the Office of the Executor.[6]

There may have been other reasons the record was useful to the Grascia, or to the appellate court judge before whom the cooks and gravediggers were to report. Especially in times of heavy mortality, the record of a death of someone with property or family claim to property may have made the books useful in settling wills and testaments. That, too, was an interest of the appellate court. Usually the court would have used the notarial cartularies, into which a notary recorded the wishes of the dying person directly, as well as the official transactions involving property. But plague years were not usual, and many notaries died.[7]

Before 1400 the Books of the Dead, the *Grascia morti,* reflect the popular interest in keeping a count of deaths, and so the recording may always have been used to monitor crisis mortality. It is quite possible, however, that a second series of registers, now lost, gathered this information before the Grascia did. The physicians' and apothecaries' guild *(l'arte dei medici e speciali)* kept a second register of deaths that survives after 1450, and the guild was also responsible for regulating gravediggers.[8]

Statutes of the guild from as early as 1314 recorded the guild's nominal control over "gravediggers, priests, or others burying the dead." After 1348 the guild expanded prohibitions against selling the clothes of the dead and extended its jurisdiction to the fees gravediggers were allowed to charge.[9] Plague had motivated tighter control, and Boccaccio's description of these unsavory individuals gives a vivid sense of why so many offices were involved with funeral and burial customs:

[In the Black Death of 1348] very few were the dead whose bodies were accompanied to the church by more than ten or twelve of their neighbors, and these dead bodies were not even carried on the shoulders of honored and reputable citizens, but rather by gravediggers from the lower classes that were called *becchini.* Working for pay, they would pick up the bier and hurry it off, not to the church the dead man had chosen before his death, but, in most cases, to the church closest by, accompanied by four or six churchmen with just a few candles, and often none at all. With the help of the *becchini,* the churchmen would place the body as fast as they could in whatever unoccupied grave they could find, without going to the trouble of saying long or solemn burial services.[10]

One of the young women in the *Decameron* urged her companions to flee the city because of these loathsome gravediggers: "We see the scum of our city, avid for our blood, who call themselves *becchini* and who ride about on horseback torturing us by deriding everything, making our losses more bitter with their disgusting songs."[11]

Rumors about abuses in 1348 included scenes of bodies cast into open pits, "sprinkling dirt over them, like cheese between layers of lasagna."[12] The vicious reputation gravediggers acquired during recurrent plagues became notorious, and so after the Black Death legislators sought to control some of the most horrifying aspects of plagues by monitoring the fees and practices of gravediggers. Nothing lessened the actual mortality, but some outrages could be avoided by supervising *beccamorti,* requiring, for example, that they respect the family's parish church preference for the burial of a loved one.

Thus the early Books of the Dead may have served many different communal needs. The lists could have been used to expedite the inheritance of money and property. Certainly the gravediggers needed restraint. Numbering the dead satisfied morbid curiosity and keeping some record of deaths may have aided the Grascia in their estimates of grain needs. Furthermore, many parish priests depended on their meager fees for the death and burial of a parishioner and had little legal recourse when unpaid.[13] Whatever their uses, the practice of keeping registers of the dead was not limited to Florence.

The 1348 statutes of a nearby town, Pistoia, hint that registration of deaths before judicial officials occurred long before surviving documents attest to the practice, and there the main concern was with listing the names of propertied citizens.[14] The rectors and bailiffs were requested to report the death of anyone in their district, "before that body is buried," to the *capitano* or the *podestà.* But the regulation did not apply to "paupers and miserable persons." Similarly, in the first surviving *Grascia morti* of 1385, only eleven of the twenty-five entries from 18 September until 31 December were identified by a full name as the law required. Twenty-four were specifically noted to be poor, which suggests that only property and status warranted full inclusion of a name.

The Tuscans preceded most cities and towns of northern Italy in keeping communal registers of deaths or burials, a practice that did not become widespread before the late fifteenth century. During the 1370s and 1380s, Arezzo, Pistoia, San Sepolcro, and Siena – other Tuscan towns – kept municipal burial records independently of any preexisting parish or confraternity lists, but when the record keeping actually began and whether it was a response to the advent of great plagues are questions unanswered by the existing records.[15]

General content of the Books of the Dead

Four books of the *Grascia morti* series of deaths between 1385 and 1449 survive. The first book stretches from 1385 to 1397, with several gaps in record keeping, and the 1406 register is bound mistakenly into this volume. The second book is a very large one, encompassing the years 1398 to 1412. Many whole years' records are missing, but the volume is dominated by the fairly careful records of the plague of 1400. The third book includes only the summer of 1424 through the autumn of 1430, but no months or years are omitted. The fourth surviving book registers deaths from 1439 to 1449. Minor gaps in the entries are common during the early period (to 1412), and longer lacunae of several years interrupt both early books: Records from 1394, 1404, 1410, and 1411 are missing.

The form and character of the actual death entries changed markedly between the early two books and the later two. In the series to 1412, a basic entry would fall under the heading of the day the death was entered and would usually provide most of the following information: a name or description of the deceased, the *populus* in which he or she lived, the parish church in which the body was buried, and, usually, the name of the gravedigger. Individual scribes influenced the amount of additional detail, some providing none at all, others some rudimentary age and economic data. For example, 23 April 1388, "Doninus Fortini, gravedigger, related that a boy or infant born this same night, son of Monardo Angeli of the quarter of Santa Maria Novella and the populus of Sancti Apostoli, died and was buried in this same church of Sancti Apostoli." Some note "a small, poor girl," "an aged pauper," "a captive in prison," "the rich wife of Gherardi," or "an infant born this night." Others give only name and surname or father's name. Nevertheless, the general tendency over the entire early period is toward an increasing use of some identifying name. By 1415 gravediggers were obliged by communal law to report name and surname of each deceased.[16]

During the period before 1412 several other minor changes in registrations of death occurred. In 1385, as mentioned above, many other items of interest to the Grascia were mingled with death entries: cooks' reports, occasional record of legal proceedings, and notice that a death was officially announced to the citizenry by

town criers or even trumpeters.[17] Other entries, lacking full names,
were identified as unusually poor, possibly constraining the
gravedigger to reduce his fees. But by 1387 the books omitted
the restatements of sumptuary laws that garnished early reports,
and only rarely thereafter do legal inquisitions appear in the record. By 1390 wedding and banquet reports vanish from these registers, and the book is solely *liber beccamortuorum,* book of the gravediggers. After the mid-1390s few deaths are listed as being announced, even in the cases of prominent Florentine citizens. After
the great plague of 1400, scribes more often report the dead in the
vernacular, and after 1405, Italian is always used in the *Grascia
morti.*

The appearance of the registers changed greatly between 1412
and 1424. The new *Grascia morti* are bound in leather with vellum
pages clipped close to the entries, much reduced in size from the
old, bulky, paper pages of the first two books. Also the entries are
pared, with the later books giving only name, parish, and place of
burial, the minimum required by statute. But the later books make
one very important addition to the record: causes of death. Very
probably the purpose of the record changed, a point to which we
shall return shortly.

Beginning 26 March 1450 a second, apparently independent, series of Florentine death registrations survives. These books were
kept by the physicians and apothecaries' guild and still describe
their purposes as controlling the gravediggers: "Here is the book
containing the notices of death of all dying and buried in the city
of Florence," it begins, "as related by the *beccamorti* or *becchini* of
Florence." The registers make no reference to the Grascia series.
Thereafter both sets of mortality books survive until 1781, each
series missing some individual books. Some scholars have specu-
lated that the physicians' guild kept better records, but no evidence has been found to show that the guild kept records before
the Grascia did.[18]

These five volumes in Florence from 1385 until 1458, four registers of the Grain Office and one of the physicians' guild, thus
provide significant data about the number, gender, age, and residence of those who died. One last feature was added to the books
in the fifteenth century: After 1424, scribes recorded causes of death
during years in which plague was either seen in the city or feared.
In plague years, the cases of plague or pestilence have been clearly

singled out by the scribe with a capital *P* in the margin by the victim's name. In nonplague years these notations accompany registrations very infrequently and without any pattern or predictable diagnosis. This makes the study of nonepidemic, ordinary mortality patterns elusive, but since other causes of death besides plague are also noted, the task is not impossible.

Frequently *di pestilenzia, di morbo,* or *di segno,* are written in addition to the *P.* All of these terms seem to be equivalent to singling out a case of plague. Table 2–1 examines the relationship between death totals after 1424, the total number of entries provided with a cause of death, and the subtotal of all the deaths labeled with a *P.* The percentage of entries showing a cause of death from any cause rose dramatically when plague cases appeared in the city. This phenomenon is much more striking in the record itself than in the table. In 1448, for example, the record for the first death from plague appeared on 19 July; before that date only 15 percent of the names listed that year were accompanied by a diagnosis. None of the entries in 1456 carried a diagnosis before the first discovered case of plague. There are a few years (1425, 1439–40, and 1450–1) in which plague lingered in Florence, causing sporadic deaths. During these years the notary continued recording many causes of death, even though few of them were from plague.

One year alone stands out as an exception to this generalization. In 1444 there were no plague cases, but almost one third of the entries indicated cause of death. This was an epidemic year, however, and Table 2–2 shows how the fear of explosive epidemic, this time from *pondi,* or dysentery, stimulated the recording of a cause of death.

In 1458 the guild book contains 70 percent more causes of death than does the Grascia list of the same year, even though the total number of registered deaths is quite close (820 and 815, respectively). The reporting of deaths in the separate registers occasionally varies according to the day recorded, but the names of the individuals leave no question that the same deaths are being registered in both books. The abundance of diagnoses in the guild register raises the speculation that the physicians' and apothecaries' guild took a greater interest in death causes, perhaps even first recorded them, but again, there is no other evidence to support this conclusion.

Table 2–1. *Reporting deaths from plague in Florence: percentages of* P *diagnoses compared to all reported diagnoses by year, 1424–58*

Year	Total number entries	Number of entries with diagnosis (%)		Number deaths with *P* diagnosis (% of those diagnosed)	
1424	[1,363]	[1,306]	(96%)	[890]	(68%)
1425	926	691	(75%)	15	(2%)
1426	756	18	(2%)	2	(11%)
1427	619	5	(0.8%)	0	
1428	473	8	(2%)	1	(13%)
1429[a]	736	108	(15%)	56	(52%)
1430	[2,955]	[2,763]	(94%)	[2,269]	(82%)
1439[b]	[624]	[405]	(65%)	[39]	(10%)
1440	616	69	(11%)	1	(1%)
1441	619	89	(14%)	0	
1442	438	49	(11%)	0	
1443	632	31	(5%)	4	(13%)
1444	826	238	(29%)	0	
1445	665	6	(1%)	0	
1446	847	1	(0.1%)	0	
1447	588	2	(0.3%)	0	
1448[a]	824	434	(54%)	136	(31%)
1449	[1,320]	[1,305]	(99%)	[925]	(71%)
1450	[1,520]	[1,403]	(92%)	[875]	(61%)
1451	723	188	(26%)	10	(5%)
1452	520	6	(1%)	0	
1453	410	8	(2%)	0	
1454	465	3	(1%)	0	
1455	482	1	(0.2%)	1	(100%)
1456[a]	650	329	(51%)	122	(37%)
1457	1,290	1,156	(90%)	644	(50%)
1458[b]	655	300	(46%)	187	(62%)

Note: Brackets indicate incomplete reporting for the year.
[a] Diagnoses and plague cases all after 1 July.
[b] Plague cases scattered in year.

There is certainly no evidence that the diagnosis reported was made or even confirmed by someone with a medical background. One suspects that the reporting gravedigger may have been required to bring back this information, no matter how the diagnosis had been made originally. It is possible that the two different scribes recording the two series did not always see the same grave-

Table 2–2. *Seasonal incidence of pondi during major pondi years*

Year	Total pondi cases	Diagnoses made from 1 July to 31 October			
		Pondi cases	P cases	Total diagnosed	% P
1425	117	106 (91%)	2	276	0.7
1430	28	26 (93%)	1,674	1,992	84
1444	51	51 (100%)	0	98	0
1450	75	74 (99%)	722	1,060	68

digger when the official reports were given, or that assistants were occasionally required to carry information to one or the other office. The diagnosis of a few individual cases in 1458 varied between the books, so presumably the Grascia notary was not simply copying the guild register.

CAUSES OF DEATH IN THE BOOKS OF THE DEAD

Nonspecific chronic ills

The diagnoses seem to have been kept in order to monitor the progression of plague within the city. When a person was ill for more than a week prior to death, "plague" was not the most likely cause of death. The record is thus deeply colored by its purpose of monitoring plague. But the other causes of death that occasionally appear in the record illustrate what else claimed the lives of Florentines, even in epidemic years. Table 2–3 provides tallies of the leading causes of death presented in the *Grascia morti* and the guild's first *Libro dei morti*. The most prominent diagnosis, plague, will require separate discussion and will thus be postponed until the following chapter.

Old age. First among the other causes, in numbers of deaths per year, is "old age." With it probably belong deaths from a few other noticeable chronic diseases, including gout, colic, and respiratory infections. *Vecchiaia,* old age, was the second most frequently cited cause of death in the mortality registers. Several studies, all using Florentine sources, have attempted to define life expectancies in the Renaissance. All agree that it was quite unusual to survive seventy years. Whether one looks at the diaries and

Table 2–3. Major "causes" of death reported in the Grascia Morti and Libri dei Morti, by year

Year	% Diagnosed	Plague	Old age	Ill-ness	Bachi	Fever	Neo-natal	Pondi	Mal Maestro	This-ico	Vaiuolo	Child-birth (mother)	Gocci-ola	Scesa	Uscita
1424	96	900	91	41	32	34	29	9	21	13	30	5	6	6	—
1425	75	14	129	38	80	96	40	117	27	14	15	13	3	13	6
1426	2	2	4	1	1	3	1	2	—	—	—	—	—	—	—
1427	0.8	—	—	—	—	—	—	—	—	—	—	—	—	—	—
1428	2	1	—	—	—	—	6	—	—	—	—	—	—	8	—
1429	15	46	15	6	6	16	4	3	1	3	47	15	1	1	5
1430	94	2,265	63	72	51	37	38	28	35	12	—	4	4	11	2
1439	65	39	65	67	35	52	17	3	16	10	32	2	3	12	—
1440	11	1	29	10	5	4	—	1	1	4	8	9	1	3	—
1441	14	—	45	15	13	7	4	2	6	2	2	1	4	1	—
1442	11	—	19	4	9	7	2	—	1	1	—	1	—	1	—
1443	5	5	9	1	1	—	2	3	—	1	—	—	3	—	—
1444	29	—	54	24	33	11	8	51	14	4	3	10	—	5	3
1445	1	—	1	—	—	—	1	—	—	—	—	—	—	—	—
1446	0.1	—	—	—	—	—	—	—	—	—	—	—	—	—	—
1447	0.3	—	—	—	—	—	—	—	—	—	—	—	1	—	—
1448	54	140	54	51	33	51	26	21	13	14	2	10	7	9	3
1449	99	889	65	44	44	16	20	—	6	14	2	6	17	1	1
1450	92	882	89	86	38	29	33	75	21	15	3	15	14	6	1
1451	26	9	51	12	20	7	7	7	6	6	13	1	8	2	—
1452	1	—	1	—	2	1	2	—	—	—	—	—	—	1	—
1453	2	—	—	2	—	1	1	—	—	2	—	—	1	—	—
1454	1	—	1	—	1	1	—	—	—	—	—	—	—	—	—
1455	0.2	1	1	—	—	—	—	—	—	—	—	—	—	—	—
1456	51	126	36	28	18	4	30	5	12	21	1	4	6	2	—
1457	90	899	102	58	27	31	67	3	18	33	3	9	17	4	—
Totals		6,219	924	560	449	408	338	330	198	169	161	105	96	86	21

letters of wealthy Florentine merchants or considers the life tables calculated from tax surveys, "old age" seems to have indicated survival only to one's fifties or sixties.[19]

In the books the actual or estimated age of the deceased is rarely stated, unless the victim reached a very advanced age. Three examples, all from 1456, illustrate this:

19 August, Filippo, who was a threader . . . was 102 years old.

27 September, Fruosina, a widow, . . . was about 100 years old.

11 October, Piero di Nardo, a fisherman, . . . was extremely old, more than 100 years.[20]

From Table 2–4 we can see that in most years women outnumbered men two to one in dying of old age. Of 891, 596 (67%) of the diagnoses, *de vecchiaia,* were of women. Herlihy and Klapisch-Zuber have shown that among females listed in the *Grascia morti,* 1424–30, old age was the second leading cause of death, whereas it was only the fourth most frequent diagnostic category among males. In all age brackets that they surveyed with the 1427 *catasto* (a large tax survey) of Florence and her territories, Herlihy and Klapisch-Zuber found that men outnumbered women by ratios averaging around 1:1.10. For all age categories except a small cluster of individuals around fifty-five years of age, the ratio of males to females was greater than one, and this included all the individuals who declared themselves to be over sixty years of age. This "masculinizing" tendency of the catasto is particularly pronounced among wealthier households. When Herlihy and Klapisch-Zuber considered literary sources such as the *ricordanze* of wealthy merchants, the picture of men surviving to old age more frequently than did women was dramatic.[21]

Nevertheless they were convinced that both the fiscal survey and the family diarists underreported the number of women alive in Florence, although for very different reasons. Because diaries were written by men in their later years, recording for their descendants the history of the family, the only deaths of women in the family journal would be those who had died younger than the author, usually in childbearing years. Male lineage was always traced, so that when a woman survived her husband, only her sons' stories would be followed in the ricordanze. Women who survived their merchant or banker husbands seldom left their own diaries.

Table 2–4. *Deaths from old age, by year, comparing death totals to percentage of female victims of old age*

Year	Total	Females	Females (%)
1424	91	62	68
1425	129	95	74
1429	15	9	60
1430	63	43	68
1439	65	42	65
1441	45	25	56
1442	19	11	58
1443	9	6	67
1444	54	43	80
1445	1	1	100
1448	54	32	59
1449	65	40	62
1450	89	62	70
1451	51	34	67
1452	1	1	100
1454	1	1	100
1455	1	1	100
1456	36	23	64
1457	102	65	64
Totals	891	596	67% (mean)

The bias of the tax survey, on the other hand, was a financial one. Families whose resources were adequate, though meagre in comparison with the greats of mercantile Florence, might need to support a widow for many years after her husband died and after her family's fortune had technically been dispensed to the male heirs. Herlihy and Klapisch-Zuber felt that a large number of such women, destitute and widowed, migrated to Florence in their later years to relieve the family's burden of caring for them. In the city they would have to rely on charity and slim handouts from relatives. Because they were truly miserable and propertyless, they were of no interest to the tax assessors.[22]

Thus Herlihy and Klapisch-Zuber argue that the disproportionate number of women among those dead of old age is one of the few records accurately reflecting the greater number of older women in Florence. Once past her childbearing years, a woman naturally had a much greater chance of survival to old age, even without the added numbers from a selective immigration to the city.

The Books of the Dead allow at least one other hypothesis to explain the imbalance in male and female deaths from vecchiaia. Popular literature suggests that a large number of other diseases, among them "dropsy" (*gocciola*), shortness of breath or difficulty in breathing (*ambascia*), catarrh (*catarro* and *scesa*), phthisis (*tisico*), chest pains (*mal di petto*), flank pains (*fianco* and *sciatica*), bladder stones (*mal di pietra*), and gout (*gotte*) were frequent companions of the elderly. Although there are not many cases of some of these ailments reported among the causes of death, for some (gotte, mal di pietra, and ambascia) all the victims are male adults. For others (mal di petto, gocciola, and scesa) the majority of victims were male: 60 percent of all cases from 1424 to 1450. With the infirmities that must have involved some infectious disease (tisico and catarro), a substantial number of the deaths were young children and the diseases thus do not seem to be afflictions simply of the elderly. But chronic diseases, especially those with symptoms that distinguished them from general old age, were the diseases of older men.

Literary evidence outside the Books of the Dead supports this conclusion that there were specific chronic diseases more familiar to adults, whether or not they were responsible for deaths. Alessandra Strozzi, writing to her son when she was only forty-two years old, regarded her affliction with *scesa* as proof that she was entering old age:

I received your letter a few days ago, on the eighth of August [1448], and I didn't answer immediately because I have had the scesa for over a month; I'm sorry. I am getting old and becoming less healthy daily.[23]

Archbishop Antoninus of Florence included a lengthy, meticulous account in his *Summa Theologica* of the multisystem failures common in old age. Many deaths, especially those of men, may have received these more refined diagnoses rather than being dismissed simply as old age.[24] Of all older persons listed as "ill" at the time of the Pisan catasto (1428–9) there was no pronounced excess of women among the aged.[25] If one does not elect to add in a large number of widowed and indigent women, missing from the survey, to the population statistics reflected in these catasto surveys, one gathers the impression that early Renaissance societies invested more interest, before and after death, in the illnesses of men. This, too, is consistent with the general "masculinizing" tendency

of record keeping – a relative neglect of women – noted by Herlihy and Klapisch–Zuber.

Long illness. The third most frequent cause of death found in the
Grascia morti tells us very little about mortality in Florence. "Long
illness," seen in a number of variations (*lunga infermità, infermità,
malattia lunga, era infermo*), is not even a diagnosis that could lead
us to conclusions about the extent of chronic illness in Florence.
The diagnosis frequently may signify no more than the fact that
the individual had been sick long enough for the certifier to rule
out death from plague. Thus the "wife of Francesco" who died 12
August 1450 was said to have been ill "long enough." A plague
death was possible if the person died within around two to six
days after the onset of illness.

Fever. The fifth leading cause of death is not much more specific
than long illness. It tells us only that infectious diseases were common. Unlike long illness, fevers do seem to occur slightly more
frequently in the spring, although this characteristic helps little in
isolating the probable causes of these deaths in modern terms. In
seven years selected because they provide nearly complete registration of cause of death, sixty-seven fever deaths occurred between 16 March and 15 June, compared with eighty-seven in the
subsequent two and one half summer months, the months most
favorable to plague. Considering that both deaths and diagnosis
of cause of death were more likely in the summer, springtime fevers are potentially very interesting. In the record, lethal infectious
diseases occurring in the spring would not be masked and confused by summer plague cases, so the clustering of deaths due to
fever in this season could reveal the recurrence of a nonplague
epidemic. The occasional combination of fever with catarro, scesa,
and mal di petto, all referring to respiratory symptoms at death,
suggests that pneumonias and other respiratory tract infections occurred routinely. But in the Books of the Dead no discrete epidemics of "fever" emerge. The prevalence in the spring points
instead to periodic, "immunizing" diseases of childhood, and respiratory diseases that snuffed out the lives of the old and the very
young. About 52 percent of all fever deaths in these years were
male and 46 percent of fever victims were children.

Diseases of little children

Fortunately, we can say much more about the infections that killed little children, because the mortality patterns among them strongly resemble those in modern developing nations. Periodic epidemic diseases and chronic unsanitary environments were responsible for killing around half of those born before they reached ten years of age.

Bachi. After plague, long illness, and old age, "worms" were the fourth leading cause of death. The diagnosis of plague, which we have not yet discussed, the obvious phenomena of chronic illness and old age, and the lists of afflictions that troubled adults seem comfortably akin to our expectations about life and death in the fifteenth century. The prominence of *bachi* among the causes of death, however, makes us realize for the first time how different was the fifteenth-century way of looking at illness from our own.

Very few serious helminthic and nematode infections, those of the worms and parasites studied by parasitologists today, are common in temperate climates, and those that are recognized as "worms" do not kill their victims rapidly. Common round worms (*Ascaris*) and tapeworms allow their victims to linger, often until their adult years. Probably most Florentine observers were not describing infection with pathogens familiar to us as worms.[26]

From the humble certifier of cause of death in Florence to the university physician writing about worms, all seemed in fact to be referring to episodes of diarrhea frequent among young children. The description of stomach worms offered by Ferrarese physician Giovanni Michele Savonarola illustrates how easily Galenic physiology accommodated this strange diagnosis.[27] Worms were generated in the stomach following an inauspicious mixture of the humors, resulting from causes like eating the wrong foods. Young children were particularly vulnerable. Children under seven years should not consume "phlegmatic and viscous foods," because these impeded digestion and because such foods invoked an opposite humoral response, that is, they exaggerated the warm, wet humors of little children.[28] Worms that remained in the stomach caused nausea and vomiting; when the worms passed further, diarrhea resulted.

Anything that slowed digestion exposed an infant to worms,

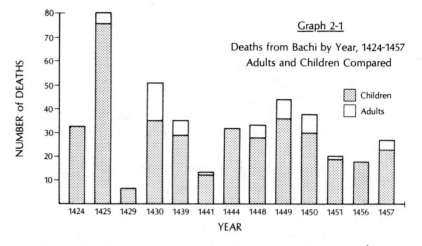

Graph 2-1

Deaths from Bachi by Year, 1424-1457

Adults and Children Compared

including cold air and strong winds. Savonarola discussed the benefits of keeping a fire in children's rooms to decrease the harmful side effects of cold air. With the attention to detail appropriate to a well-trained physician, he specified the most suitable woods for burning.[29] He advised mothers to take precautions in spring and fall, keeping the digestive tract free of the leaden weight of improper foods by careful attention to diet and through the use of purges. The recommendations were typical and understood by most well-to-do Florentines. Giovanni Morelli went so far as to pass along his own preventive for worms, purging with rhubarb preparations.[30]

The individuals who died from worms, according to the Florentine Books of the Dead, are analyzed in Graph 2–1, including all the years in which more than 10 percent of the recorded deaths carried any diagnosis at all. The shaded areas further represent the individuals who were probably dependent children. As the graph shows, over 85 percent of all victims from worms were children.

At times the preference for little children is quite dramatic. In the very small number of cases where age at death was specified in the record, the victims of bachi were mere infants:

3 July 1430, Biagio d'Antonio Mazochi . . . was six months old.

13 Jan. 1449, Manetto . . . was three months old.

2 July 1424, the baby boy of Martino . . . was two months old.

17 July 1424, the little girl of Rosello, painter . . . was one month old.

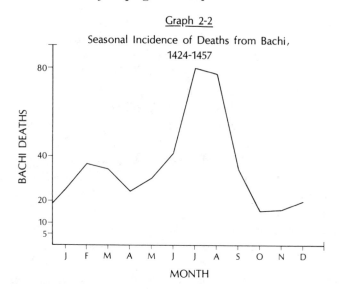

Graph 2-2

Seasonal Incidence of Deaths from Bachi,
1424-1457

20 March 1425, a baby girl . . . three weeks old.

12 April 1425, a baby boy . . . two days old.

Reasoning that the scribe bothered to record age only because the victims were unusually young, we could conclude that this list represents the exceptions. But it certainly also indicates that "worms" were an acceptable cause of death in early infancy, again suggesting that a literal understanding of "worms" to explain these deaths misses the mark. Most children less than six months old would have little or no exposure to intestinal parasites especially if they were swaddled and nursing.

Bachi victims were usually children. Neither sex was at a greater risk (53 percent of the deaths were of males). The season for worms was not, however, the spring or fall. As Graph 2–2 illustrates, bachi deaths were most likely to occur in the summer months with plague (July and August). The graph presents aggregate numbers, by month, of all bachi deaths recorded between 1424 and 1458.

Nevertheless the graph may be deceptive, because summer plagues motivated cause-of-death reporting and all diagnoses thus tend to rise in the summer months. Moreover, in some years (e.g., 1424 and 1456), the only record we have begins during the mid-summer. In other years (e.g., 1430 and 1449), diagnoses end suddenly in October. In the plague year of 1449, 93 percent (41 of 44) of the bachi victims died before June 15, but in the following year, 95 percent of the cases fell between 16 July and 1 October. We must conclude that bachi could be associated with a seasonal rise in incidence, yet need not be linked to the summer infections.

The clinical and epidemiological picture of bachi resembles the syndrome called "weanling diarrhea" by experts in the health problems of lesser developed regions today.[31] During the early months of an infant's life, breast feeding provides fully adequate caloric intake in addition to its immunological benefits.[32] When fed only breast milk an infant will be protected from a multitude of common infections, notably intestinal pathogens. But, from the onset of weaning, diarrhea repeatedly challenges the infant. A mild amount of gastrointestinal dysfunction and subsequent weight loss is common when solid foods are first added to the infant's diet, and this response is normal even in healthy infants fed sterile foods. When supplements, often cereals, are administered under deficient sanitary conditions, the diarrhea may be accentuated and prolonged by the onslaught of many microorganisms. Intestinal pathogens are readily transmitted to and from other children in the family. After every such episode, the child risks developing longer-term malnutrition.

The counsel wealthier Italians received in the fifteenth century was to allow a child to nurse at least one year, up to two years for a more prized male child. Communal statutes required a wet nurse to keep a child thirty months, but from this we should not conclude that breast milk would be the only nutrition provided. A cautious parent would spend much time selecting a suitable wet nurse, one who met prescribed physical and moral descriptions.[33] How many supplemental, calorie-rich foods the child may have been allowed after the early months depended in part upon the material resources of the mother or nurse. A better paid nurse, thus charged with a greater responsibility for the health of the child, could afford the supplemental water mixed with sweet wine, the rich broths, and the fruit mixtures and special cakes recommended for children at weaning. Many mothers of necessity nursed their own children and weaned them early in order to take on paying nurslings; still others could ill afford supplements and thus prolonged breast feeding.

After the first six months or so, breast milk will increasingly fail to meet the total caloric requirements of the growing child.[34] Although fully adequate in protein and still protecting the infant immunologically, milk alone will retard the infant's growth and development and lead the child eventually to a state of primary caloric malnutrition. Here again, infection and diarrheal disease may exacerbate the underlying problem of malnutrition, and each bout with diarrhea will leave the infant closer to protein-energy malnutrition. The good health and growth of children at this very vulnerable stage largely depend upon preventing infections. Where this fails, diarrheal disease can provide the most serious threat to young lives after they have survived the neonatal period. Along with respiratory infections, ordinary diarrheas are the most common causes of death among children in less developed nations today.

Weanling diarrhea usually begins acutely between four and thirty months of age, subjecting the child and his or her caretakers to frequent, progressive, semiliquid stools (three to twenty times a day). In areas were malnutrition and poor sanitation prevail, over a third of the affected individuals also pass some blood or mucus with the diarrhea. Fever is not a prominent symptom, but the child is irritable and colicky throughout the usual four- to five-day course of illness. Dehydration can cause a more rapid course to death, especially in a younger child, and this may help to explain why summer was the season of greatest bachi mortality.

One brief comparative example may be cited to show how diarrheas of early childhood could be responsible for much of the normal infant mortality in preindustrial Europe. Stephen Hatvani's statistics, collected and analyzed in the eighteenth century, describe mortality patterns in his native Debrecen, Hungary, then a town of 20,000.[35] Hatvani concluded that infant and child mortality, especially in the first five years, was the most crucial obstacle to longevity. A five-year average of infant deaths during the first year of life showed his contemporaries that diarrhea was the single most important problem of infancy and accounted for a staggering 229.5 deaths per thousand infants per year. There is little reason to suspect that the situation was not similar to Florence in the fifteenth century, and so the recorded deaths from bachi may be a significant clue to understanding normal early childhood mortality.

Whether calorie depleted (primary malnutrition) or subjected to recurrent diarrheal disease (secondary malnutrition), many children must have indeed suffered from a watery, mucoid diarrhea that looked like small "worms" to observers. The infection and death of some Florentine children while others were spared may well have depended upon their socioeconomic status, but this is difficult to prove with existing data.

Pondi and uscita. Bachi was a different diarrheal disease from the other acute diarrheas that afflicted Florentines. Pondi usually implied a "heaviness" and was a popular term for the Latin *tenesmus,* meaning a gripping or cramping in the gut. Acute dysentery would be the best general translation in modern terms. *Uscita* referred to much the same severe, explosive diarrhea (it means roughly "exit of the gut"), although it seems to be used only with reference to very young infants. Very few cases of uscita appear in the death registers, so for purposes of discussion we will consider only pondi.[36]

Fifteenth-century observers recognized pondi well, though they seldom described epidemics. Pondi also was predominantly a disease of children. Fifty-one cases of pondi death were registered in 1444, and forty-five of them were children. Yet the chroniclers and diarists are silent about the epidemics. The only outbreak of pondi vividly described by a Florentine observer, Giovanni Minerbetti, is that of 1390. It could easily be distinguished from the epidemic of "pestilential pustules" that same year:

Toward the end of July of the year 1390 the infirmity of pondi began in Florence, and physicians considered it a branch of pestilence. This malady was tenacious, lasting well over a month, and most of those who had the disease died of it. It was a foul, unpleasant affliction, and he who contracted it spewed out blood, soiling the entire house in which he lived. Those who suffered also had great discomfort; their bodies were wracked with pains. It killed many men, women, and children and lasted until late September.[37]

The *Grascia morti* reflect only the barest outline of the sudden epidemic that the chronicler described. From mid-March until early July the record shows a steady daily death rate (2.4 to 2.7). Then the count soared to 10, then 15, per day in late July. A gap in the record intervened until late August, at which time the daily deaths had fallen to four. By the end of September, until late December, the deaths per day were a mere 1.6.

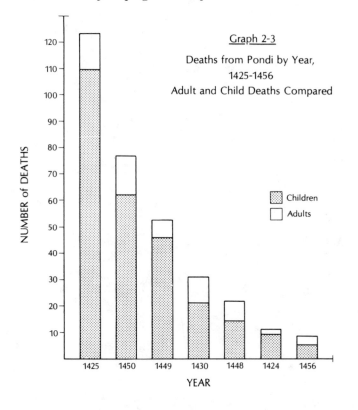

Graph 2-3

Deaths from Pondi by Year,
1425-1456

Adult and Child Deaths Compared

The *Grascia morti* do not document a high adult mortality, how-ever, so perhaps Minerbetti exaggerated in an effort to depict the high morbidity of pondi. Adults do suffer dramatically from acute dysentery, but they usually can prevent the severe dehydration that so rapidly kills young children. Even wealthy gentlewomen like Alessandra Strozzi could suffer from this unpleasant afflic-tion.[38] But few succumbed as did the very young. Graph 2–3 shows the rather large proportion of children among the pondi and uscita deaths. More so than bachi, however, there was a pronounced seasonal incidence of pondi epidemics: late summer. Graph 2–4 compares the seasonal occurrence of pondi during several epidem-ics. The one year in which no cases of plague appeared, but in which causes of death were nonetheless registered (1444), illus-trates that pondi epidemics occurred independently of plague.

Decreasing numbers of victims with increasing age, taken to-gether with a distinctive seasonal and periodic incidence, fit the pattern of dysentery, and the hot, dry Florentine late summer was an ideal time for the fecal-oral spread of infections. Less developed

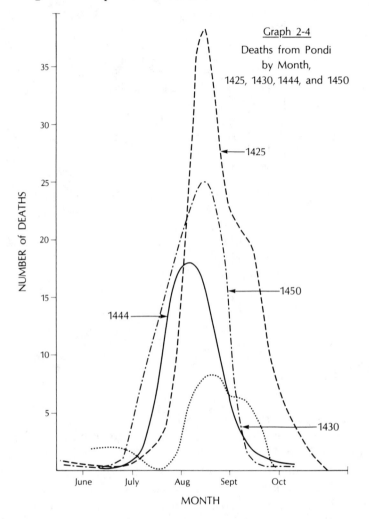

Graph 2-4

Deaths from Pondi
by Month,
1425, 1430, 1444, and 1450

NUMBER of DEATHS

MONTH

regions today experience a cyclic recurrence of epidemic dysentery, about three times in ten years. Were diagnoses more uniformly available in the *Grascia morti,* perhaps the pattern of pondi deaths would resemble this "periodic endemicity." No one organism now accounts for all the flare-ups in a locale; in fact, several pathogens are often responsible even in the same epidemic wave. *Shigella* species, the most common cause of bloody diarrheas, *Salmonella* organisms, *Escherichia coli,* and viral gastroenteritis with secondary bacterial infection are now likely causes of an epidemic dysentery, and there is no reason to suspect that they were not equally common in Renaissance Florence. Where poor sanitation and undernutrition prevail, the young are the most vulnerable, even though all age groups suffer.[39]

Miscellaneous diagnoses

The remaining diagnoses could be gathered into two separate categories for the purpose of discussion. First are the killers of little children, causes of death that seldom claimed the lives of adults. Second are diagnoses that probably included infectious diseases we would expect to see in epidemic form.

Foremost in the first category is *mal maestro*. Literally "master disease," mal maestro must have referred to any convulsive illness of undetermined duration. Savonarola warned his audience of mothers and midwives that mal maestro was particularly grave in the neonatal period. He held the mother's milk responsible for producing the disease and advised that she follow his dietary advice closely. His discussion supports the hypothesis that mal maestro was usually a disease of nurslings. Savonarola's use of the term *maestro* for the umbilical cord, *maestretto,* may hint at a popular explanation for the disease: obvious infection at the cord site.[40] Modern medicine suggests a very likely explanation in neonatal tetanus or neonatal sepsis. Early-life infections commonly end in seizures.

The diagnosis of mal maestro seems to indicate in most cases at least one episode of seizures prior to death. The record does not indicate which cases may have been chronic seizure disorders and which cases were only a terminal episode of tonic-clonic seizures. Notary Ser Lapo Mazzei, lamenting his son's chronic illness from mal maestro, described an affliction that recurred every two months for over twenty-five months.[41] Future masters were warned to make certain that the slaves they purchased were not affected by mal maestro.[42] Such examples support an argument that true epilepsies were included in the diagnosis. Nevertheless the general pattern is quite different.

Seizures claimed a surprising number of victims, surprising because mal maestro, like bachi, is a diagnosis that has little directly translatable meaning to modern medicine. As with worms, it is difficult to accept the dictionary translation of epilepsy at face value. Just once in the causes of death an alternative meaning epilepsy, *mal di caduta* ("falling sickness") was offered to explain this cause of death further.[43] The diagnosis would be better translated as convulsions instead of epilepsy. It has two common causes in early childhood: dehydration, usually following diarrhea, and febrile seizures, often due to overwhelming infection.

The cases of mal maestro deaths are heaviest in the summer months, possibly because of the summer bias in all cause-of-death registrations: seasonal rise is depicted in Graph 2–5. A startling 95 percent of these cases were children; furthermore, 14 percent of the overall total were babies. There were only a handful of cases with specific indication of age at death, but in this small sample there are two medically distinct categories. First were those specifically under the twenty-eight days of age that constitutes the neonatal period: there were three babies eight or nine days old. Cases in the second category were slightly older – two to four months old. Some were also listed as being "at the nurse," but no age was recorded.

For somewhat older infants, severe dehydration commonly results in convulsions, and central nervous system infections such as meningitis could equally well explain a fifteenth-century diagnosis of mal maestro. But unlike pondi, there were never enough cases of this disease in any one year to suggest its epidemic character. So there is little to suggest that this affliction was due to any one type of infection, much less any one group of pathogens. Some combined diagnoses, mal maestro and bachi, or mal maestro and uscita, further encourage the conclusion that mal maestro designates the victims of early life infection and sepsis. Infants of well-known Florentine families appear among the lists of victims of mal maestro, whereas it is difficult to find Francesco di Matteo Palmieri, Fillipo Lippi, Giovanni Pitti, and the like among the fathers of pondi, bachi, and uscita victims.

The hazards of the neonatal period were not limited to the infections thus far discussed. In the major epidemic years neonatal deaths (not including those from mal maestro or from bachi) included eighty-eight premature infants, either "born before the time" (*nacque innanzi al tempo*) or "not born at the right time" (*non nacque al tempo*). There seems to be little distinction between these two diagnoses. Eleven were actually listed as aborted fetuses, probably over six months' gestation since the sex of the child was specified. Eight died during childbirth, and four cases of *mal di trassinato* may

Graph 2-5

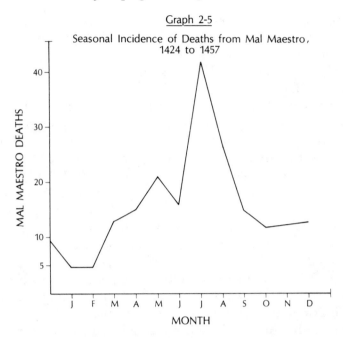

Seasonal Incidence of Deaths from Mal Maestro,
1424 to 1457

MAL MAESTRO DEATHS

40
30
20
10
5

J F M A M J J A S O N D

MONTH

also refer to deaths during the delivery. We know, because their age in days was recorded, that an additional forty-nine babies died in the neonatal period. Eleven more died because they were unable to nurse (*per non poppare* or *non poppava*). Florentines tended to baptize any child quickly, in order to save its soul, as an example from Gregorio Dati's diary vividly illustrates:

At the third hour of Thursday, 19 March 1405, Ginevra [his wife] gave birth to a female child of less than seven months. She had not realized that she was pregnant, since for four months she had been ailing as though she were not, and in the end she was unable to hold it. We baptized it at once in the Church of S. Giovanni. The sponsors were Bartolo, Monna Buona, another lady, and the blind woman. Having thought at first that it was a boy we named it Agnolo Giovanni. It died at dawn on Sunday morning 22 March, and was buried before the sermon.[44]

A category of childhood deaths of potential interest to epidemiologists is that relatively small group of children who smothered in bed, by their mothers' sides or at the wet nurse. They are usually referred to with the same word meaning "drowned" (*affogò*). These deaths, presumably from suffocation, may include very early reported cases of the sudden infant death syndrome

(SIDS), more familiarly known as crib death. A previously healthy infant is inexplicably found dead in its bed and the postmortem evaluation gives no obvious cause for the child's demise. Records earlier than the nineteenth century have not been studied in an attempt to trace the history of SIDS.[45]

Two historical associations with the Florentine data, however, minimize the hope that this syndrome can be seriously considered as a solution to the entries like "affogola la balia" (the nurse smothered her.) First is the curiosity that the diagnosis begins to appear with any frequency only toward the mid-fifteenth century. The earliest case is not truly smothering, but the death of an "infant girl of Barto di Lapo" by an ill-intentioned nurse ("per cattività della balia"). Thereafter one case of smothering appears in 1444, three in 1448, two in 1449, and one in 1450. Eight were recorded during the half-year for which diagnoses were given in 1456, and eleven more followed the next year. It is possible that a change in attitude toward that practice was emerging at midcentury, making infanticide more widely practiced.

The number of cases here is too small to draw any conclusion from the early Books of the Dead. Several researchers have pointed to a growing concern for the health and welfare of children, a concern that was reflected in a boom of hospitals and foundling homes dating from the end of the fourteenth century. What Herlihy has called a "new concern for the survival of children" was fairly widespread in French and Italian cities of the fifteenth century.[46] Whether this was due to a larger number of orphans and foundlings after the ravages of epidemics, the books do not tell us. They instead seem to show that infants and children were more vulnerable in the face of these epidemics than were adults.

Trexler holds that the origins of foundling homes lay rather in the "widespread infanticide and abandonment of children."[47] Though frugal city funding policies often regarded the care of infants as a church responsibility, both church and state seem to have increased their campaigns against the mother or wet nurse suspected of killing a child. The late fifteenth and sixteenth centuries, Trexler argues, saw increasing church and secular prosecutions of infanticide. The length and austerity of penance for any mother so accused increased during that time. After 1517 parents who kept a child with them in bed could be excommunicated if the child died. By the sixteenth century special wooden cribs with "little arches" over them were being used by cautious wet nurses. A hole carved out of the casing permitted only the breast to the infant. Later, even nurses were sometimes required to use these ingenious contraptions. Such a shift in attitudes toward the evil nurse can certainly be seen in Matteo Corsini's mid-fifteenth-century accusation that a certain Monna Piera, wife of Chaio in San Cassiano, killed his little son Horlando.[48]

But Trexler argued also that infanticide was more commonly practiced on female infants and demonstrated their higher death rates over the male infants brought to a foundling home in the 1440s and 1450s. Among "smothered" babies in the Books of the Dead, there is not a similar imbalance. The sample is quite small, but from 1444 to 1457 eight boys and five girls supposedly suffocated at the nurse. Furthermore, when we examine the cases of all smothered babies, no marked tendency for female children to die emerges (Table 2–5). If anything, there is a slight male bias in these few cases, similar, in fact, to the male bias seen in SIDS cases.

Foundling homes may have had different attitudes toward the survival of male and female children, but the first small series of smothering deaths in the city mortality registers does not suggest that well-paid wet nurses, or parents whose children died at home, had similar biases in reporting the casualty. Perhaps the interest in this diagnosis as an accusation was rising. Perhaps also, there was an interest in reporting cases of child deaths that were not due to plague.

The second broad category of miscellaneous diagnoses, infectious diseases that frequently reach epidemic proportions, reveals the most unexpected feature of the causes of death in the *Grascia morti*. Smallpox ranks tenth among the causes of death, just behind *thisico* (phthisis), a very rough diagnosis including tuberculosis. Neither of these major infectious diseases claimed many lives in early Renaissance Florence, at least during the plague years. Similarly, chronicles, diaries, and legislative reports did not report many deaths from these causes during the nonplague years. It is impressive that most of the infectious diseases regarded as common during the last two or three hundred years rarely deserved mention in the fifteenth century.

Savonarola declared that *varole* (for the Florentines, vaiuolo, or pox) and *fersa* (*rosolia* in Florentine, for measles) were common

Table 2–5. *Cases of Smothering in the* Grascia Morti

	Smothered at nurse	Smothered in bed	Smothered by mother's side	Died at the nurse
Male	8	4	2	9
Female	5	1	1	4

among children under seven years. Before the sixteenth century, however, physicians did not clinically distinguish between measles and a variety of other rash–producing diseases such as scarlet fever and rubella (German measles).[49] Savonarola also described smallpox as a rather benign, almost necessary, disease of children, purging and purifying the blood. Possibly a clinical distinction was not made between smallpox and chicken pox (*varicella*).

But even if we assume that smallpox was endemic in this society, its ravages were negligible in comparison with plague. Possibly it was not the same virus that afflicted Europeans two centuries later. Few years saw many deaths from vaiuolo in Florence, but there are discrete summer epidemics in 1425, 1429, 1439, and 1451 that peak in August. Fourteenth-century chroniclers had noted at least two epidemics of smallpox in Florence (1336 and 1363), but there are no accounts of the disease in any later literary source from Florence. At the worst, smallpox seemed to claim no more than fifty victims in an epidemic year, so it seems no wonder that this was not a greatly feared infection.

Perhaps a relatively nonvirulent strain of smallpox was responsible for these epidemics and virulent smallpox entered Italy at some later date. Perhaps smallpox was, like measles, poorly differentiated from other infections, particularly varicella or even from "plague pustules." This would mean that plague deaths were conflated with smallpox mortality, and that the major killing disease, plague, was often misdiagnosed.

NORMAL YEARS AND PLAGUE YEARS

Whether one looks at scattered accounts of plague epidemics in Florence among the chroniclers and diarists of the fifteenth century, or whether one uses the record of deaths in the *Grascia morti* and the *Libri dei morti,* the mortality pattern is of sawtooth, crisis mortality. The most serious limitation to a full understanding of

Table 2–6. *Seasonal deaths per day during nonepidemic years,*
1424–58

Season	Median	Mean	Standard deviation
January– 15 March	1.4	1.5	±0.4
16 March– 30 April	1.6	1.7	±0.5
May– 15 June	1.4	1.4	±0.3
16 June– 31 August	1.6	1.9	±1.0
September– October	1.5	1.6	±0.5
November– December	1.4	1.4	±0.4

periodic infections – and ordinary mortality – in Florence is the lack of any information on morbidity or illness that did not result in death. Without such data the best epidemiological analysis we can offer is a look at normal, seasonal changes in mortality.[50]

Table 2–6 summarizes the average deaths per day calculated from six arbitrarily chosen seasons. The seasonal periods were chosen in order to provide time periods large enough that deaths-per-day averages would not differ between years solely because the sample size was too small, but short enough to reveal unreported mortality-producing epidemics in the city. A "normal" year reflected slightly exaggerated mortality rates during the summer and early fall, and increased deaths in the early, but not the later, spring. Perhaps as important, the normal year did not show increased mortality in the November to December, or in the May to 15 June periods.

In Table 2–6, records of thirteen years between 1424 and 1457 document "normal" nonepidemic years. The large standard deviation of normal summer deaths-per-day disappears if two of the thirteen years averaged in the death rates are considered to be epidemic years. In 1427 and 1446 summer deaths were substantially elevated, well beyond the normal rate, as Table 2–7 shows. These averages have been further compared in this table to the known nonplague epidemic year of 1444, a year of summer dysentery

Table 2–7. *Seasonal deaths per day during epidemic years, 1427, 1444, 1446*

Season	1427	1444	1446
January– 15 March	1.8	1.3	1.4
16 March– 30 April	2.1	1.6	2.6
May– 15 June	1.1	1.7	1.7
16 June– 31 August	4.1	4.3	4.1
September– October	2.2	3.1	2.5
November– December	1.7	1.6	1.8

(pondi).[51] All three of the summer death years compared directly in this table show a rise in deaths from 16 June through October that was greater than that expected in a nonepidemic year, and thus the data can be used to support ahypothesis that 1427 and 1446 were additional minor epidemic years not cited in either cause-of-death entries or in chronicle accounts. The 1427 and 1446 statistics also suggest that there were unreported epidemics in the early spring season, again because the mortality levels exceeded those normally expected.

Markedly elevated winter death rates do not appear in any year, with or without cause-of-death notations, to suggest the independent appearance of lethal winter pestilences such as influenza. The year 1427 saw European-wide influenza, but many of the epidemics occurred in the summer months, at least north of the Alps.[52] A gentle rise in deaths over a longer period of time might reflect less acute epidemic flare-ups, but without the companion cause-of-death citations, it is difficult to say what disease or diseases, if any, may have been responsible for increases in the mortality rate. One might expect that childhood infectious diseases, such as measles, mumps, chicken pox, or whooping cough, would contribute to early spring rises in deaths. Similarly a greater number of adult, especially "old age," victims may reflect late winter rises in respiratory diseases. The lack of dramatic increases in mortality rates from such epidemics does not suggest that such afflictions were uncommon or unimportant, only that they cannot be easily distinguished in the mortality data.

A GENERAL PICTURE OF FLORENTINE HEALTH AND DISEASE

Florentine economic prosperity in the fourteenth and fifteenth centuries depended upon local industries, particularly the wool trade, and the far-reaching markets Florentine merchants had established. Geographically Florence's location on the Arno River allowed her wool industry a competitive advantage over Tuscan neighbors, because the hill towns had less generous, predictable water supplies. But the river was often torrential in spring and autumn, and usually sluggish in the summer. Because business activity was restricted and because ordinary water supplies were limited and often polluted, the annual summer drought made daily survival difficult in this season for many Florentine laborers even without the presence of epidemic diseases. Although winters could be fairly cold and wet, attended by coughs, catarrhs, and other respiratory diseases that victimized the very old and the very young, the summer drought was by far more threatening for the majority of Florence's inhabitants.

Not surprisingly the spectrum of diseases reported in the Books of the Dead reflects the ordinary infectious causes of death that claimed heavy tolls among the very young. Most disease was infectious, and many individuals had to traverse a difficult microbiological battlefield only to be cut down after childhood by plague or some other febrile disease. Children probably had to face periodic viral epidemics such as smallpox, measles, whooping cough, influenza, and dysentery, all of which contributed to mortality.

Plague looms so large in the early Renaissance centuries that it is easy to forget that many other epidemic and endemic diseases existed, and probably added to the mortality of plague years. But even with these fairly good records it is difficult to piece together the evidence reflecting ordinary mortality. If a nonwealthy adult died from some other cause than plague, it was not likely to receive much attention. Miscellaneous afflictions are occasionally cited as causes and the scattered diagnoses help to support the picture of "periodic epidemicity" described in the first chapter. Other epidemics formed a constant backdrop to the drama of plague. They were expected visitors.

Although many diseases may have preyed selectively on the young, the poor, and those unable to leave an unhealthy Florentine summer for a safer retreat, the kinds of infections that killed them suggest further that securing adequate nutrition was an added obstacle to survival. Both malnutrition and poor sanitation suffuse this picture of fifteenth-century urban mortality.

Neither can we ignore the fact that none of the other diseases, epidemic or endemic, seems to be responsible for heavy mortality in the fifteenth century. The absence of noticeable epidemic mortality from smallpox, typhus fever, influenza, and the lack of good fifteenth-century descriptions of chronic suffering from tuberculosis and venereal disease are puzzling. This "missing mortality," lacking from both the literary accounts and the registers of deaths, raises two separate questions for discussion in the following chapters. First we must examine in some detail the extent to which diagnoses of plague may have been inaccurate. Then we must consider the historical significance of the chroniclers' perception that plague and only plague was important.

3

Plague in Florence

There are many different problems involved in making a retrospective diagnosis of the cause or causes of past epidemics.[1] The individuals whose "true" cause of death we seek lived five hundred years ago, in a different culture and in a different ecological setting from those in today's Florence. The words describing illness are embedded in a system of medical diagnosis that shares little with our own classifications and explanations. To understand what effects plague actually had in Florence from 1348 to 1460 we will, for the moment, ignore the context in which the diagnosis of plague was made in individual cases, and we will assume that "plague" refers to *Y. pestis* infection. This chapter will first examine the characteristics of Florentine plagues from 1348 to 1460, without attempting to argue that these epidemics and modern plague have a direct correlation.

Even without comparing medieval and modern plagues we can see that fifteenth-century plagues differed in three major respects from those of the fourteenth century: mortality rates, seasonal peak of mortality, and noticeable clustering of deaths. Thus epidemics of plague changed over the course of a few generations, in a way that contemporaries would have noticed: They became less virulent. But during the course of the century from 1350 to 1450, the very witnesses to these events changed their own perceptions of how to recognize plague and how to confirm individual cases of the infection. When we examine closely the individual cases of plague recorded in the Books of the Dead, we find some reason to doubt that "plague" always refers to *Y. pestis* infection.

Epidemiologically the best resolution of the dilemma between "plague" and "plagues" in fifteenth-century Florence is to assume that witnesses had little diagnostic sophistication and that a "plague" was a mortality crisis due to many infectious causes, including *Y. pestis*. Historically the best resolution of the dilemma is to understand that the growing perception of "plague" as a contagious disease was one that was reinforced with each epidemic.

DEMOGRAPHIC BACKGROUND

Florentine population changes in the late Middle Ages were much the same as those of other European cities from 1250 to 1500. Short-term, episodic fluctuations of war, famine, and epidemic mortality crises gave every locale its own particular demographic history, but generally until the early 1300s cities tended to absorb the surplus rural population of countrysides that had grown far too populous. Throughout Western Europe both urban and rural areas were beginning to experience widespread subsistence crises before the Black Death of 1348.[2]

Economic hardships and demographic decline were certainly as important features of Tuscan rural society, as elsewhere, in 1300. The generation living in Florence before 1348 had witnessed rapid population growth at the turn of the century. The walls of the city had to be extended twice during the fourteenth century to gather in a population which probably reached a peak of 120,000 by the late 1330s.

A severe famine in 1327–30 fell hardest on the overpopulated countryside, but Florence herself did not suffer greatly until political and demographic crises enhanced the subsistence shortfalls of the early 1340s. The pestilence of 1340 left over 15,000 dead, a new economic crisis followed the collapse of the Bardi and Peruzzi banking houses, the despotism of Walter of Brienne added to the city's deep-seated political unrest, and the famine of 1347 seemed a fitting close to the disasters. It was instead only the beginning. During the spring and summer of 1348, the first plague in Florence arrived to claim as many as 50,000 lives out of a population now under 100,000.[3]

This staggering decline in population was not permanently reversed for over a century. Between the Black Death and 1427, Florence lost between 1 percent and 1.25 percent of her population annually. The longer perspective shows just how great was the demographic collapse: Between 250 and 325 people lived in Florence in 1338 as compared to every 100 alive in 1427. After eight plagues, in 1427, 27 percent of Florence's preplague population survived, living in the larger city's shell.[4]

Nevertheless after each of the five major fourteenth-century plagues, immigration from countryside to city helped Florence to reequilibrate to a population of around 60,000.[5] As the countryside became further depressed during the early decades of the fifteenth century, the city total fell and the first major fiscal survey of 1427, the catasto, revealed only around 37,000 city inhabitants. Finally in the 1460s Florence's population once again began to climb, at a gradual growth rate of 0.4 percent per year.

In Florence, as elsewhere in Western Europe, demographic stagnation characterized both urban and rural areas during the first century after the advent of bubonic plague. Only a few researchers believe that plague independently caused the depression of the early fifteenth century, but most admit that the economic depression of these years cannot be fully explained without reference to the virulence and frequency of *Y. pestis* outbreaks. Nevertheless everywhere in Europe the plagues of the fourteenth century were more destructive than in the following half-century, so plague alone could not have been responsible for the lag in recovery until the mid-fifteenth century.[6]

In order to argue that plague epidemics were causing more damage than they could have by a simple periodic extraction of people from the landscape, many demographic and economic historians have looked to the ages of plague victims to explain why the decline was so profound. After extensive demographic analysis of the 1427 tax survey, Herlihy and Klapisch-Zuber suggested that plagues may have been particularly lethal to little children. Although plagues tended to stimulate birth rates during the years immediately following an epidemic, recurring epidemics and heavy losses in the years before peak adult fertility could have contributed to the century-long recession.[7]

MORTALITY RATES OF MAJOR AND MINOR PLAGUES

Judging from the Books of the Dead, the absolute numbers of deaths during Florentine plagues declined during the early fifteenth century: Plagues after 1424 killed many fewer people in Florence than they did in the fourteenth century. Of course, fewer inhabitants lived in the path of plague, so absolute totals may not reflect mortality rates. The city population of Florence probably did not exceed 40,000 throughout the 1420–60 period, so the 3,000–

4,000 deaths in peak plague years of the early fifteenth century disclose overall mortality rates under 10 percent. In comparison, the deaths of no fewer than 12,000 city inhabitants in 1400, out of a population of around 60,000, are at the 20 percent level. The later plagues were less virulent.

Chroniclers and diarists also reflect a decline in plague virulence by speaking of epidemics as though they were more a nuisance than a serious threat.[8] Many of these references to plague, sometimes a single account about plague in the city, show how peripheral to important events recurrent plague became. For example, Matteo Corsini noted casually in 1438 that his third child, Ginevra, was not born and baptized at home "because we had fled the plague, there being several deaths from it in Florence." The plague of 1430 barely received notice by contemporaries, competing for their attention with the recent Milanese wars, new fiscal efforts to make the state solvent, and political intrigue. When Filippo Rinuccini sat down to write his family's memoirs at midcentury, he recalled the truly spectacular plague of 1400, and he noted that the 1411 epidemic was quite "minor" compared to that of 1417, which had claimed the lives of his father and other important Florentines, but the epidemics since that time did not arouse his interest. The conscientious Florentine archbishop, Antoninus, felt it was important to record the major plague visits of the century, but the 1424 and 1430 episodes escaped his notice.

Perhaps the plague had become all too familiar to deserve description. But there is more than a hint that plague in the early fifteenth century was actually less threatening, even though it recurred more frequently. Other infections competed with plague for victims among the disadvantaged populations unable to flee the city, but the record of their ravages comes only from nonliterary, archival sources. The Florentine registers of mortality reveal important aspects of fifteenth-century plague that escaped the chroniclers and diarists.

SEASONAL CHARACTERISTICS OF MINOR PLAGUES

The *Grascia morti* registers reveal much the same sawtooth mortality pattern implied by the references to epidemics made by chroniclers and diarists. The numerous lacunae in the mortality registers mean that using this source alone would also have given

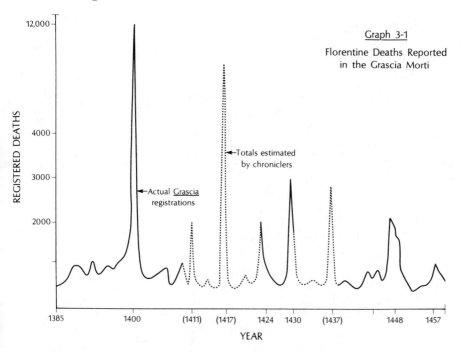

Graph 3-1

Florentine Deaths Reported
in the Grascia Morti

as incomplete picture of early fifteenth-century epidemics in Florence as would the use of only literary sources. The only additional
information given by the Grascia record is that of the 1444 pondi
epidemic. Graph 3–1 charts the absolute totals of deaths drawn
from Grascia records, with estimates from the chroniclers sketched
over the periods of missing registers.[9] Nevertheless the same
impression of less virulent crisis mortality emerges in the comparison of plagues after 1417 with those before that year.

The less virulent, minor plagues of the early fifteenth century
also differed from the major plagues in the season of peak mortality. In the fourteenth century the season of plague was predictably
May to September in Florence. The worst months of the plagues
of 1348, 1374, 1383, and 1400 always fell in midsummer, July and
August.[10] In all the fourteenth-century plagues the crisis had largely
subsided by October.

These summer plague peaks could be readily compared with the
seasonal peak of another major mortality crisis of the fourteenth
century that was certainly not plague. The season of nonplague
epidemics often differed from the midsummer plague season. Burial
monuments purchased in the Dominican Church of Santa Maria

Table 3–1. *Burials in Santa Maria Novella, fourteenth-century epidemic years, by half-month*

	March		April		May		June		July		August		September		October		November	
Plague years																		
1348	—	—	—	—	—	—	11	20	16	6	2	—	2	—	—	—	—	1
1361	3	2	4	2	1	7	17	13	44	16	8	3	—	—	—	—	—	—
1374	—	1	1	—	—	1	3	3	7	6	11	12	10	6	1	2	10	2
1383	—	1	6	2	—	2	4	6	32	37	30	17	11	9	4	4	1	2
Nonplague years																		
1340	7	11	7	8	20	37	44	15	3	—	—	—	—	—	3	—	—	1
1331	1	4	9	7	3	3	—	4	1	1	—	—	—	—	—	—	—	—

Novella during the fourteenth century illustrate the difference well.[11] Table 3–1 shows the data derived from the record of burials, divided into half-month totals. The record is of the burial of adults, and clearly demonstrates the June–July rise in burials during plague years. The sole exception, 1374, in which the peak of mortality appears to have occurred later in July and August, was the only fourteenth-century plague accompanied by widespread famine.

In sharp contrast is the pattern of the 1340, nonplague pestilence, where the burials in Santa Maria Novella reflect an earlier seasonal peak, in late May and early June. Bubonic plague did not appear in western Europe before the end of the 1340s, so the pestilence of 1340 in Florence was due to another cause or causes. Even without the certain knowledge that plague could not have been responsible for the 1340 mortality, the seasonal peak of deaths confirms its nonplague character.

Not until 1400 do surviving *Grascia morti* lists help document the actual course of a large-scale plague epidemic within the city. After a late winter respite, in March and April the death count in Florence began to climb back to the ominous 6–8 per day seen the previous fall (see Graph 3–2). The last week in April the rate reached over 8 deaths a day, and by mid- to late May close to 50 a day were being reported by the gravediggers. As elsewhere in Tuscany, July was the worst month in 1400.[12] On 5 July, the last full day before a gap in the record, 202 names were presented to the Grascia notary; on 14 July, when the record resumes, 187 were reported. Thus at the epidemic's peak during these nine days, 1,738 names were entered, an average of 193 per day (see Graph 3–2a). With the worst of the epidemic in early July, the 1400 epidemic well illustrates the May-to-September pattern of great fourteenth-century plagues. Although not as dramatic or devastating as the original plague of 1348, the 1400 epidemic nevertheless ran the same seasonal course in the city.

During cycles of minor outbreaks, as plague appeared in the city (1429, 1448, 1456) cause-of-death citations suddenly accompanied the death registrations. During the early months of a minor plague outbreak, summer and fall mortality rates were slightly elevated when compared to "normal" years, with a continued slight rise in deaths-per-day during the winter months. In the actual plague years (1424, 1430, 1449, and 1457) that followed the "beginning" plague years, the spring rise in deaths occurred during the late spring season of May to 15 June.

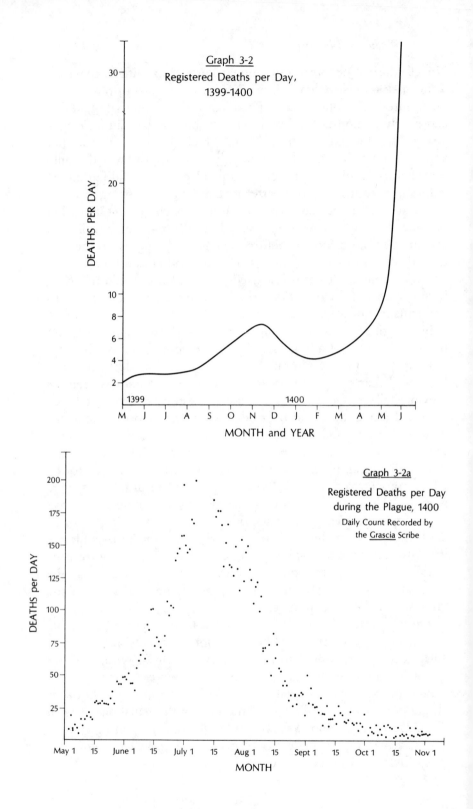

Graph 3-2

Registered Deaths per Day,
1399-1400

DEATHS PER DAY

1399   1400

M   J   J   A   S   O   N   D   J   F   M   A   M   J

MONTH and YEAR

Graph 3-2a

Registered Deaths per Day
during the Plague, 1400

Daily Count Recorded by
the Grascia Scribe

DEATHS per DAY

May 1   15   June 1   15   July 1   15   Aug 1   15   Sept 1   15   Oct 1   15   Nov 1

MONTH

Graph 3-3

Deaths per Day in Non-epidemic and Plague Years,
by Season, 1424-1458

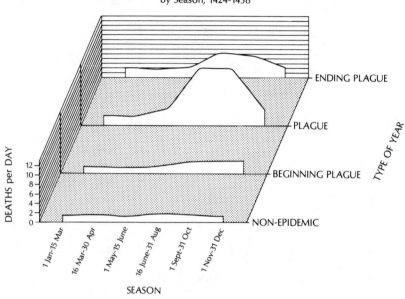

Graph 3–3 compares this phenomenon to the "normal year" described in the previous chapter. The peak of deaths in minor plague years occurred later in the summer than in the major plague years of the fourteenth century, and elevated mortality rates extended into October and November. In years following minor plagues, death rates returned to normal in the spring, but rose slightly during the summer and early fall seasons.

Graphs 3–4 through 3–7 show the seasonal rise in deaths during minor plague years. Mortality was greater during the two fifteenth century plagues that peaked in the summer, rather than in September and October (1430 and 1449).

GEOGRAPHICAL DISTRIBUTION OF PLAGUE

Florence was not evenly settled. Six parishes (San Lorenzo, San Frediano, Sant'Ambruogio, San Niccolò, San Piero Maggiore, and Santa Lucia Ognissanti) accounted for over 50 percent of the population of late fifteenth-century Florence. The largest single parish was San Lorenzo, but the area around the parish of San Frediano

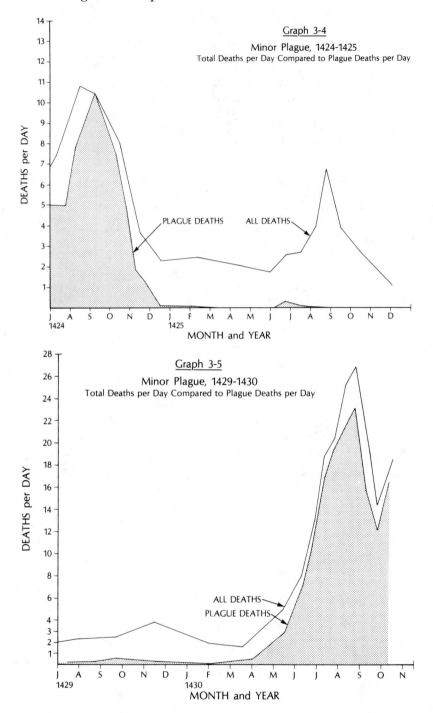

Graph 3-4

Minor Plague, 1424-1425
Total Deaths per Day Compared to Plague Deaths per Day

Graph 3-5

Minor Plague, 1429-1430
Total Deaths per Day Compared to Plague Deaths per Day

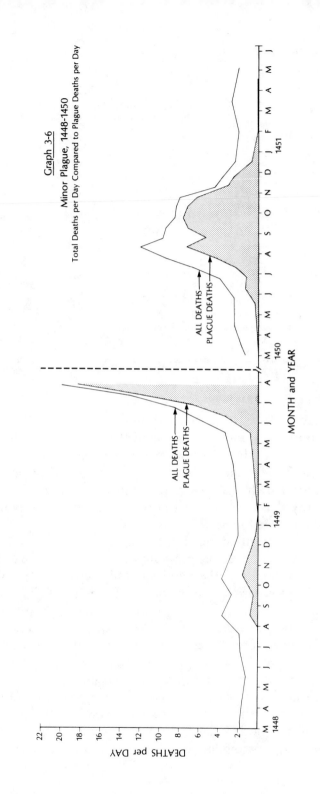

Graph 3-6

Minor Plague, 1448-1450

Total Deaths per Day Compared to Plague Deaths per Day

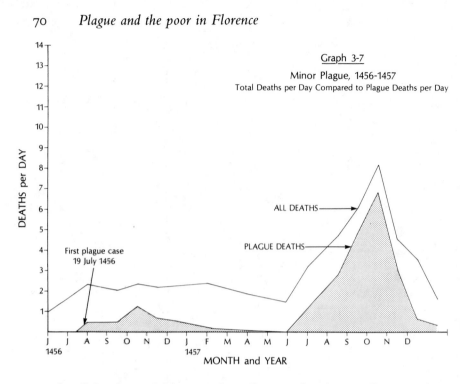

Graph 3-7

Minor Plague, 1456-1457
Total Deaths per Day Compared to Plague Deaths per Day

south of the Arno River was heavily populated as well. For administrative purposes Florence was divided into quarters, three north and one south of the river bisecting the city, and into further divisions of *gonfalone* – the ancient standard-bearers of justice – four to a quarter. Parish churches were assigned to each gonfalone district in a way that did not necessarily reflect the physical and human geography of Florence.[13]

Florence was arbitrarily divided into units of governmental administration that overlapped the geographical boundaries of parish populations. The Books of the Dead faithfully report the parish population to which each victim belonged, but that information cannot be used as a proxy either for economic status or geographical location, even if we were to assume that most deaths occurred at home. (The books record where burials, not deaths, occurred.) Even though they lived side by side, there were significant differences in the physical surroundings of rich and poor, the former living in spacious, even palatial, rooms, the latter in one-room hovels. Already in the fifteenth century expansion in housing was usually vertical, not horizontal, and the less privileged classes of course had to resort to crowding to solve most housing problems.

Samuel Cohn, Jr., in his *The Laboring Classes of Renaissance Florence,* grouped the parish populations of San Frediano, Santa Maria in Verzaia, San Pier Gattolino, San Jacopo sopr'Arno, Santa Felicità, San Felice in Piazza, and Santo Spirito together into a "cluster," as a way of reconciling geographically the confusion of parochial and administrative districts in Florence, an area roughly corresponding to the streets and neighborhoods shown in Map 3–2 (below, p. 76). This area, most of the quarter of Santo Spirito, remains today much as it was in the fifteenth century. Although many Florentine historians hold that there was nothing resembling a ghetto, or a wealthy subsection, within Florence at this time, according to Cohn this "cluster" of parishes did become a predominantly working-class district during the early quattrocento, a character it was to retain into the twentieth century.[14]

Presenting an accurate historical description of the geography of Florence in the fifteenth century – the distribution of population within the city, within parishes, within gonfalone, within quarters of the city – if possible at all can only be done in years of fiscal surveys, such as that of the catasto of 1427. Both epidemics and immigration could have altered the picture radically in a very short time. Thus to compare the geographical distribution of plague cases in different epidemics, we may not be able to reach any definitive conclusions about how plague actually spread in the fifteenth century. The comparison does, however, reveal general observations about plague mortality that could have been as apparent to fifteenth-century bureaucrats as they are to us.

Table 3–2 compares the two minor plagues of 1424 and 1457 to the major epidemic of 1400, revealing another distinguishing characteristic of minor plagues. Although the evidence is not quite as strong in 1424 as in 1457, a higher percentage of all deaths in the city occurred in the large, heavily populated quarter of San Giovanni. Close to half of all deaths during the summer of 1457 occurred in this one quarter. During peak plague months, in whatever season that peak occurred, the geographical clustering of deaths characterizes minor more than major plague years. Furthermore, in normal years, and in years following plague, no similar geographical concentration is evident in city death statistics. Thus one may hypothesize that in minor outbreaks of plague, the disease may have been confined to limited geographical sections of the city to a much greater extent than in the severe plague years.

Table 3–2. *Deaths in the quarter of San Giovanni, among total Florentine deaths (in %)*

Season	1400	1424	1457
January–15 March	47	—	43
16 March–April	65	—	53
May–15 June	46	—	51
16 June–July	36	37	62
August	33	45	50
September	36	47	46
October	39	39	51
November–December	28	38	50

Table 3–3. *Death totals in 1400: percentage totals in the quarters of San Giovanni and Santo Spirito*

Week	City total	San Giovanni (%)	Santo Spirito (%)
3–10 May	87	58.6	20.7
11–17 May	141	57.4	19.8
18–24 May	208	51.9	18.3
25–31 May	278	50.7	28.4
1–7 June	343	44.9	28.6
8–14 June	542	37.6	37.3
15–21 June	550	42.3	30.5
22–28 June	887	39.3	31.3
29 June–5 July	1,177	35.7	31.9
20–26 July	1,015	34.3	28.1
27 July–2 Aug.	966	32.5	25.3
3–10 Aug.	746	32.4	32.6
11–17 Aug.	459	36.1	22.2
18–24 Aug.	253	33.2	32.0
25–31 Aug.	233	30.0	26.2
1–15 Sept.	341	33.4	28.7
16–30 Sept.	203	40.4	25.1
1–15 Oct.	118	41.5	22.0
16–31 Oct.	92	35.9	21.7
Overall	9,486	37.4	29.0

In 1400, no area of the city was spared. Table 3–3 charts the weekly course of death registrations during the spring and summer of the major plague of 1400. Despite an early preponderance of deaths in San Giovanni, by the peak weeks of plague the quarter

Table 3–4. *Death totals in 1430: percentage totals in the quarter of Santo Spirito*

Weeks	City total	Santo Spirito (%)	Plague among deaths in Santo Spirito (%)
1–15 May	64	37.5	67
15–31 May	101	43.6	82
1–15 June	133	51.9	94
16–31 June	196	53.1	91
1–15 July	293	57.3	93
16–31 July	329	34.3	87
1–15 Aug.	354	39.5	84
16–31 Aug.	463	28.1	87
1–15 Sept.	248	37.9	85
16–30 Sept.	222 (est.)	24.3	78

accounted for only 30–40 percent of the citywide total. The second most populous quarter of Santo Spirito accounted for 20–32 percent of Florentine deaths. After the first week in June, the disease apparently was dispersed throughout the city.

During the minor plague of 1430 (Graph 3–5 and Table 3–4), in contrast, the normal seasonal peak of death registrations appeared highest before late August in the quarter of Santo Spirito. Over 50 percent of all deaths from June through mid-July were counted in this one section alone. Although the seasonal onset of exaggerated mortality was only slightly later than in 1400, the disproportionate progression of deaths in isolated sections of the city distinguishes this minor plague with 22–26 deaths per day at the epidemic's peak, from the major 1400 plague with 200–250 deaths per day at its height.

The minor 1430 plague year record includes the names of streets on which many of the victims died. Thus the dispersal of deaths during the first two months, the weeks when the quarter of Santo Spirito was so heavily affected, can be mapped. Maps 3–1a to 3–1d illustrate the biweekly totals of deaths west of the Via Romana, the main street running from the Ponte Vecchio south to Porta Romana. Each dot represents one death from plague, each x a death from some other cause. When the death notice was not accompanied by a street name, but by a parish and place of burial

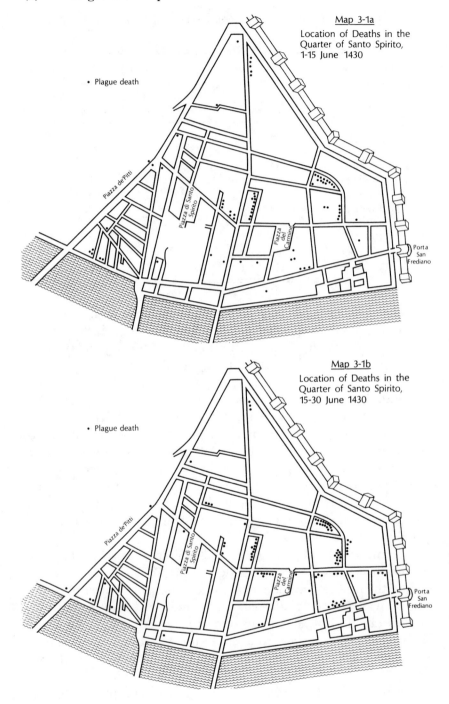

Map 3-1a
Location of Deaths in the
Quarter of Santo Spirito,
1-15 June 1430

• Plague death

Map 3-1b
Location of Deaths in the
Quarter of Santo Spirito,
15-30 June 1430

• Plague death

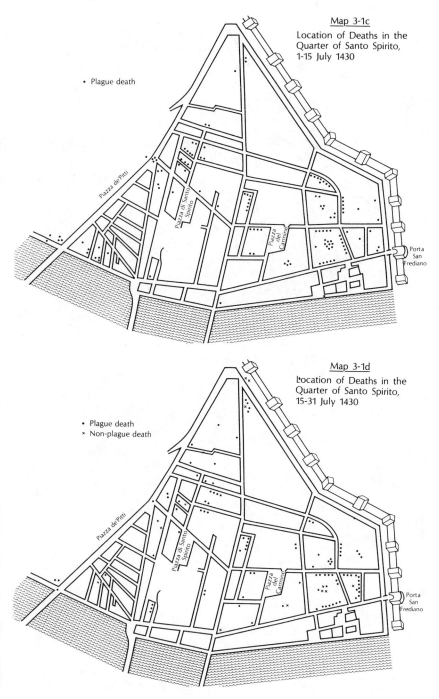

Map 3-1c
Location of Deaths in the
Quarter of Santo Spirito,
1-15 July 1430

• Plague death

Piazza de' Pitti

Piazza di Santo Spirito

Piazza del Carmine

Porta San Frediano

Map 3-1d
Location of Deaths in the
Quarter of Santo Spirito,
15-31 July 1430

• Plague death
× Non-plague death

Piazza de' Pitti

Piazza di Santo Spirito

Piazza del Carmine

Porta San Frediano

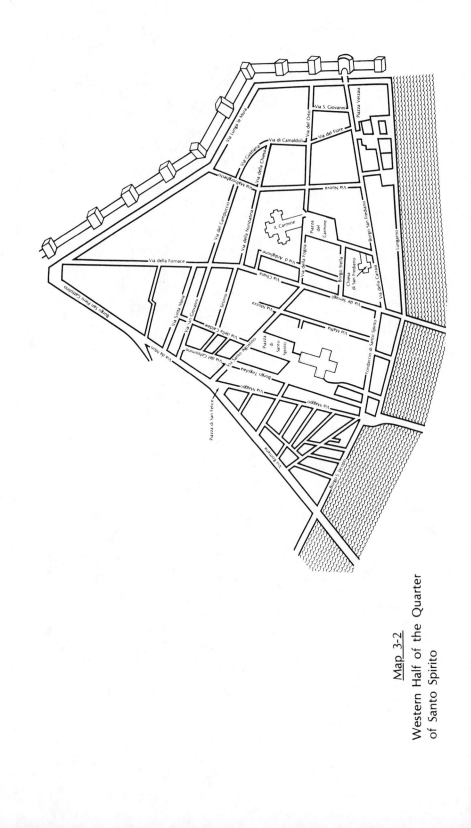

Map 3-2

Western Half of the Quarter
of Santo Spirito

only, the symbols are placed in the middle of a block, rather than along the street.

The progression of deaths even through this one city subsection was not uniform: Deaths clustered first in the most western part, around the church and gate of San Frediano, in the working-class parishes of San Frediano and Santa Maria in Verzaia, and along certain streets even within this limited space (e.g., Via Gustiana, Via Ardiglione, Via di Camaldoli, and Borgo San Frediano on Map 3–2).[15] As the plague marched through Santo Spirito, eventually the whole quarter was affected, although clumping of deaths was still evident.

One street could be taken as an example of the extremely local dissemination of minor plague. Borgo Tegolaia shows an apparent clustering of plague deaths within families, a pattern much like that revealed by the cases of plague isolated during the first few months of the 1456 epidemic. As Table 3–5 shows, four households along this short narrow street suffered more than one death. Many streets in Santo Spirito, as well as in other districts of the city, seemed to be local plague foci during the summers of minor plagues.

Though unique in providing street names, the 1430 record is not alone in suggesting the localization of deaths during summer epidemics. The seasonal and geographical distribution of deaths from 1439 to 1457 is summarized in Appendix II, focusing there on the populous quarters of San Giovanni and Santo Spirito. In 1448–50, during the late spring season, the heavy San Giovanni mortality rate resembles the bias toward this quarter that the 1400 numbers showed. During the summer season, however, Santo Spirito again had higher mortality rates. In the late summer and early autumn period, a similar bias toward these two populous districts emerges in the epidemic years of 1444, 1448, 1450, and 1457, but not in normal years.

From the greater numbers of cases in epidemic years it is clear that the epidemic waves passing through Florence in the early fifteenth century hit the populous working-class districts with disproportional severity. In the minor plague years documented by the *Grascia morti*, intracity and intradistrict clustering of fatal cases was more evident than in major plague years, such as 1400. During minor epidemics, furthermore, the disease appeared to choose its victims either by some person-to-person communication or by

Table 3–5. *Deaths in Borgo Tegolaia, summer 1430, showing the clustering of deaths geographically and in households*

1. Household of Federigo di Lodovico Folchi, burials in San Jacopo
   11 July, Francesca – *P* diagnosis
   1 August, Giovanna – born premature
   3 August, Monna Sandra – *P*
   16 August, Federigo himself – *P*
2. Household of Simone di Lorenzo, burials in San Jacopo
   16 July, Brigida – infirmity
   10 August, Alexandra – *P*
3. Household of Andrea d'Andrea, parish of San Jacopo, burials in Santa Felice in Piazza
   7 August, Ermellina – *P*
   8 August, Ginevra – *P*
4. Household of Dato, who is a wine vendor, burials in San Jacopo
   3 August, unnamed son – *P*
   17 August, Meo, who stayed with Dato – *P*
   17 August, an unnamed child who stayed with Dato – *P*
   24 August, Mea – *P*
   29 August, Zanobi – *P*

Other deaths, all on Borgo Tegolaia:
28 July, Matteo, son of the rector of San Donato in Poggio – *P*
5 August, Bartholomea, of Goro, bucklemaker – *P*
9 August, Alexandra, of Simone di Stefano – *P*
23 August, Giovanni, of Piero from Siena – *P*
27 August, Ginevra, of Aghostino di Tedaldo – *P*
9 September, Ginevra, of Ricciardo di Stefano – *P*

dissemination from a common source. This pattern undoubtedly appeared frequently during major epidemics as well. But although many members of a family might die in the space of a few days during a major plague, the tremendous numbers of dead in all sections of the city inevitably obscured whatever "local effect" may have been present.

INDIVIDUAL DIAGNOSES OF PLAGUE

There is no evidence, external or internal to the Books of the Dead, that educated physicians aided the gravediggers or others diagnosing cause of death. The process may have resembled that used in Mantua in the mid-fifteenth century, employing a variety of communal officials and medical consultants to decide the cause of death in difficult cases (see chap. 1). But no surviving letters, statutes, or other documents show how Florentines certified a death from plague. It seems likely that the gravediggers or priests, possibly even the family and neighbors of a deceased person helped in the process, without needing any formal medical opinion as to the nature of a reigning pestilence. The diagnoses always appear in vernacular, Tuscan Italian, not in medical Latin, and, as we have seen, many of the causes refer only to symptoms the deceased bore in the final illness, or to the length of time he was ill. Identifying deaths from plague was initially the reason the causes of death were entered, but nothing in the record says how the information was then used.

In addition to the large *P* beside the name of each person dead from plague, most of the victims carried another diagnosis. *Morbo, pistolenza,* and *di peste* were the general vernacular terms used for plague or pestilence; *di segno* ("of the sign of plague") was the only diagnosis that hints at greater specificity. It was not used uniformly and accompanied only some *P* victims. No recognizable pattern of these deaths allows us to do more than speculate about what the signs of plague were. The Mantuan records described in Chapter 1 suggested that several decades later than these early Florentine records there was little concensus about a single sign, or group of signs, characteristic of plague.

Since the great 1348 plague laymen and educated physicians did not mean the same thing when they referred to the "signs" of plague. Laymen tended to refer to clinical symptoms of plague in an individual, and physicians, at least in formal plague tractates, tended to describe "signs" of plague as epidemiological and ecological portents of a coming epidemic. The popular description of plague signs given by Giovanni Boccaccio in the *Decameron* leaves no doubt that bubonic *Y. pestis* ravaged Florence in 1348, and the long passage is quoted here to show a popular version of the signs of plague:

It did not act as it had done in the East, where bleeding from the nose was a manifest sign of inevitable death, but it began in both men and women with certain swellings either in the groin or under the armpits, some of which grew to the size of a normal apple and others to the size of an egg (more or less), and the people called them *gavoccioli* [*bubboni*].

And from the two parts of the body already mentioned, within a brief space of time the said deadly *gavoccioli* began to spread indiscriminately over every part of the body; and after this, the symptoms of the illness changed to black or livid spots appearing on the arms and thighs, and on every part of the body, some large ones and sometimes many little ones scattered around. And just as the *gavoccioli* were originally, and still are, a very certain indication of impending death, in like manner these spots came to mean the same thing for whoever had them.[16]

The "sign" is clearly the bubo, although livid patches might be the token visible to the gravedigger. The sign furthermore indicated imminent death, usually within three days.

Medical treatises dwelled on three additional signs of plague, but they were remote predictors: celestial events, terrestrial weather disturbances, and any evidence of localized corruption of the air and water. Not until late in the fifteenth century, and thereafter consistently in the sixteenth century, do plague tractates deal with the "signs" of plague in an individual patient.[17]

In the Books of the Dead the clustering of plague within households and limited geographical districts is more obvious now than clinical "signs" that may have influenced fifteenth-century diagnoses of plague. The outbreak of plague in 1456 dramatically illustrates this phenomenon. As indicated in Table 3–6, the earliest reported fatal plague case of the year occurred on 19 July. "Papino di Salimbene" was a carpenter's son in the district near Santa Maria Novella (see Map 3–3). (Papino is presumed to be a child here because of the death of a "Bartolino di Salimbene" on 26 July, in the same district and parish church.) For over two weeks plague cases clustered in the districts of Santa Maria Novella and San Piero Maggiore, parishes separated by over a mile of crowded, winding streets. With only one exception, all plague fatalities occurred within the families of carpenters (*legnaiuoli*), in two circumscribed geographical areas. During the first two months of plague in 1456, from 19 July to 18 September, 75 percent (25 of 33) of the plague deaths occurred in just nine families, only one of which resided outside the two affected districts.

As with the Mantuan cases one of the criteria for a diagnosis of plague may have been multiple household deaths, since the families of other tradesmen were not involved. It is improbable, but

Table 3–6. *All plague deaths reported in Florence, July–August 1456: the clustering of deaths within parishes and households*

Santa Maria Novella (SMN): 13 cases; 9 households, of which 5 were carpenters
    19 July –   Papino di Salimbene, carpenter
    22 July –   Nanna, daughter of Giunta, carpenter
    23 July –   Lorenzo, son of Sirafino di Lorenzo del Biado
              –   Simone, son of Francesco, carpenter
    26 July –   Bartolino di Salimbene, carpenter
    29 July –   Giunta di Bartolo, carpenter
    7 Aug. –   Andrea, the son of Francesco, carpenter
    8 Aug. –   daughter of Lorenzo d'Antonio
    9 Aug. –   Francesco di Bartolo
    19 Aug. –   Chaterina, a little girl who stayed with Mona Mea in the house of Tano, carpenter
    21 Aug. –   Francescha, daughter of Lorenzo d'Antonio
              –   Isabetta, daughter of Berto del Chiaro
    27 Aug. –   son of Filippo di Livo, spitiale alla palla

San Piero Maggiore [SPM] – 6 cases; 2 households, both carpenters
    22 July –   Antonio di Piero, carpenter
    24 July –   Giunto, son of Betto de Francesco, carpenter
    3 Aug. –   son of Antonio di Piero, carpenter
    4 Aug. –   Brigita, daughter of Betto di Francesco, carpenter
    5 Aug. –   the wife of Antonio di Piero, carpenter
    9 Aug. –   daughter of Antonio di Piero, carpenter

San Brancatio – 2 cases; same household (a carpenter's)
    24 July –   Giuntura, the little daughter of Domenico di Zanobi, carpenter
    26 July –   Domenico di Zanobi, carpenter

San Felice in Piazza – 2 cases; same household
    15 Aug. – daughter of Lorenzo di Bindo, builder
    16 Aug. – son of Lorenzo di Bindo, builder

San Simone – 2 cases; 2 households
    18 Aug. – Lorenzo di Michele
    19 Aug. – daughter of Martino

Others:
    6 Aug. –   the slave of Jacopo Ridolfi, in the parish of San Jacopo sopr'Arno
    29 Aug. – Zanobi di Nicholo di Checho, buried in Santa Croce

Map 3-3
Plague-affected Districts in Florence, 1456

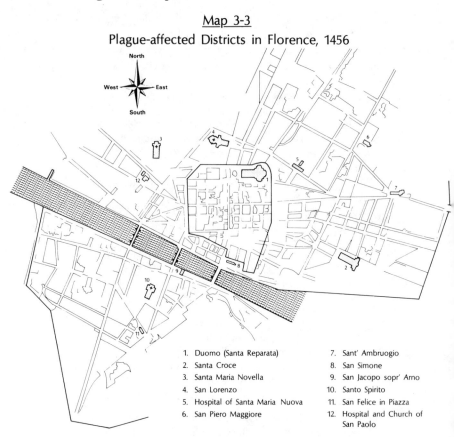

1. Duomo (Santa Reparata)	7. Sant' Ambruogio
2. Santa Croce	8. San Simone
3. Santa Maria Novella	9. San Jacopo sopr' Arno
4. San Lorenzo	10. Santo Spirito
5. Hospital of Santa Maria Nuova	11. San Felice in Piazza
6. San Piero Maggiore	12. Hospital and Church of San Paolo

not impossible, that rats and their fleas would single out just these individuals. Whatever signs were found on the bodies, if any were, it seems obvious that links in household deaths played a role in the attribution of these deaths to plague. Familial, occupational, and intradistrict dissemination of disease suggests contact-borne infection, or spread from a common source.

Once a death in a household was declared a plague death, subsequent deaths in the family might automatically be called plague without further inquiry or investigation. In September through October of this year (1456), two additional families lost six and eight members, respectively. In each family the initial death of a child preceded those of the other victims by about two weeks. Table 3–7 illustrates how the diagnosis of "worms" in these two families was revised once other family members died. Once again, the possibility that the deaths were due to flea-borne plague cannot

Table 3–7. *Cases of plague in two families, 1456*

P deaths in the family of Donato Berghamino, barber, parish church, San Tommaso, buried in San Lorenzo	P deaths in the family of Nardo Maestro, buried in Santa Maria Novella
22 September: girl of Donato Barbiere (diagnosis of "worms" canceled)	10 October: a little girl, "Bartolomea," of Nardo Maestro (diagnosis of "worms" canceled)
5 October: girl of Donato Barbiere called Berghamino	23 October: Antonio, Nastasia, and Domenicha, children of Nardo Maestro
5 October: another girl of the same man	
6 October: Donato di Giovanni called Berghamino, barber	24 October: Orsino and Caterina, children of Nardo Maestro
6 October: Girl of the same Donato	
8 October: Francesco di Donato Berghamino, barber	27 October: Giovanni and Jacopo, children of Nardo Maestro
6 victims in 16 days	8 victims in 17 days

Source: Carmichael, "Plague Legislation in the Italian Renaissance," 517. *Bulletin of the History of Medicine* 57 (1983): 517.

be dismissed, but some other communicable disease that is directly transmitted among family members would be a more likely explanation of this pattern of deaths. One is even tempted to speculate that an incubation period of about two weeks might further characterize the malady that claimed these lives, but such a conclusion is hardly warranted on the basis of two cases.

It is likely that the diagnosis of plague was often awarded without any further confirmation once a second member of the family had died soon after the first. There is no way to know whether individual cases were investigated among Florentines too poor to have family names; occupations are not consistently recorded by the scribes. But an example of deaths in a relatively wealthy family shows the same household clustering. Between 19 April and 24 April 1430, four members of the Strozzi family reportedly died with "fever." Three more deaths occurred between 29 April and 7 May, as Table 3–8 shows, and only then were the deaths attributed to plague.

Failing to revise the "fever" diagnosis of previous Strozzi family deaths may mean that a social stigma was associated with dying

Table 3–8. *Deaths in the family of Barla di Stagio degli Strozzi, 1430*

Date	Individual	Diagnosis
19 April	Lisa, daughter of Barla	Fever
20 April	Monna Cosa, wife of Barla	Infirmity
21 April	Caterina, daughter of Barla	Fever
22 April	Agniesa, daughter of Barla	Fever
[24 April	Bindo d'Uberto degli Strozzi	Fever][a]
29 April	Tita, daughter of Barla	Pestilence
7 May	Margherita & Giovanni, children of Barla	Pestilence
12 May	Madonna Maddalena, who was the wife of messer Luchino Visconti, "Casa degli Strozi"	No diagnosis

[a]Not specifically Barla di Stagio's house; but same *populus,* same burial as other Strozzi deaths.

from plague, and that a wealthier family was able to escape the label for a longer period of time. The example may also mean that "fever" was of less concern to diagnosticians than was "worms," and there is some evidence to suggest that "worms" frequently preceded plague.

Diarist Giovanni Morelli was concerned that worms were most dangerous to children in years when plague was expected.[18] Experience in at least some plague years upheld this popular theory. Moreover, worms was virtually the only diagnosis from 1424 to 1458 that was repeatedly subject to revision and reconsideration. There are four instances of plague replacing an original diagnosis of worms, but there are no overwritten diagnoses among the more common diagnoses of long illness, or old age, and no instances where a diagnosis of plague was revised. There is only one case of "fever" being replaced by "plague."

An entomologist, Robin Bernath, has suggested to me the possibility that flea larvae could have been what looked to observers like tiny worms.[19] Larvae usually hatch from eggs after a few days' incubation in warm, humid air, and fleas usually lay eggs after a blood meal in some organic debris, so that the larvae can meet their iron requirements. This does not seem to be a probable explanation of the worms diagnosis, but the fact that fleas carry other bacteria besides *Y. pestis* and can expose a host to many different kinds of diarrhea-producing diseases may be of significance. Diarrhea was relevant to the diagnosis of worms. Although fifteenth-century medical thinking understood the generation of worms as linked to corruption of humors, and rather like "a canary in a coal mine" for signaling the subtle corruption of the ambient air that led to plague, the association of plague and worms may not have been entirely determined by medical theories.[20]

CONTAGION AND THE MINOR PLAGUES

On the basis of normal *Y. pestis* ecology, it is difficult to explain the clustering feature of the minor plagues. The evidence better supports a contagious or common-source spread of disease. It is unlikely that a burgeoning epizootic among rats in a city would have been so geographically restricted.

It seems more likely that the recurrence of disease in one family or subsection may have been due to some bias in the way plague cases were identified. The recorders may not have confirmed the plague cases when they heard of successive deaths in a family and may have merely assumed the presence of plague. In addition, the flight of richer families may have left the city unevenly populated so that only particular groups were exposed to plague infection.

If the localization is a real feature of minor plague, however, two mechanisms could have been responsible for the limited, contagious spread of disease: transmission by human fleas and plague pneumonia. The first, occasionally invoked in historical and medical explanations, is that during the fifteenth century the human flea, *Pulex irritans,* became the more important vector in transmitting *Y. pestis* among persons in close physical association.[21] Although neither as effective nor as efficient a vector as the rat flea, human fleas could play an important role if present in considerable numbers, as might occur among people with multiple layers of clothing covering unclean bodies.

Undoubtedly plague could be and probably was occasionally spread by human fleas. Even close to death, humans infected with plague do not have blood concentrations of bacilli dense enough to infect fleas frequently, but the human flea will feed indifferently on human or rat. Blood levels of *Y. pestis* in an infected rat are concentrated enough to infect any flea, but the rat flea, *Xenopsylla cheopis,* has more difficulty ridding its system of the infection.[22] *X. cheopis* so prefers the rat host that it will not feed on humans unless deprived of rat blood. All these conditions and preferences suggest that if the human flea was an important vector in the fifteenth century minor plagues, it probably depended on alternate, infected rat hosts as well as humans.

Neither is it likely that pneumonic plague made any significant contribution to the minor plagues. First, none of the recorded epidemics took place during the winter, or even a cool season, when conditions prevailed that would have supported airborne, droplet dissemination of *Y. pestis.*[23] Second, if pneumonic plague was responsible for many of the plague cases, then the characteristic bubo would usually be absent. To verify the presence of pneumonic plague, one would have to have great faith in the diagnostic sophistication of the gravediggers or other certifiers of a cause of death, for these individuals would have to distinguish plague pneumonia from all other primary and secondary causes of hemoptysis (coughing or spitting blood).

Pneumonic plague occurs usually as a secondary complication of bubonic plague infection, or as a primary infection acquired directly from someone suffering from pneumonic plague. In the latter case, airborne droplets teeming with the encapsulated *Y. pestis* are coughed or sneezed out of the respiratory tract of a moribund plague sufferer and absorbed directly onto a mucous membrane of another person. Case fatality rates for primary pneumonic plague infection approximate 100 percent.

During the twentieth century pneumonic plague has been a relatively uncommon complication of bubonic plague infection in individuals (only 5–15 percent of all bubonic cases progress to secondary plague pneumonia), and rarely has the documented chain of infection been appreciable.[24] One might imagine that in the absence of an arthropod vector those persons nursing or caring for a plague sufferer, or those in unavoidable proximity to a person with secondary lung infection, might become exposed to the bacillus directly. The clinical course to death is quite brief, a matter of a few days at most, and a single individual would have little chance to infect large numbers of other people with primary pneumonic plague.

Furthermore, pneumonic plague epidemics that have occurred in the twentieth century not only occurred in winter months, they took the lives of adults with much greater frequency than the lives of children, a picture that contrasts with the Florentine data. During the very large, fourteenth-century epidemics of plague, especially in 1348, witnesses frequently described pneumonic complications of bubonic disease. But in massive plague epidemics one would expect an increase in the absolute number of cases of secondary pneumonic plague, and with poor segregation of victims, at the peak of the epidemic many further cases of primary pneumonic plague. The soaring death rates at the height of a bubonic plague epidemic and the descriptions of hemoptysis among plague sufferers are not, however, part of the record in fifteenth-century plagues.

WERE THE MINOR PLAGUES TRUE PLAGUE?

However many individual cases of misdiagnosis occurred, one must first analyze this seasonal difference between major and minor plagues as if *Y. pestis,* the causal agent of bubonic plague, was principally responsible for all the epidemics. If bubonic, flea-borne plague was predominantly responsible for the mortalities, three possible explanations might account for the relatively minor plagues of the fifteenth century. First the hotter, drier month of August, because of its decreased humidity, may have restricted the mobility and reproduction of the rat fleas within the city. The optimal temperature and humidity requirements of the flea for reproduction and survival, and the cyclic recovery of rat populations during the early spring, may have imposed further biological restrictions on the later-season transmission of plague to humans.[25] These complications of plague ecology will be further elaborated later in this section.

Second, an increased frequency of plague in the first half of the fifteenth century may have further limited spread of plague within the city. Rat populations, also decimated by plague, may not have had the time to recover their numbers if more frequently beset by infected fleas.[26] The optimal flea vector for the propagation of bubonic plague is the flea of the black rat, so the numbers of fleas besetting human populations would depend on the size of the rat population. Some instances of human bubonic plague no doubt were due to other means by which fleas were transmitted to the cities (e.g., by grain transport or by the clothes of travelers), but this cannot account for the majority of plague cases.

Third, the bacillus itself could have been less virulent in the early quattrocento. Study of plague epidemics in the twentieth century has shown that the virulence of the bacillus is stable or even increases within individual epidemics. That is, the relative ability of the microorganism to multiply within host tissues does not tend to decrease in the course of a particular epidemic.[27] The evolution of less virulent strains, however, can occur randomly, so one might explain the decline in fifteenth-century plague mortality without invoking the development of an "immunity" in the general human population. The actual case fatalities from *Y. pestis* would decline with less virulent strains, but it is also possible that the nutritionally deprived, more vulnerable members of society might have succumbed to other secondary infectious diseases while recovering from a less lethal strain of plague.

From all this one might easily surmise that virtually any event or combination of events external and exogenous to human societies may explain the decline in plague mortality in the early fifteenth century, or even the disappearance of plague two centuries later. Although it is difficult to know in modern medical terms what actually happened in human plagues of the early fifteenth century, the fact that contemporaries perceived them to be less threatening is historically important.

The ecology, epidemiology, and clinical symptoms of *Y. pestis* are so complex that almost any fifteenth-century evidence – whether fragmentary or abundant – could be made to conform to a retrospective diagnosis of "true plague." Given the lack of sophistication attending diagnoses of plague in the early Renaissance, however, it appears that individual diagnoses may well have accommodated evolving notions about the contagion of plague, the likelihood of household and other contact cases, and the rapid progression from health to death that were widely accepted "signs" of the disease. In the general climate of the early fifteenth-century experience with less lethal *Y. pestis* outbreaks and especially with the absence of the upper classes from the affected urban centers, it is historically more useful to see the characteristics of minor plagues as a problem separate from seeking an answer to the unanswerable question of why, ecologically, these plagues were minor. Whether they were truly due to *Y. pestis,* totally or in major part, mattered little to those whose "experience" of "plague" was framed and shaped by these urban epidemics. The conclusion a Florentine observer could have drawn by the mid-fifteenth century was that plague was usually contagious and that it was predominantly a disease of the poor.

4

The social effects of plague in Florence

Significant changes in normal sanitary legislation and in plague controls came during the fifteenth century, not during the years of major plagues. Florentine legislators by the mid-fifteenth century were convinced that plague was a contagious disease best controlled by segregating and isolating potential sources of infection. By the end of the century they were equally certain that poorer people, especially migrants and beggars, were carriers of the disease. There was a deepening conviction that poverty and plague were linked threats to the security of the state. The novel plague legislation formulated in this period helped to ensure that poverty and plague would be lasting companions.

DEMOGRAPHIC SIGNIFICANCE OF MINOR PLAGUES

Historians who have studied individual plagues have disagreed markedly in their conclusions about which individuals were most likely to fall victim to plague during a human epidemic, for the records that they have used to document mortality give no consistent answer to the problem. In a classic study of plague mortality in London during the late sixteenth century, Hollingsworth and Hollingsworth found that adult males died with a significantly greater frequency than did adult females or children. Ell supported this conclusion with a detailed discussion of how human immunities to plague are formed. On the other hand, Domenico Sella carefully compared losses, by parish, during the Milanese plagues of 1630, with the age structure of the population before the plague, and demonstrated the heavy losses among children. Ell studied Venetian mortality during the same plague and found dramatic losses among adult women. Herlihy and Klapisch-Zuber's analysis of Florentine demographic history and Zvi Razi's study of an English manor from 1348 to 1400 both found persuasive evidence for heavy mortality among children during plagues. In striking contrast to Ell's medical model is Razi's evidence of the differential survival of young adults. In sum, there seems to be no universal agreement in the evidence or among investigators that plague always behaved in a predictable fashion. At times plagues claimed young adults, sometimes the men, often pregnant and lactating women; at other times heaviest mortality occurred among young children or the aged.[1]

The Books of the Dead give strong evidence of heavy mortality among dependent children during the early fifteenth century. The overall losses of children appear to have been somewhat greater in minor plague years than in the years of major plagues. Table 4-1 shows that during epidemic years more than 70 percent of those dying from all causes were children. Particularly in 1430 the relative losses of children exceeded the percentages that would be expected if plague alone were the principal determinant of mortality patterns, since there is no reason that bubonic plague would selectively affect the young. Although in most years male victims slightly outnumbered female, the differential mortality is not striking, as Graph 4-1 reflects.

Herlihy and Klapisch-Zuber found that only about 3 percent of the Florentines surveyed by the 1427 catasto were infants less than a year old. In fact, children younger than fourteen comprised only 40 percent of the total population.[2] But in a preindustrial society such as this, one would normally expect about half of the total mortality to be concentrated in the cohort under age seven. Thus in all years, children under fourteen years should appear more often than adults in the death registers. In 1439, a year following the long, unrecorded plague of 1437-38, deaths among children comprised 51.1 percent of the entries. Of the plague deaths recorded during this year, however, 66.7 percent (24 of 36) were undoubtedly children. Because dependency is not always cited, both these figures underestimate actual deaths among the young.

True bubonic plague tends to affect all members of a population equally, without regard to state of nutrition, if all members are equally likely to be infected. This statement must be qualified by Ell's recent reviews, arguing that normal human differences in immune status according to age, sex, and availability of serum iron can enhance the growth of microorganisms in healthy, young adults.

Table 4-1. *Child victims among total deaths, epidemic years, 1424–58 (in %)*

Season	Beginning plague years		Plague years			Ending plague years				Nonplague year
	1448	1456	1424	1430	1449	1425	1439	1450	1457	1444
Jan.–15 May	46.0	41.9	—	34.2	34.2	32.3	—	—	42.7	38.7
16 March–April	35.7	31.2	—	68.3	40.3	36.5	47.4	42.9	57.1	43.1
May–June	37.5	47.2	—	75.8	69.1	34.7	57.9	40.0	30.0	47.4
16 June–July	55.5	50.6	73.5	84.2	82.5	51.5	59.6	59.7	70.8	68.6
August	65.4	50.6	73.8	77.5	78.2	62.5	65.7	74.7	68.7	75.9
September	55.8	50.7	75.3	84.6	—	48.5	71.2	74.8	66.7	51.3
October	69.6	50.7	72.5	83.9	—	37.1	55.2	69.4	60.4	37.0
Nov.–Dec.	44.8	53.7	53.3	—	—	34.4	37.3	56.8	56.8	42.3

Note: Calculations represent Number of dependent females × 100%
⎯⎯⎯⎯⎯⎯⎯⎯⎯⎯⎯⎯⎯⎯⎯⎯⎯⎯
Total number of females

Graph 4-1

Deaths from Plague by Year
Male and Female Deaths Compared

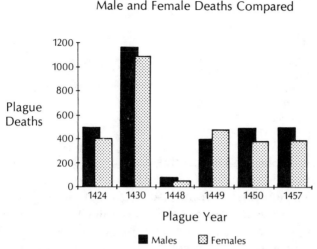

Ell shows as well that certain previous infections help to protect individuals because they acquire a cross-immunity that serves well against plague infection.[3] Nevertheless many of these well-taken objections must be set aside because we lack information about individual patient histories and because most of the valuable data pertain to population-level phenomena.

It seems reasonable also to suppose that children were not more likely targets for rat fleas than were adults, even though we could imagine circumstances under which this was not the case. Table 4–2 suggests that in a major plague, 60–70 percent of overall mortality occurred among children, a fact easily explained by assuming that the delivery of food and normal sanitary care was disrupted and that the individuals needing these services most (children) succumbed to secondary infections.[4] During minor plagues, overall losses of children were not much greater than in major plague years, but the percentage of children among the plague victims soared. During the minor plagues, children were disproportionately affected by whatever was being diagnosed as "plague."

During the month of July 1449, 65.7 percent of all the *P* deaths registered were children. But only 123 individuals were specifically registered as dependents, and 117 of these children (95.1 per-

Table 4–2. *Child victims among all deaths during a major plague year, May through October, 1400 (in %)*

May	65.8
June	70.4
July	62.8
August	64.1
September	54.8
October	50.1

cent) died of plague. During this plague year only six diagnosed deaths of children carried a diagnosis other than plague. In 1439, in contrast, only 11.3 percent of child victims were plague cases. Graph 4–2 shows the causes of death for all children during 1439, illustrating that fever, smallpox, and diarrheal disease alone claimed over 30 percent of the children who died, and as many again were not diagnosed at all. Prematurity, death in the neonatal period, and mal maestro accounted for another 10 percent. Since it is not likely that this full spectrum of other diseases among children disappeared during plague epidemics, many plague deaths, especially of children, were either misdiagnosed cases or unconfirmed plague deaths. Viewed from a perspective of five hundred years, the devastating effects of a plague outbreak would still be great, but the recognition that many deaths were not due directly to *Y. pestis* should be emphasized.

The very high percentages of children who died during the plague summers undoubtedly disguise the other epidemic and non-epidemic diseases that tended to claim youthful lives. The weight of modern medical evidence does not support the contention that children are and therefore were more susceptible to plague. Furthermore, no long-lasting immunity is conferred on individuals who recover from bubonic plague, so those who had lived through another plague should not have been protected any more than the children. Children are more susceptible to infections, malnutrition, and fluid losses than are adults who do not receive adequate care, and if they were simultaneously subjected to some of the common "immunizing" diseases of childhood, they had even less chance of surviving the summer. Thus the Books of the Dead lend

Graph 4-2

Causes of Child Deaths, 1439

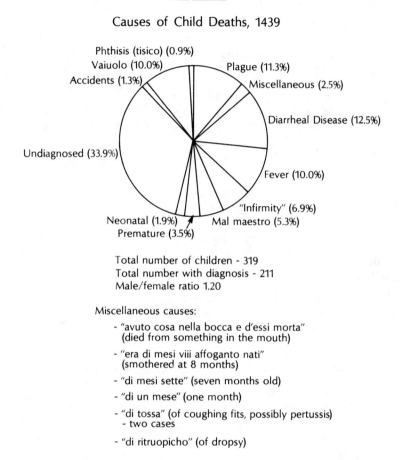

Phthisis (tisico) (0.9%)
Vaiuolo (10.0%)
Accidents (1.3%)
Plague (11.3%)
Miscellaneous (2.5%)
Diarrheal Disease (12.5%)
Undiagnosed (33.9%)
Fever (10.0%)
"Infirmity" (6.9%)
Neonatal (1.9%)
Premature (3.5%)
Mal maestro (5.3%)

Total number of children - 319
Total number with diagnosis - 211
Male/female ratio 1.20

Miscellaneous causes:

- "avuto cosa nella bocca e d'essi morta" (died from something in the mouth)

- "era di mesi viii affoganto nati" (smothered at 8 months)

- "di mesi sette" (seven months old)

- "di un mese" (one month)

- "di tossa" (of coughing fits, possibly pertussis) - two cases

- "di ritruopicho" (of dropsy)

support to the demographers' suggestions that by affecting the age distribution of the reproducing population minor plagues continued to have an important effect in stalling population recovery.[5]

Nevertheless, whether minor plagues were too frequent or too rich a mixture of infections to allow population recovery in the early fifteenth century, their undeniable effect was the way they shaped Florentine attitudes about the causes of pestilence. Legislators' actions, based on their experience with these minor plagues, radically changed traditional sanitary legislation in the area of plague control.

LEGISLATIVE SIGNIFICANCE OF MINOR PLAGUES

Traditional sanitary legislation

Leonardo Bruni, humanist chancellor of Florence from 1406 until
1444, singled out cleanliness among the city's special virtues:

Indeed, it seems to me that Florence is so clean and neat that no other
city could be cleaner. Surely this city is unique and singular in all the
world, because you will find there nothing that is disgusting to the eye,
offensive to the nose, or filthy under foot. There the great diligence of
all inhabitants ensures and provides that all filth is immediately removed
from the streets, so you see only what brings pleasure and joy to the
senses. Therefore, in its splendor Florence probably excels all the cities
of the world.[6]

Many Florentines similarly boasted that the city was "cleaner,
healthier, and more beautiful" than its neighbors, and the testi-
monies are a surprising contrast to modern notions of medieval
stench and squalor.[7]

Florence possessed a considerable body of sanitary legislation,
and much of it seems to have originated in the thirteenth century,
the century of Florence's greatest growth.[8] Most of the legislation
was written with an understanding of preventive health measures
dictated by Galenic medical concern for purification of water and
air, so it concerned the general areas of street cleaning and the
supervision and sale of meats, fruits, and fish. Overseers for each
judicial district of the city were to enforce the cleaning of streets
and piazzas and ensure that the city sewers were cleaned twice a
year. In years of epidemic or famine, the governing body, the
Signoria, had to appoint extraordinary controllers to continue normal sanitary surveillance, but in other years much of the legislation was left to individuals or to guilds to enforce. Most medieval
law saw street cleaning as the responsibility of those whose property faced the street.[9]

Fines and restrictions dominate communal statutes that survive
from the 1320s. A citizen must not construct channels for rain-
water drainage of his property such that the water emptied onto
the property of another. Those living beside the river must construct underground passages to the water for the disposal of human wastes. No sick animal may be watered at the communal
fountains. It was forbidden to throw human refuse out of a lodg-

ing before the third sounding of the communal bell at night (about
11 p.m.). No one except butchers may keep pigs or ducks in the
city. Manure could not be sold in the city. Neither dyers nor
butchers were allowed to empty filthy water or waste onto the
streets. The guildsman must either transport refuse out of the city,
or construct sewers from his home leading to the river. Butchers
were required to have an underground sewer in their residence for
draining blood or animal parts. (Though casting viscera of such
animals onto the streets was expressly forbidden by the statutes,
they could be emptied into the river.) Practicing trades which generated fetid odors was discouraged, "since the city of Florence must
be cleansed of such odors by which the air is corrupted and pestilential illnesses arise."[10]

Naturally the mere presence of such extensive legislation does
not prove that it was actually enforced. There are no comprehensive judicial records from this time or records of fines collected.
Only a handful of grievances reached the Signoria during the fourteenth century. Neighbors in an alleyway near the river complained that the area had become hazardous to their health, since
it was now marshy and filled with garbage. Residents near the
western wall of the city complained that sanitary conditions were
so bad that some had become ill.[11] These examples are rare, even
beside the usual petitions in the same province that argued for
street repairs because they would beautify the city or ensure safe,
efficient passage of merchandise. It is unlikely that sanitary legislation was of major concern to the upper echelons of Florentine
government during the early fourteenth century, but sanitation
was, at least, an acknowledged component of good government.

Outside the realm of statute law but within the working legislation of the commune was the provision of city physicians to the
poor. Magistro Jacopo de Urbe, "bonesetter," occupied this position in Florence for thirty years before the Black Death, and two
of his sons succeeded him during the 1350s. He received a meager
five florins a month for his extensive services, and twice had to
petition the Signoria to obtain a horse to take him to patients in
the surrounding district. Nonindigent citizens could easily avail
themselves of the services of a large number of physicians in the
city. Florence seems to have attracted sizable numbers of physician
migrants even though it possessed no medical school.[12]

Ordinarily prisoners were given medical care at communal expense even though the physician's duties included administering "justice" by the removal of hands, feet, or limbs. Similarly necessary was a continual vigilance against lepers entering the city, and statutes called for hired guards at the gates to prevent their entry. The commune supported the leprosarium as well. Communal leaders were more likely to extend charity, in both moneys and grain, during famine and epidemic times than they were under the everyday circumstances of hiring public physicians.[13]

Although we might now regard it as a form of "moral sanitation," the legislation regarding control of prostitutes and sodomites within the city also was included in traditional sanitary legislation. This was not because the city leaders felt that certain diseases were sexually transmitted, but rather because the activities of such individuals were offensive to God. Controls were necessary in order to

rout out evil and crime that can befall the city of Florence from the dishonesty of these women, living and working every day in the city, because in their shamelessness they commit many sins offensive to God and to the honor of the said city, and in their lasciviousness they form a bad example to others.[14]

Other aspects of moral sanitation included statutes to keep men's and women's days at the baths strictly separate, in order to reduce sin and vice resulting from "clandestine mixture of the sexes."

Moral legislation was linked to sanitary legislation during epidemic years before and including the Black Death.[15] Before 1348 the control of prostitutes and sodomites was enforced most rigidly when a crisis reminded the city leaders of their sanitary duties. This type of legislation held a prominent position in preplague crises and it survived the advent of new sanitary laws in the fifteenth century. Moral legislation tended to be embellished and updated more than were the older street-cleaning and meat-selling regulations.

Crisis legislation during and after the Black Death

Florentines knew that the plague had reached and destroyed Messina, Sicily, by October 1347, and that Pisa was stricken by winter. Traditional sanitary legislation was proclaimed anew through the streets of Florence at least once a month from January to May.[16]

Citizens were ordered to clean up streets and piazzas, to scour their homes, to keep animals out of the city, and to illuminate the streets at night. Butchers were reminded of the restrictions on the slaughter of animals and the sale of fresh meats. Prostitutes and sodomites were ordered out of the city. When these measures failed to prevent the entrance of plague, a 500–lire fine was imposed on travelers from Genoa and Pisa, the two hardest hit coastal towns, and vendors of used clothing and other goods were forbidden to sell the possessions of infected persons. Prostitutes were once again forbidden access to the city.[17]

By 11 April 1348, enforcement of the legislation seemed ineffective in the face of impending plague. An unusual step was taken: Eight prominent citizens were appointed as a special health commission, instructed to rigorously enforce sanitary laws. This included the forcible removal of "all putrid matter and infected persons, from which might arise or be induced a corruption or infection of the air." A skeleton crew of leaders desperately tried to maintain order and enforce sanitary measures throughout the summer.[18]

The creation of a sanitary commission was a temporary crisis measure provoked by the Black Death. But there is no record of another such "health board" in Florence until the end of the fifteenth century. In the interim the huge body of sanitary law had undergone little or no change, either in wording or in the amount of fines that could be levied. Novel sanitary measures to deal with plague were limited to minimizing social disruption during an epidemic, to obtaining information about the spread of plague, to dispensing charity toward those unable to leave a plague-ridden city, and to discussing the feasibility and advisability of constructing a plague hospital.

Florentines first posted guards during the plague of 1383. "Because of the current plague in the city of Florence," the new legislation read, "a large number of citizens are absent from the city, fleeing the pestilence." Worried about the "peaceful security" of Florence, legislators decided to hire soldiers and archers to protect the properties of absent citizens.[19] According to a chronicler, Florentines tried to curtail flight from the city. Since the "little people" (*popolo minuto* or *gente minuta*) could not leave, leaders feared that this faction would stir up new conflicts like those of the recent Ciompi revolt. Because the rich left anyway, next the priors tried to prevent any departure without their express permission. This failed as well. They then tried to tax those leaving and those who had already gone. When objections were raised, the priors contended that they needed the money to hire soldiers so that the state would remain stable.[20]

The fear of revolt must have risen with the number of deaths from plague. By July the chronicler seemed sure that the "little people" were stirring up rebellion. A treatise was discovered, allegedly written by these people. Because so many had fled the epidemic, the tract was said to have argued, those remaining might be able to call back some of the banished political dissidents and, with the popolo minuto, take over. A rally was held, and an unspecified number of people marched across the city from Sant' Ambruogio to the gate to Prato, beyond the Church of Ognissanti. According to several contemporaries the 1383 mortality was severe (reaching up to 400 deaths per day or more).[21]

There being now so few citizens remaining in Florence [July 1383], a brigade of Ciompi plotted . . . an uprising the night of Saint Mary Magdalene [July 22, the anniversary of the original Ciompi revolt of 1378]. They went throughout the city crying "Long live the twenty-four guilds and the Guelfs!" And they raised the banner of the guilds. But with the help of God and the provisions of the *signori* and the *Otto,* and the services of Messer Cante da Ghobbio, *capitano,* the rebels were seized following this, and were decapitated; thereafter the *signori* kept good watch and honorably ended their administration without any other incident.[22]

The plague of 1383 rekindled fears of armed conflict like that of the Ciompi revolt of 1378. Then artisans and day-wage laborers in the large wool industry had briefly dominated city politics, burning the houses of several wealthy citizens in their one-month show of power. Enraged patricians vowed never to allow their ascendancy again. After the 1383 plague, the hiring of guards became a regular feature of Florentine plague defense.[23]

By this fourth plague, flight to a healthy city was commonplace among wealthier citizens. The chancellor of Florence in 1383, Coluccio Salutati, was particularly disturbed by how many left, since he did not think that flight ensured survival. Prevailing medical theories of the corruption of the air made flight illogical. More important, he maintained, God alone determined the hour of one's death.[24] Experience with plague defeated the belief that flight was a rational response. Why, he asked, did the plague spare some in a household and not others? Why did the old die at some times and at others the debilitated? And especially, he wanted to know, *what* corrupted the air? If the winds, the swamps, or a failure to bury the dead caused the corruption, why were different cities and towns in a polluted region affected unequally? There was an instance where the plague was raging in Pisa, whereas outside the walls of the city all were healthy. Could walls separate healthy from infected air? Experience of the plague, Salutati concluded, showed that God alone determined the hour of one's death. He urged friends and fellow citizens not to flee the capricious epidemics.

Nevertheless most who could did flee. One of the reasons that Florentine diarists and chroniclers describe epidemics of the early fifteenth century so poorly was that they did not witness the events.[25] Those who stayed became convinced that a place was infected once a death from plague occurred and flight from that place offered some hope. Goro Dati described his intracity flight:

The pestilence was in our house, as God who provides all good things so willed, and began with our servant, Paccino, at the end of June 1420. Then three days later our slave Marta [was stricken], then the first of July my daughter Sandra, and 5 July, Antonia. And thus we all left the house and went opposite [*dirimpetto*] and in just a few days Veronica died. So we left there and went to Via Chiara, where the illness took Bandecca and Pippa. They both went to paradise on the first of August; all had the sign of pestilence. It ended, and we returned to our house.[26]

Flight was rational only if one knew where plague had not broken out. There is little Florentine evidence for the use of a network of information about plague outbreaks, but the evidence elsewhere in northern Italy shows that even tiny towns kept informed about safe and proscribed cities. But even as early as 1383, fleeing Florentines seem to have carefully chosen two cities that were not affected by the widespread plague outbreaks that year.[27] By the mid-fifteenth century such information gathering was standard plague procedure.

In 1448 the Signoria first used the word "contagion" to describe the plague. They appointed additional priests to hear confessions and administer the sacraments, four physicians and four barber-surgeons, forty women and twenty men to attend the sick, partic-

ularly the indigent, and they considered the necessity of a special
hospital for plague patients.

Much of the novel effort was designed by Florence's archbishop, Antoninus, who was more concerned with the administration of needed charity to the poor than with the spread of
plague. His request for a lazaretto casually referred to the contagion of plague; his plea was for better administration of food and
medical care. With the city nearly evacuated, not only by the ar-
istocracy but also by middle-class citizens, many poor were un-
employed and destitute. Antoninus persuaded the Signoria to al-
locate 3,000 florins, and with some of the money he hired young
people to seek out the sick and see to their needs.[28] Because he was
much more concerned with the lack of Christian charity the fear
of plague engendered than with plague's contagious spread, Antoninus presented the request for a plague hospital in the context
of helping the poor and needy.[29]

Similarly the isolation hospital proposed in 1464 was a work of
charity to "placate almighty God and persuade Him to be merciful
to this people and preserve them from such pestilential disease."[30]
The large hospital of Santa Maria Nuova continued to be used
temporarily for plague patients during the epidemic years, but with
plague victims deliberately segregated from other sick persons.
Legislation proposed the construction of a lazaretto specifically to
control the contagious spread of plague, arguing that "receiving
and caring for these stricken [endangered] those ill from other infirmities." Five citizens, together with the rector of Santa Maria
Nuova, were to take charge of the lazaretto project in a search for
land and funds that was to last fifteen years.[31]

In 1464 the Florentine Signoria also aggressively designated
plague hospitals for Pisa and Livorno, conscious that these maritime towns were likely to meet plague cases before Florence did.[32]
All these provisions, the priors and their colleagues argued, would
show the world that Florence was more charitable than any other
city and could provide for sick and healthy, for wanderers, and
"all sorts of miserable persons." Florence would take in plague
sufferers, "even though this be perilous to those who govern [and
though the city] be abandoned and deserted by all."[33]

The most persuasive argument for spending money on the
plague stricken was the growing conviction that plague was spread
more by contagion than by corruption of the air. Charity had

meshed with communal motives for building a lazaretto in 1464, but by 1476, when the commune was again exploring possible resources for completing a new hospital, the Signoria was clearly aware that their efforts were being directed to only one social class.

In sum, during the first century after 1348 legislative responses to recurring plagues were surprisingly slow. Generation after generation traditional sanitary laws were recopied, unchanged. Controlling the disruption plague outbreaks caused in the lives of influential citizens occupied the attention of legislators for a century after the Black Death. Most of the attention of the ruling elite was directed to protecting person and property during the plagues. But by the mid-fifteenth century legislation began to address the control of plague itself, through control of infected persons. Very quickly this new approach to plague adjusted its focus to the social problems of the day.

SOCIAL SIGNIFICANCE OF EMERGING PLAGUE LEGISLATION

The plague hospital, called the *spedale del morbo,* was first used during the epidemic of 1497. By the end of the fifteenth century a gradual change in plague controls and sanitary legislation resulted in a mature system of epidemic surveillance and control, employing many separate units of the Florentine government and recalling to service the idea of a "health board" first used in 1348. From 1493 until 1498 Florence was under the threat of plague, though a full-scale epidemic like that of 1479 never occurred. The story of their preventive measures well illustrates the contemporary association between plague and poverty.

On 12 April 1493, the Eight of Watch and Ward, usually acting as a secret police in political matters, wrote scathing letters to the Consuls of the Sea in Pisa, and to the captains overseeing the Florentine countryside.[34] "We have taken no less wonder than displeasure [at your actions] having ordered you . . . [to keep] . . . good watch of and provision for plague, and to be vigilant and diligent that no one from a place suspected of plague pass through." Both the captains and the consuls were held responsible for the "quantity of ruffians" [*marrani*] who arrived at the city gates on the road from Pisa. The officials, together with "principal citizens," were disturbed at the lack of prudence displayed by those whom they held responsible to keep "such kind of people and in such numbers" away from the city.[35]

The Eight had reports of plague from Naples, Volterra, and the swampland near Pisa, and had so informed the sea consulate 27 March 1493, charging them to take every precaution to keep Pisa and Livorno free from infection.[36] Notices continued through the summer of 1493, and alarm grew because Rome was infected. The Signoria delegated special powers and funds to another committee, usually in charge of foreign affairs, to oversee the city's defense against the *morbo per contagione,* giving them "most ample and liberal authority" to act as they saw fit within the jurisdictional compass of Florence.[37] As long as the plague was in Rome, they had special license to act.[38]

Early in March 1494 the Signoria created an extraordinary commission, a *balìa* of five citizens "pro la cura della peste," reminiscent of the original 1348 health board and the 1464 hospital committee. Unlike the officers used in the previous year, they had no responsibilities other than keeping plague out of Florence. During their six-month term they were occupied solely with communicating to field representatives, dispensing licenses for passage through their territory or entry into the city, securing information as to the spread of plague, and condemning violators of their proclamations.[39]

Like their predecessors this commission felt that some travelers were a greater threat to the health of the city than were others. Gatekeepers were warned on 10 April to keep out "scoundrels, swindlers and the poor, or other people on foot who came begging"; on 16 April a widow and her family were banished for having recently visited Rome.[40] But although bans multiplied against markets, festivals, processions, and even against the movements of clergy, others of greater political importance to the state were awarded license to enter, though they traveled unabashedly from plague-infested regions.[41]

The committee moved swiftly and efficiently in its communications with the leaders of smaller Tuscan towns. A case of plague in Monte Varchi drew their immediate attention, and they instructed the local vicar to investigate and organize strict watch so that infected persons did not mingle with others. Of course, their needs for food and spiritual comfort were to be met, but the vicar was to give nearly daily notice of the progress of infection within the town.[42] Roads were blocked, and even though plague did not appear to have taken hold of the town, inhabitants were still forbidden festive celebrations for religious holidays.[43] The committee saw to all details, from imprisoning those selling food or clothing to poor travelers on the highways, to collecting and killing dogs – thought to be plague carriers.[44]

The committee considered plague to be contagious, and moved quickly to contain each newly reported case in the *contado* so that "the contagion of this disease not be spread to other persons."[45] Consequently, many letters demanded of informants and officials that effort be spent in diagnosing each doubtful case in their areas. Once a case was diagnosed with certainty, not only was the family isolated, but officials were instructed to spare no effort in ascertaining that the contacts of the ill person were segregated from the general community. The vigilance only gradually relaxed after information reached Florence that cases in Rome were lessening and that the plague there was ending in "noncontagious fevers."[46]

The care and responsibility assumed by the five men in charge went unlauded by chroniclers and contemporary historians. No cases of plague occurred within the city, and the numerous instances of insulted worthies, as well as efforts to smuggle friends and family into Tuscany, suggest that the committee aroused not a little resentment. The bans were lifted in September 1494.[47]

Since scattered notices of nearby plague cases continued, by early March of 1496 the Signoria chose to create another group to deal with plague, now called the plague officers, *Ufficiali del morbo*.[48] They suspected that plague had already begun in many places in the countryside but thus far no cases appeared within the city walls. The officials were to serve until October, supervising care for the sick poor and seeing that those individuals did not mingle with others. All was done in the absence of actual plague in the city. Sporadic cases in Florentine territories continued as the summer progressed, but plague did not take hold. More troublesome that year, reported a diarist, were the "French boils" resembling smallpox that afflicted chiefly adults.[49] (This was one of the early reports of syphilis, the "great" pox.) Not until December were cases of plague discovered within Florence.[50] Famine followed in early 1497; prices of foodstuffs soared. On 19 March the chronicler tersely noted that "more than one child was found dead of hunger in Florence."[51]

Girolamo Savonarola's inflammatory preaching stirred up much political turmoil in Florence this year, so the Signoria took advantage of fears about plague, little substantiated by actual cases, to control his preaching in the city. Early in May they forbade any large convocations, especially for sermons, since such assemblies increased the danger of plague.[52] Instead of plague, "pestilential fevers" were at work, "making [people] rave and lose consciousness, and when that happened they died in two or three days." On 1 June:

Many people died of fever after being ill only a few days, some in eight days and some in ten, and there was one man who died in four days. It was said that during these last days of the waning moon there were 120 cases at the hospitals and in the city together. It was also said that there was a touch of plague at the hospital. Ten or twelve cases went there each day and 24 have died just lately at Santa Maria Nuova. At the same time there was another trouble, the spiritual discouragement and physical weakness, which caused the poor to be indifferent as to dying; and numbers of them did die, in fact. Everyone said, "this is an honest plague."[53]

Excommunicated on 18 June, Savonarola could offer his followers only a written "spiritual" regimen against the worsening epidemics.[54] Hunger, fever, and plague continued through the summer and fall, lessening gradually with harvest and winter.

The Ufficiali del morbo survived well into 1498, and their activities included expelling the suspected poor just ten days before the ill-fated Savonarola was hanged and burned. The diarist lamented:

The officers of the plague went into the hospitals and drove out the unfortunate sufferers; and wherever they found them in the city they sent them out of Florence. They were actually so cruel as to place hempen rope with a pulley outside the Armorers' Guild to torture those who tried to return. It was a brutal thing and a harsh remedy.[55]

The officers of health became a permanent institution in Florentine government after the plague of 1527.[56]

The gradual commitment to a contagion theory of plague, and to a near certainty that the poor were most frequently the carriers of plague emerged before 1500 in Florence. The need for accurate information about occurrences of plague, the necessity of protecting properties during plague, and the general need to provide some form of charity and community services during a crisis were all present in the previous century of major plagues, but no system of plague prevention and control emerged.

Control of some individuals – poor, wanderers, beggars, "ruffians" – and not others (cardinals and ambassadors, for example) was seen as integral to the control of plague in a way that was not envisioned in 1348. Possibly this aspect of plague control was but an extended, well-developed form of the moral sanitation that greeted epidemics of the fourteenth century, forcing out prostitutes, sodomites, and others who offended God, but by the end of the fifteenth century it was expressly linked to the spread of plague rather than to pleasing God. The shift in perspective can be seen as a secularization of older moral laws, but it fit well in the emerging legislation to control the spread of plague. The minor plagues of the fifteenth century had seemingly provided critical experiential data to support the theory of contagion, and the safe flight of Florentines during plague years undoubtedly added to both their certainty of plague's contagious spread and to the likelihood that the poor would die in greater numbers than the well-to-do. The establishment of isolation hospitals only reinforced this link between plague and poverty.

5

Plague controls become social controls

In 1348 Italian communes immediately responded to the threat of epidemic by enforcing traditional sanitary laws. When these failed, they enacted extraordinary crisis measures to minimize social disruption. Finally, they sought in desperation simply to maintain order through the disaster. As much as a century later little had changed in this sequence of responses, despite the frequent recurrence of plague.

Then in the mid-fifteenth century, as if by consensus, Italian legislators decided to isolate plague sufferers by building or designating a lazaretto (pest house). The emphasis on special hospital care shifted from the mere provision of charitable services to isolation of the ill and their contacts. Once hospital isolation of plague sufferers became routine, lawmakers phrased their concern for plague control in terms that betrayed their conviction that plague was a contagious disease. By the end of the fifteenth century health boards were widely considered to be necessary bureaucracies in overseeing the enforcement of sanitary law in times of crisis. And, as we have seen, this new legislation had become tinged by the consciousness that poorer persons were more frequently the victims and the carriers of plague.

PLAGUE CONTROLS IN 1348

Pistoia was one of the Tuscan hill towns within the sphere of Florentine influence, a town that provided many immigrants to Florence. No later than March or April of 1348 plague had penetrated the surrounding district.[1] The Council of the People met sufficiently regularly until June to record all their efforts to stifle plague's progress. On 23 May 1348 they forbade entrance to the city of any "matter of the illness" (*materia infirmitatis*) from the epidemic reigning in the countryside, referring to both people and goods. Furthermore, communication with Lucca and Pisa, towns known to be already infected, was forbidden, except by consent of the council. Gatekeepers were assigned to enforce this legislation.

In Pistoia the particulars of epidemic control are much more explicit in the surviving records than they are in Florence. Used clothing, specifically linen rather than wool, was barred from city trade, and articles confiscated from violators were to be publicly burned. Dead bodies had to be placed in wooden caskets "so that no *fetor* could escape," and had to be buried at least two and one-half arms' lengths deep into the ground. No dead bodies could be transported into the city for burial. Citizens were warned not to associate with the families of victims or enter the house of a victim, and all mourning activities and visits were restricted to "immediate" family. (The deaths of nobles, lawyers, judges, physicians, and other notables could continue to command a greater mourning display.) These crisis measures were set beside a reiteration of traditional legislation: restrictions on the sale of fresh meats, particularly during the summer months, on the slaughter of pigs, on the burning of unused animal flesh, and on the cleaning and tanning of animal hides inside the walls of the city. There is also a hint in the council's proceedings that Pistoians kept a record of all who died.[2]

By June the Council found it "almost impossible" to assemble a quorum of elders and to continue official provisions. Records disappeared after 27 June, following attempts to revise the number needed for passing new legislation. The last known ordinances before 27 June were directed toward sanitation and funeral display.[3] No bell ringing should accompany burial of the dead, no funeral processions could follow the deceased to the church. Mourning was restricted to immediate family and relatives on the mother's side only. Sixteen men for each district were hired to extract the dead from their houses and deposit them at the church for burial. The public porters would be paid from communal funds so long as they gave written notification of the burial, consigned by the priest, monk, or hospital rector at the burial ground. The council still enjoined "good men" to carry and bury the poor without remuneration. The number of candles burned for the dead would be severely limited, and churches were to curtail the use of torches.

Elsewhere in Tuscany, Luccans proscribed travelers from Genoa and Catalonia as early as 14 January 1348 – though to no avail.[4] The Perugians, according to a local chronicler, even boasted a team of physicians dissecting plague victims to ascertain the causes of plague. No record of public health measures in Perugia survives from 1348, but a chronicler noted that physicians counseled their private patients to be careful of diet and to ingest prophylactic medicines (especially purgatives) that would prepare the body to withstand corrupt air.[5]

Venetian officials, far removed from Tuscany, also created a special health board to deal with the Black Death. A three-man commission concentrated their efforts on sanitation just as had Florentines (see chap. 4, "Crisis Legislation During and After the Black Death"). With even more reason than the Pistoians had, they worried about health measures in burial.[6] New cemeteries had to be consecrated quickly to receive all the bodies; boatmen were needed to transport them. Burial pits needed to be dug to a minimum depth of five feet.[7] As in Lucca and Pisa, ill foreigners were quickly perceived to be a source of infection, especially when the epidemic began to worsen. Incarcerating travelers and burning their goods, including the boats carrying them, became possible penalties for infraction of the new rules.[8]

Historians who have studied or reviewed these events in the history of public health often note rightly how similar the actions taken against the plague of 1348 were to those taken during large, well-documented sixteenth- and seventeenth-century epidemics. However, such a telescoped view overlooks three important features of this history. First is that the "prototype" health boards of 1348 were not recalled for a hundred years. Second, in later centuries the motivations and justifications for sanitary policy were analyzed piecemeal by both legislators and physicians in a way that was not attempted during the 1348 disaster. Finally, physicians and legislators were, by 1500, not motivated by the same reasons when they subscribed to particular sanitary policies, even when they agreed on the measures to be taken.

PLAGUE CONTROLS AFTER 1348

Real changes in sanitary legislation began with the initiation of quarantine, but that measure was not used on the Italian mainland before the fifteenth century. Venice's small Adriatic colony, Ragusa (now Dubrovnik), adopted in 1377 a thirty-day period of isolating travelers and their goods. The isolation applied to all travelers, not just those coming from a locale where plague raged. Thus the quarantine isolated healthy individuals and their goods in order to halt the extension of infection. The original quarantine was not motivated by an early appeal to contagion as an explanation of the spread of disease. It was instead a passive waiting and watching for a hidden epidemic. Legislators fully expected the air to become locally infected if plague was incubating aboard ship. The Ragusans, utterly dependent on sea trade and having little commerce with the mainland, could be reasonably sure that plague was transported to the city from outside. No other obvious source of infection existed. In the original quarantine, no traveler's good health was taken for granted and no provisions were made for the isolation of plague stricken individuals once plague appeared. The original legislation contained no explicit defense of a contagion theory; even in Ragusa measures to isolate the ill did not appear until the mid–fifteenth century.[9]

The external origin of plague was less apparent to inhabitants of inland cities or of ports having extensive communication with inland hinterlands than it was to the Ragusans. Most cities did not develop anything like a quarantine before the fifteenth century. Two exceptions are worth mentioning, for they show that a single, powerful ruler could enforce unpopular legislation isolating well individuals. In both cases, however, the rulers were convinced that plague was contagious and could be carried by healthy individuals who traveled from a region where plague raged. Thus they did not defend the quarantine as a passive defense against infection. Not surprisingly, in both Milan and Mantua the ruler's belief in plague contagion dictated the adoption of additional measures to isolate those suffering from plague as well.

Within the space of a few months, and several years before Ragusa's quarantine, Bernabò Visconti of Milan and Ludovico Gonzaga of Mantua took unusual steps to defend these two cities from epidemic. The Milanese proscription was earlier (17 January 1374) and is fairly well known.[10] Bernabò Visconti wrote to an official in Reggio in Emilia the measures that he thought were most useful to control plague in the city. Priests would view the ill in their parishes and notify inquisitors of the nature of the disease. The stricken would be sent outside the city walls. All of these provisions operated on the basic presupposition that plague was a contagious disease, and so it was treated just as leprosy had been in the preceding centuries.[11] Visconti's ordinance even admits that he wished to preserve Milan and its territory "from contagious maladies."

Ludovico Gonzaga decreed sometime in 1374 that any Mantuan who passed through a place where the great mortality raged could not then reenter the city. Those who violated the new law risked death.

And it shall be cried out and commanded . . . that any person of the vicarates of Borgoforte, Luzara, Suzara, Gonzaga, Rozolo [Reggiolo] or any other part of Mantuan territory, or who even lives in the Mantuan domain, whether male or female, of whatever status great or small, is forbidden to enter any territory in which there be the epidemic or mortality, under penalty of death; . . . and citizens are obligated to make a denunciation of violators to the vicars. Furthermore no one living in Mantuan territory may receive or lodge any person coming from a territory where the epidemic rages, under penalty of death for so violating.[12]

The vicars, themselves under threat of death if they disobeyed, were additionally obliged to enforce this legislation, burning transgressors' goods and houses. There was no specific mention of a fixed period of isolation, as there was in the Ragusan quarantine, but the Milanese and Mantuan examples did apply to all citizens.

The early Mantuan and Milanese examples suggest that tyrants had uncontested, unqualified authority over their cities. Neither ruler apparently listened to conflicting medical opinions, and neither apparently considered astrological explanations for the appearance of plague. Gonzaga and Visconti had the power to do something that was politically and economically unpopular and that violated medical counsel as well.[13]

By 1400 anyone passing through Mantuan territory needed official license (a *boletino*) to travel during plague times.[14] As early as 1374 Bernabò Visconti had designated official guards to prohibit anyone from a plague region entering Milan.[15] His successor, Giangaleazzo Visconti, exercised an even greater power in extending preventive plague bans. By August 1397, Giangaleazzo banned all travelers coming from plague-ridden Belluno.[16] As the great plague of 1400 approached, the proscriptions escalated.

Giangaleazzo appointed one trusted official to coordinate all his bans, proclamations, and plague-relief measures. First, all the towns in Visconti domain were proscribed as they became plague infected.[17] Each town had to obey trade and travel restrictions and actively provide assistance to its infected citizens. One of the Visconti circulars, dated 10 January 1400, shows the extent of the duke's power and concern:

We have heard with some displeasure that there are many cities and regions of our territory where the disease had once fallen, and where for some time the plague then ceased, so long that the cities deemed themselves free of plague; and after a little while the plague then flared up again, striking down many men, women, and children. And it is thought to have come out of other sources, either from citizens or from outsiders who have stayed in some infected place and then reentered this city. But others explain that it came from those houses in which the disease had formerly appeared, thence proceeding to the rest of the city and countryside which had remained healthy. [By this latter explanation] those returning to the infected houses made no attempt to disinfect or fumigate the houses and so the disease was easily disseminated. Therefore we command that you take mature and discreet warning concerning these infected homes.[18]

Giangaleazzo augmented preventive plague measures to include the fumigation of houses where plague had occurred. He was also clearly unwilling to accept halfway quarantine measures as citizens had done. He ordered that "suspects" or survivors of plague households should be transported out of the city to houses (*mansiones*) of recovery, and he severely restricted fairs and festivals that would increase the association of the sick and healthy.

Once plague broke out in Milan, however, most of the duke's provisions aimed only at managing the crisis. In 1399 Giangaleazzo ordered that Milan's city gates be closed during the plague assault, as he frequently did when war made Milan vulnerable to foreign invasion, but there is no evidence that he allowed guards to protect the property of absentee citizens. He tried to ensure a supply of foodstuffs, since he thought that famine could lead to further plague. He ordered that the sick be carried to hospitals, and when the plague worsened he forbade the well to leave, demanding that they assume the jobs of the sick and dead.[19] Wagons to collect the poor and transport them to hospitals had been employed since 1396, and they were used extensively during the plague. The sick lived in fear of the rattle of carriages.[20]

All the Visconti legislation was based on the ruler's belief in the contagious spread of plague. It was not a program widely imitated in 1400 or in the generation that followed because it was costly and difficult to enforce, but more importantly because most northern Italians in 1400 did not believe in the contagiousness of plague. A contagion theory acceptable to university-trained physicians needed to explain precisely what could be transmitted by contact. Even Galen had ultimately rejected the notion of invisible particles or substances passed from one body to another, in favor of a generalized corruption of ambient air that could corrupt body humors. Giangaleazzo died of a "pestilential fever" in 1402, and his successor, Gian Maria Visconti, continued to enforce his program of plague control. However, the measures were abandoned by the time of the plague of 1406 in Milan. There was no comparable legislation to fight plague in Milan until 1424, and then the provisions did not stem from the Visconti Duke or his personal secretaries.[21] In the generation between 1424 and mid-century, widespread interest in controlling the spread of plague emerged throughout northern Italy.

Under Filippo Maria Visconti's rule (1412–47) official bans began to appear from the "Vicar of Provisions," the "Twelve of Provision," and the "Commissioner of Health." In other words, the plague controls in the fifteenth century became separated institutionally from the duke and his retinue. Consequently the commission turned more attention to Milan's needs. It prohibited change of habitation within the city during a plague, as well as the movement of household goods; houses where someone had died of plague had to be aired out thoroughly. The commissioner's office may have been a relatively permanent one since references to the office are scattered among Milanese notices from 1424 to 1447.[22]

Without the influence of Giangaleazzo Visconti, Milanese legislation developed at the same time as the beginning of extensive plague bans throughout northern Italy. In 1422 Forlì officials proscribed travel from at least fourteen different towns identified as infected.[23] The Perugians proclaimed in 1424 that no citizen could lodge a foreigner coming from a place suspected of being plague ridden.[24] In mid-July 1424, the council of Udine banned all travelers from infected places, except those who had the express license of the council.[25] The Venetian senate even sent out warnings to galley captains to avoid places infected with plague.[26] Similarly in Mantua the Gonzaga lord issued the same sort of plague restrictions many city-states were finding necessary in 1428: No one could harbor an outsider traveling from a plague site; no citizen could leave and return home if he traveled to a plague region; and no one from a plague-infected house could move elsewhere.[27]

By midcentury, legislation banning commerce with infected places was widespread and extensive. The Gonzaga of Mantua commanded an impressive information network, including information about large territories and major commercial cities along with reports from tiny villages in the immediate vicinity of Mantua. Detailed information continued to be proclaimed from March 1447 until plague finally reached Mantua on 27 March 1451:

The illustrious *principe* . . . with a singular displeasure and bitterness has learned that a death from a contagious illness has occurred within Mantua; and wishing, with humble supplication to almighty God as well, to make full provisions which will preserve the city from further malady . . . he will have proclaimed that no one may presume to visit any infirm person or his immediate family without the express license of the court . . . . Moreover, every day at evening, the *Cavi de Compagnia* must present written notice of the sick in their district to the *Ufficiale de la bolete,* and insofar as it is known, of what cause the person suffers, and what needs each sick person may have for provisions.[28]

Apparently Mantua continued to be well staffed with physicians. The marchese felt that many died needlessly in July because medical attention was not sought soon enough. Physicians, for their part, complained that public baths and games increased the number of infected persons.[29]

During the subsequent years, Mantuan officials continued to gather information about plague outbreaks. To give some idea how accurate the marchese's information could be, on 24 July 1456 the public criers announced that Florence was now infected, but "not greatly."[30] They knew and reported to the citizens of Mantua that there were a few plague cases in just two parishes of Florence (see chap. 3, "Individual Diagnoses of Plague"). The Mantuan record says that several other cases were in the large hospital of Santa Maria Nuova, for which no Florentine record now survives.

In sum, mid-fifteenth-century bans on travel and trade from plague regions were the first real innovations for inland cities and towns.[31] These measures are based upon the basic quarantine idea (i.e., segregating persons and merchandise to prevent the progress of plague into a territory), but the restrictions were limited to those people and goods that have passed through a plague region. True maritime quarantine was not feasible for inland cities and towns. The measures also may have provided a network of information about safe regions and cities.

THE EVOLUTION OF TRUE PLAGUE CONTROLS

The second major innovation in plague controls before the mid-fifteenth century was the development of bureaucracies to protect the properties of those who fled the infected cities. Before the mid-fifteenth century, guards were not hired expressly for the purpose of controlling the spread of plague.[32] Just as the information network may have served their flight from plague, so the increased use of guards supports a conclusion that flight became the dominant response to plague among the privileged classes of the early Renaissance. The Florentine motive governing the use of guards was neither charitable nor defensive against outside aggressors. These guards were now used to staff the city gates and rebuff those traveling from plague areas. The Ciompi revolt was unique to Florence and appears to have been a sufficient stimulus for this new use of plague guards.

Venice saw no conflict comparable to that in Florence, but its progressive use of plague guards can be traced in the minutes of the highest governing bodies.[33] In 1348 the Greater Council of Venice called on hired nightwatchmen to help supervise their surveillance of incoming goods and travelers, because it suspected those travelers might bring further infection into the city.[34] In the fifteenth century these very same nightwatchmen were used to patrol the waters and arrest looters, in other words, to supervise a watch over the personal property of those absent from the city during plague.

Boatmen to patrol the goods and houses of absentee merchants became a regular feature of Venetian plague defense by the mid-fifteenth century. The rationale given for hiring guards in 1456 illustrates how the measure was thought useful:

Since many nobles and other good citizens have fled the city on account of plague, such that the city is practically vacant, it is necessary to provide custodians of the city because so many dangers and inconveniences might otherwise occur. Especially [we must protect] homes left without any custodian from thieves and evil men, just as has often been done by this council in similar cases. Thus we decree that sixteen boats will be armed with four men in each boat, governed by four captains.[35]

The following year first eight-, then twelve-, then the full sixteen-boat patrol was reinstated in the spring. In the heat of summer fines were again ordered for boatmen sleeping on the job, and sixteen additional men were hired to watch over the costly merchandise in shops near the Rialto, "so that crimes may be prevented." Guards were casually added to the normal patrol as the plague worsened.

Just as in Florence with the Ciompi episode, the Venetian defense of properties in 1456 and 1457 coincided with a fear of disruption by a disenfranchised remnant within the city. The coming of plague was linked to the arrival of Albanian and Slavic immigrants to Venice, hungry job seekers who crowded the public squares and porticoes.[36] Throughout the fifteenth century Slavic peoples had been steadily moving into Venetian colonies on the Adriatic, and their migrations were stepped up with the push westward of the Ottoman Turks. In the mid-fifteenth century a sizable number of the refugees descended on cities in eastern Italy, and the ruling patriciates obviously resented their presence. In 1455 Venetians justified dispersal of the immigrants by citing the public health nuisance they created:

Whereas many men, women and children from Slavic territories have come to this city in extreme poverty and misery, and many of them are sick; and whereas they have retired, scattering themselves to the arcades of palaces and to San Marco; it was provided that they should go to stay in one of the communal buildings near San Blasius. And so they did. But as their numbers grew, so did the number of them infirm, such that there remained little doubt that their refuse and odor would infect both the places and the people nearby. After this the whole city [would be infected], especially with spring coming . . . Wishing to avoid every inconvenience and considering that every possible provision be made that the city, God willing, be preserved from pestilential plague (*morbo pestifero*), [we recommend] that these poor be removed from the building . . . and the Slavs who are sick be sent to the lazaretto so that they will be fed and cared for. . . . Those others who want to leave the city and live somewhere else should be given a quarter of a ducat.[37]

The lazaretto was used to segregate a social group, not to isolate plague cases. The following summer (1456) brought famine. The Council of Ten feared the "danger and great confusion" food shortages could produce in the city, so they redoubled efforts to secure more Sicilian grain.[38] With the proclamations of plague that summer and the next, the council found it relatively easy to rid the city of immigrants on the grounds that they had brought the plague to Venice.

Albanian and Slavic refugees were also the targets of plague controls in other eastern Italian towns. In Recanati, on 30 December 1460, the city legislature proclaimed that the immigrants should get out before the coming January festival.[39] In the same years Perugians ordered that "every Albanian, whether man or woman, who has come here *within the last three years,* has now three days to pack up and leave the city and countryside. Violators risk the loss of their belongings, two lashes each, and a year in prison" (emphasis mine).[40] Among the plague provisions in Jesi in 1467, all Albanians who had come to settle in the territory during the previous ten years were banished. The measure accompanied more usual plague restrictions on trade and travel, placing guards at the city gates, limiting festivals, procuring physicians, and opening two new hospitals. The epidemics, however, did not come until 1470; the period during which these individuals were seen as infective was well beyond the normal quarantine. When the "pestilential influence" arrived, in small measure during the years 1470 to 1473, and viciously after 1479, the leaders of Jesi found the territory "infested with Albanians and Slavs who, fleeing the Turk, brought the plague and other calamities with them to the Italian lands which sheltered them."[41] The bans, like those of Perugia and Recanati, were renewed in 1479.

The development of a lazaretto or plague house was an essentially different idea from the passive quarantine. The earliest permanent lazaretto isolating plague sufferers was created by the Venetian republic in 1423, "because our city is infected by pestilential illness almost every year." The senators decided to reconsider their entire plague defense program, and, if it were deemed necessary, build a separate hospital. The illness was blamed on foreigners coming from pestilential regions. Unless some provision were made the steady flow of travelers and merchants would ensure continual infection; banning travelers from unhealthy regions thus became a popular measure. These aggressive bans were dependent upon the quarantine idea and exactly contemporary with the rest of northern Italian restrictive legislation. Violators of the trade and travel bans would be incarcerated, as would those citizens who housed them. But, the legislation continues, such regulations might not suffice to keep out pestilence, so funds to build a hospital needed to be set aside. Any persons from Venice or the immediately surrounding *terraferma* "in whose houses one has become ill with pestilence," can be sent to this hospital so that their needs might be attended. A prior, prioress, female attendants, and physicians would be supplied at communal expense.[42]

Besides commitment to the quarantine idea, charity was the fundamental aim of this legislation. The lazaretto was designed to facilitate care of the ill during the plague. In 1430 the senate reflected that the designation of a hospital had been most useful, but their efforts had been somewhat dampened by the clergy's refusal to attend the sick, a refusal governed by their "fear of excommunication or other irregularity" incurred from higher authority if they should visit the lazaretto. The senate decided to intervene in church matters to the extent of writing to influential cardinals, perhaps even to the pope himself. The lazaretto was now defended as a measure that would protect the city from further "contagion" but it was still an institution whose main purpose was charitable relief to the sick.[43]

Ferrara's plague hospital was established with the same charitable intention as was the original Venetian lazaretto.[44] As Table 5–1 suggests, however, most communities decided to build plague hospitals in the mid-fifteenth century, fully a century after plagues began. Florentine discussions of the use of an isolation hospital originally had been in the context of providing charity, and another major example contemporary with the Florentine decisions shows the same starting point.

Milan was briefly governed by its own citizens at the end of the 1440s, and one of the first tasks assumed by the new "captains and defenders of the liberty of Milan" was those prophylactic measures in plague prevention that the previous Visconti government had supported. An official in charge of preserving the health of the city was appointed, and he took over or continued normal surveillance, including the registration of suspicious deaths. From December 1447 to October 1448, a time when there was no direct

Table 5–1. *The decision to build a*
lazaretto: northern Italian cities in the
mid-fifteenth century

City	Year of Legislation
Venice	1456 [1423]
Ferrara	1463 [1436]
Florence	1463 [1448]
Milan	1468 [1450]
Mantua	1450
Genoa	1467
Siena	1478
Ragusa	1464
Parma	1468
Udine	1464
Recanati	1462

Note: Brackets indicate that an older
hospital was designated as a plague
hospital, temporarily, during the crisis.

mention of pestilence near Milan, the republic also combined sanitary and charitable needs the way its predecessors had by assign-
ing a hospital and salaried physicians to a villa at Cusago, all "in
service of the poor and the infirm." The office of health seems to
have had charity as its only motive for administering to the poor,
for no mention of segregating plague cases accompanies its efforts
to secure the new hospital. In fact, two locations to which they
transported the sick poor were assigned, one outside the city (Cusago) and one inside. Neither was a plague hospital.[45]

As the plague once again invaded Lombardy, this situation
changed. Milanese territories were definitely infected by March
1449. Bans and announcements similar to those of Mantua accompanied active surveillance of the plague's movement. At the same
time famine worsened, and administrators linked the progression
of famine to the growing fear of plague, so they redoubled efforts
to transport the poor to a place where they could be more easily
fed. When the plague finally hit in full force in 1451, however, the
governors of the board of hospitals that controlled the Cusago
retreat were forced to use the institution for the first time as a
refuge for the plague stricken. One contemporary historian esti-

mated that up to 30,000 died that year; thus the desperate need for a large facility such as that at Cusago seems to have dictated its first emergency use as a lazaretto.[46]

The proposal to construct a true lazaretto, rather than merely designate a previously existing hospital as one for plague sufferers, was not made in Milan until 1468. Construction did not begin until 1486, and the plague hospital was not completed until 1488.[47] The timing of Florentine and Milanese decisions that a plague hospital was necessary, the delays in finding money and land, and the final contruction are almost identical in the two cases. Similarly Genoese elders made a decision to build a lazaretto in 1467, although their hospital was not completed until 1512.[48] As Table 5–1 shows, Venice, Siena, Parma, Udine, Cremona, Recanati, even Ragusa – all decided during the 1460s and 1470s that a plague isolation facility was necessary.[49] Shortly after the mid-fifteenth century, most of the legislators of northern Italy found that a lazaretto was necessary to meet their needs for plague control.

PLAGUE LEGISLATION FOR THE POOR

Just as in Florence, the re-creation of health boards occurred elsewhere in northern Italy during the later fifteenth century (see Table 5–2). And just as in Florence, the bureaucracies created to manage public health all evolved policies of plague prevention and control that selected one social class as the predominant vector of plague contagion. Some were temporary, some permanent, but the decision to re-create health boards was made at virtually the same time everywhere in northern Italy, just as had been the decision to build a lazaretto.

From their inception in 1348, more than a century of plagues went by before the idea of health boards was again seen as sound. An early example from Siena can illustrate the point.[50] In 1463 the general council of the city created a temporary committee of the "officials of the guard" and assigned funds to deal with impending plague. As in Florence the main hospital (here Santa Maria della Scala) was assigned the obligation of caring for all who fell sick within the city. The officials were to insure that no citizen who fled Siena because of the plague could thereafter return if he or a family member became ill. The officials were to enforce preventive travel bans, identifying offenders for prosecution. Foreigners

Table 5–2. *Timing of the creation of temporary (crisis)*
and permanent health boards: northern Italian communes
in the fifteenth century

	Temporary	Permanent
Milan	1424	1448
Venice	1459	1486
Siena	1462	1486
Florence	1464 or 1496	1527
Pavia	1450	1485
Lucca	1481	—
Cremona	1480	—

had to prove that they came from a healthy place, although mule drivers and courtiers were deemed harmless if they stayed in town only one night. It then became the chief task of the committee to deal with exceptions to the rules:

Considering that it is difficult to provide for all possible cases that may arise in these matters, as would be (for example) the arrival of cardinals, ambassadors, and other worthy persons, to whom the above [restrictions] would not be intended, it will be provided that concerning this matter of the plague the *signori,* captain of the people, the master standard-bearers, and the nine of the guard shall have complete authority and power to make whatever provisions they deem necessary throughout the city and countryside in order to preserve the city from plague.[51]

One hundred gold florins, a meager sum considering all that the officials would need to do (e.g., pay guards and dispense alms), was allotted.

These regulations are much different from those Sienese leaders undertook earlier in the century, in 1411. Bans then were like the first efforts in 1348, including ordering a procession to seek God's mercy (at least one man per household had to participate), and severely limiting mourning and funeral displays. The acceptance of passive quarantine bans on travel and trade had finally led to the development of a commission to enforce these bans, and to see to necessary exceptions to the rules.

The Sienese Nine Officials of Watch and Ward in charge of all particulars affecting the health of the city were a permanent institution from 1486.[52] Siena thus developed a magistracy that was consistently revitalized for epidemic years at the same period in time as did her Tuscan neighbors Pistoia (1496), Lucca (1481), and Florence (1494–6). To the north Cremona had a commission in 1480, Pavia in 1476–85, the specific timing depended upon the arrival of plague in a region.[53] Most of the semipermanent magistracies developed after the great pandemic of 1476–9.

The development of these boards has been amply documented by Carlo Cipolla, and the examples could be multiplied from his discussions.[54] What he does not discuss is the degree to which new health magistracies were focusing their attention on potential carriers of plague. This change in policy and attitude in public health administration can be illustrated with Venetian attitudes to a traditionally marginal group, prostitutes, once the object of "moral sanitation."

In the same year in which Venetians created their first, temporary *Provveditori alla sanità* (in 1459), the supreme governing council gave some attention to the public behavior of prostitutes.[55] The magistrates restricted the women's business networks in taverns, citing both the general shame incurred by the city with such open solicitation, and the rather specific hazard of fire that the ladies created in their frequent carrying of lighted candles to mattresses upstairs. In 1486, the prostitutes had come under the official jurisdiction of the newly re-created Provveditori alla sanità, and the officials now addressed the health menace prostitutes were seen to create. Several people denounced these women to the new office, claiming that "prostitutes living in various places throughout the city are the greatest cause of infection," because they do not discriminate between healthy and infected customers.[56] "It is clear to our office [the Provveditori] that a house can retain the infection two or three days after one dies of plague," and thus they drew out the danger of allowing prostitutes to continue normal business arrangements during times of plague. Well before plague actually arrived the magistrates herded the women into a Rialto warehouse, punishing the noncompliant with incarceration, fines, and public whippings.[57] To defend their policy as rational plague control misses the point that it should have been equally rational in 1459 or even in 1348. Plague controls evolved to encompass prostitutes during the later fifteenth century for social rather than medical reasons.

The association of contagion with prostitutes was not unique to Venice. Spoleto in 1484 forbade citizens' receiving prostitutes into their homes or businesses, on the grounds that they could thereby limit the sources of contagion.[58] From 1485 until the end of the century prostitutes were outlawed in Perugia and Siena as well, "for fear of plague." Proclamations in Mantua at this time declared that the prostitutes were a recent problem: "This city cannot abide the ignominy of becoming newly a brothel and receptacle for ruffians. [Thus it is decreed that no one shall lodge a woman of ill repute within the city.]"[59] Here no contagion was mentioned, but the sentiments of moral reform were typical of the 1480s and 1490s. The Franciscans especially were at work to clean up the spiritual environment of northern Italy, and prostitutes formed a good target. The interesting novelty is the use of contagion legislation to enhance reform efforts.

Nor were the women the only object of the lawmakers' censures. In both Siena and Perugia indigents and itinerants were suspected of being plague carriers. In the slightly earlier Sienese law of 1485, the temporary health board reestablished a protocol for street cleaning, closed the city gates, required that when a priest or notary visited the sick he must notify authorities, and demanded that all those who had contact with a plague sufferer or victim wear a white cloth as a sign of infection. In addition they added that foreign beggars were the most likely to fall ill, and they drove out "all prostitutes and their ruffian men, and loafers who had come to Perugia in the previous twenty days."[60] Perugian officials specially deputized to control the plague promulgated bans in 1485–7 that were similar to those in Siena. They banned prostitutes, "ruffians," loafers, and mendicants, all "for fear of plague."[61]

To further contribute to preventive public health measures, the Venetian Provveditori alla sanità tried to label the new outcasts with the traditional color of socially alienated groups. To know better who the dangerous individuals were, and to prevent their inadvertent association with Christians, towns in northern Italy had frequently resorted to laws that required Jews to wear a large yellow O or Star of David on cap or shoulder.[62] Similarly lepers in the distant, pre-1348 world had been identified by yellow crosses that warned the healthy not to pass too closely. Prostitutes were often labeled with yellow and even, in one instance in Venice, the passive member of a male homosexual pair was dressed in yellow for the witnessing of the gruesome execution of his lover.[63] "Ruffians who are staying in the city must wear the color yellow" seems to have been a Venetian symbol of the way socially undesirable individuals were made the target of preventive plague controls.

Just as was done with the prostitutes, it is necessary that male and female ruffians who are in the city be known to all, because they are the source of many evils. That is, others are persuaded by their example to live in their disgraceful fashion. So the [Provveditori] by the power given them by the senate, have deliberated and decided that all these ruffians who are staying in the city must wear the color yellow. Thus they will be recognized by everyone. Violators will be whipped from San Marco to the Rialto, and then banished forever from the territory.[64]

The Provveditori seemed to assume that the ruffians knew who they were in order to comply with the regulation. The order was repeated later in the spring, with the further pronouncement that prostitutes must also wear yellow.[65]

The older category of "moral sanitation" was transformed in the deepening commitment to the concept of contagion that legislators of the late fifteenth century made. The Provveditori might have cast back to older traditions, but the magistrates were looking for more direct links between "ruffians" and plague than an offense to God.

Ruffians, beggars, prostitutes, and foreign travelers who lacked official license to travel were now seen as the probable carriers of plague. Many of these people had been dealt with in the past with appeals to morality and Christian charity; now reliance on the concept of contagion and the state necessity to control plague allowed these marginal groups to be seen in a new and dangerous light. The revealing attempt of the Provveditori alla sanità in Venice to label outcasts with the traditional color of alienated groups symbolizes the transition that was taking place.

Plague did not create the need for controlling the poor and propertyless. The causal relation may have been exactly the reverse, with the growth in demands for city charity, the rise in population, and widespread migrations of hungry people stimulating bureaucratic efforts to control the poor by any means possible. The connection made between plague and poverty was real nevertheless, and it is difficult to know which problem was more acute to late fifteenth-century leaders.

Once the connection was made the methods chosen to combat

epidemics certainly worsened the chances of survival for disadvantaged groups or classes. Isolation of the ill in their homes, with some communal aid if they were lucky, or especially if they were taken to a pest house, increased the likelihood that a wide range of infectious diseases could be transmitted. Other cities had become certain by 1450 that plague was contagious, probably because they too had seen contagious spread of disease and infection among the poorer classes. Flight of the wealthy was a chronic problem, or a habitual solution by that time, and few but the poor stayed in the city to welcome the plague. Experience thus confirmed that poverty and plague were related. With the advent of plague-isolation hospitals the connection between death and poverty could only have grown stronger.

Conclusion

In this book we have examined in some depth why it was that during the mid-fifteenth century, and not fifty or even one hundred years before, novel plague controls began to appear in Florence. The answer offered was that the lesser plagues of the early fifteenth century were mixed epidemics that preyed on the very young and the malnourished. Although plague is not ordinarily a contagious disease, many of the other infections present during these miserable years were transmitted by human contact. The absence of wealthier citizens from infected cities further ensured that the economically least-advantaged segments of the population, unable to flee the city and often unable to draw a day's wage, would be exposed to many infectious diseases. Furthermore, the literate elite who described these plagues often had little direct experience on which to base their conclusions. Thus midcentury legislators could easily be persuaded that the feared plague was contagious, and that the poor were its principal victims.

One sequela of their conviction was the building or designation of pest houses to isolate the infected. It is probable that from their inception the lazaretti did not house all plague victims. Wealthier persons were probably "quarantined" in their homes. Once isolated in a minimally supported, understaffed, ill-kept, overcrowded pest house, a person was more likely to die, the natural assumption being that he or she died of "plague." Legislators were thus provided with ongoing experiential data to confirm the wisdom of controlling plague through the control of poorer persons.

Of course, there are other possible explanations. The later fifteenth century in northern Italy was one of population recovery and widespread changes in migration patterns. Le Roy Ladurie, looking at southern France, called it a "Malthusian Renaissance." Certainly the cities, fed by rural overpopulation, grew rapidly, and the social problems attending that growth suffused every aspect of traditional city life. The Franciscans found newly sympathetic audiences for the control of sodomy and prostitution, and doors briefly opened to Jews during the previous century were once again shut tight. Army after army trampled over Italy inflicting further miseries on the countryside. It is quite possible that rapid urban growth dictated the legislative concern with control of those who might cost the city precious resources. Then, too, the church was gradually withdrawing funds from many charitable enterprises. The popular contagion theory, in this context, was one that could readily organize and focus some of the concerns the elite expressed, and govern some of the changes it feared.[1]

This alternate explanation, that plague legislation derived more from changing social convictions about poverty than from experience with plague, is sketched in barest form, needing the attention of a social historian rather than a medical one. Moreover, plague experience in one city did change between the fourteenth and early fifteenth centuries and that experience was probably common to a larger geographical region. Both practical experience and lay opinion were important to legislative change and to changes in medical thought.

Medical historians have long held that the Black Death was responsible for stimulating profound changes in public health legislation. But the standard outline of sanitary "events" telescoped in their rapid accounts of medical progress tends to ignore most of the context in which plague provisions occurred. Thus Hirst credits the epidemic disease of the fourteenth and fifteenth centuries with precipitating the development of medical ideas of contagion. "Natural" explanations of plague origins, he contends, gradually replaced the "supernatural" and by 1546 the first medical treatise on contagion was published by Girolamo Fracastoro.[2]

But even though ad hoc sanitary commissions had greeted the pandemic of 1348, mobilizing governmental forces in northern Italy to take steps to clean up their cities and thereby decrease the sources of infection, such aggressive programs designed to lessen the dreadful loss of life were not undertaken again in most Italian cities for over a century. When, in the second half of the fifteenth century, towns began to adopt measures directly controlling the sick, their efforts reflected a belief that plague epidemics were contagious not only through the medium of the air, but also through individuals who carried pestilence from one place to another.

The notions of contagious spread of disease through contact with an infected substance or person, and of the movement of epidemics with the movements of peoples, had been empirical observations made by many chroniclers, diarists, and learned men of the first century after 1348. Yet by the end of the fifteenth century, all persons traveling from areas of plague were not equally feared as carriers of disease. Plague legislation, while being defended on the grounds of "contagion," nevertheless reflected the efforts of communal bureaucracies to deal with a social as well as a medical problem connected with epidemic disease, namely, treatment of the poor in times of plague.

I have already suggested that, historically, cause and effect in the evolution of a theory of contagion may be hopelessly confused with the reasons for isolating one social class. Revel pointed to the fundamental logical gap that separates medical theories of corruption of the air and empirical theories of contagion. On the one hand corruption of the air implied a need for purification and control of the sources of infection, but one had to stretch the theory to its limits to explain transmission of disease by human vectors.[3] The theory of contagion was attractive, but it demanded some explanation of the mechanism by which the contagion could be disseminated, and some answer to what was actually transmitted. The existence of a substance or material of contagion seemed absurd to fifteenth-century viewers, since it required admitting the existence of particles that could not be seen.[4] Furthermore the contagion theory could not explain why contact with an infected person was not uniformly fatal.

The emergence of trade restrictions, lazaretti, and the medical surveillance of plague cases suggests that the contagion notion, however derived or defended, was stimulating much-delayed efforts to curb the spread of disease. Presumably one would like to find influential medical spokesmen who supported the contagion theory contemporary with the adoption of legislation. As Vivian Nutton has recently shown, the idea of contagion was familiar to medieval and Renaissance physicians in a widely read Galenic treatise on fevers. Galen had briefly considered the possibility that "seeds" of disease existed. However, one looks . . . in vain for any mention of the seeds of disease among the many Western discussions of the causes of the Black Death, but although contagion and miasmata are both invoked, they are regarded as sufficient explanations in themselves, and the process of their formation goes without comment.[5]

Nutton carefully traces the concept of contagion in works by Renaissance medical authors, beginning with the *Epidemiarum antidotus* of Marsilio Ficino, a work written in part in response to the terrible pestilence of 1479 in Florence. All the other authors from whom Fracastoro "borrowed," without citation, wrote later than this.

Isolation practices may have increased local death rates while decreasing the local dissemination of various pestilences. The fact that charity to the poor was also a strong motive behind mid-quattrocento official provisions in plague years tends to support the latter causal relationship, that is, that plague controls led to theories of contagion rather than the reverse. Thus the development of medical support for a contagion theory came after the lay governmental efforts to deal with the social effects of plague.

Until Fracastoro published his landmark *De Contagione et Contagiosis Morbis* in 1546, discussions of contagion by physicians remained thoroughly Galenic, however much mention of plague and contagion crept into the texts. In fact, physicians tended to follow Galen in emphasizing the individual patient's responses to an altered environment: "The hypothesis of causative seeds was a philosophical luxury for the intellectual practitioner; it did not lead, either in antiquity, the Renaissance, or even down to the mid-nineteenth century, to the cure of disease by the elimination of these tiny agents from a diseased body."[6]

However, in the realm of public legislation, the contagion theory had significant social and behavioral consequences with which everyday practitioners in the Renaissance would have to deal. One begins to wonder if ordinary physicians of the sixteenth century, in the wake of these legislative changes in plague control, became increasingly sensitive to the subtleties of theory that would help them to distinguish a case of noncontagious fever or pestilence from contagious, isolable plague. These questions are, of course, beyond the temporal bounds of the present study.

Fracastoro, an aristocratic, armchair physician, seems to have been successful in defending the contagion notion because he was willing to adopt something of ancient atomistic theories that Galen had rejected. His greatness as a medical thinker, according to Nutton, lay in his "systematic application of the contagion idea to a variety of diseases."[7] For the average practitioner, his emphasis on the precisely similar clinical characteristics of individual diseases, whether or not the diseases were caused by unique, poisonous seeds, helped to focus diagnostic attention on individual diseases as well as on diseased patients.

But Fracastoro could be seen to have written a medical defense of a long-accepted popular theory of plague contagion. This first medical treatise devoted to contagion theory made assumptions about the social nature of plague that were as important as his assumption that unseen particles could exist and be transmitted from one body to another. Fracastoro discusses which individuals were most likely to carry plague and to die from it. To sixteenth-century physicians who had to differentiate one of the newer pestilential fevers from the dread plague diagnosis, Fracastoro's statements about the social context of a diagnosis of plague were probably of equal importance with his theory of contagion.

The plague mostly spreads by passing on the contagion from one person to another, and less by means of a tainted condition of the air, whereas the infection that we are discussing [typhus] is spread more by a taint in the air than by transmission from one person to another.

Now the nobility, on account of their wealth and other conveniences which the populace lacks, can take greater precautions against the sort of contagion that is transmitted from one person to another; but they can defend themselves less well than the populace from the contagion that depends on the air, since that sort of contagion, though common to all, is more prone to attack those who are rather delicate and less robust, and those who are more full-blooded and of less dry temperament, and the nobility have these characteristics because of their luxury and life of ease. The populace, on the other hand, are more robust and of drier temperament, because they exert themselves strenuously, and their diet is more frugal.[8]

Fracastoro had not only formulated intellectual defense for the contagion theory, he had reiterated nearly a century of legislators' convictions that the plague was a disease of the poor. His conclusions about plague and poverty faithfully reflected the popular fears of his day.

Appendixes

I: LIMITATIONS OF THE BOOKS OF THE DEAD AND THE MEANS FOR ESTIMATING NUMBERS OF CHILDREN

Some individuals were systematically omitted from the municipal death records, which is not immediately apparent when perusing the document. No bias toward social class, occupation, section of the city, or sex emerges; thousands of children, many regular and secular clergy, even *sconciature,* or aborted fetuses, appear in the lists. But all the registered deaths were reported by beccamorti. In particular, hospital patients or residents and clerics and monastics were not usually buried by communal gravediggers.[1] Only a handful of exceptions can be noted even in years of heavy mortality.[2] For the period before 1348, Pardi estimated that a minimum of 1,500 clergy members lived in Florence, and though their numbers were smaller in the period studied here, we can assume that the mortality experience of the clerical population of Florence is not systematically represented in the Books of the Dead.[3]

The extent to which the burials of the wretchedly poor went unrecorded by the Grain Office is simply unknown. Although beccamorti were enjoined to bury the poor at no charge, for the sake of Christian charity, it is possible that confraternities, such as the Misericordia and the confraternity of San Frediano, performed many of these services. Private burials also would have been omitted, but since so many of the wealthiest Florentine families are registered in the lists, the omissions here are probably not significant. Most of the advertent omissions from the records thus far noted were deaths among adults.

Thus the greatest source of omissions from the Grascia lists is the hospital deaths. Among these institutions, several were devoted to the care of infants and children, and the death rates for the very young were high. It is possible that hospitals kept their own records of burials by the late fourteenth century, but none now survive. Records of deaths were certainly kept by the mid-fifteenth century, and separate death books for male and female patients at the large hospital of Santa Maria Nuova exist from 1470.[4] The admission books for the foundling hospital of Santa Maria degli Innocenti have survived from the mid-fifteenth century.[5]

At the beginning of the quattrocento most of the hospitals of Florence were quite small, caring for under twenty-five lodgers, many of whom were not ill. With around 250 beds for the sick, Santa Maria Nuova was by far the largest hospital. The older tradition of housing poor travelers was still the major responsibility of these institutions. During the sixteenth century, only 3–4 percent of San Paolo's patients actually died in the hospital in a non-epidemic year.[6] During the plague of 1400, 8–10 died daily in Santa Maria Nuova at the peak of plague, roughly 4 percent of the hospital population.[7] These figures may be typical of adult hospital mortality in an era when hospital care was not typically medical in orientation, and when no attempt was made to segregate patients from nonpatients.

But adults in hospitals like Santa Maria Nuova and San Paolo, as well as in the numerous "hospices," did have a much better chance of survival than did small children in such institutions. Three major Florentine hospitals were responsible for the care and feeding of infants and foundlings: San Gallo, Santa Maria della Scala, and Santa Maria degli Innocenti. As early as 1319 Santa Maria della Scala supported 60 infants, and by the end of the century up to 150 were regularly assigned to nurses. San Gallo had only 38 children at nurse in 1377 but may have increased its census by 1400.[8] Santa Maria degli Innocenti, officially established in 1445 to support 90 children, was probably in operation before the 1420s.[9] Before the mid-fifteenth century, therefore, hospitalized foundlings did not account for a large number of potential omissions from the Books of the Dead. After that time, however, dramatic growth in foundling homes surely increased the numbers of non-registered child deaths.[10]

Before this period of accelerated growth in foundling institutions, the omissions of very young children from the *Grascia morti* formed a constant, but probably small, percentage of deaths. During crisis times there were undoubtedly waves of sudden admissions to foundling homes.

Another possible source of either inadvertent or deliberate inaccuracy in the death registers is the commonly found underreporting of females. Early registers (1385–1412) may indeed underregister females, as the following table shows:

Table A–1. *Sex ratio of deaths in nonplague years, 1400 excepted*

Books	Years	Males	Females	M/F
G.M. 1	1385–90	1,675	1,313	1.26
G.M. 1–2	1391–99	3,315	2,890	1.15
G.M. 2	1401–09	2,485	2,216	1.12
G.M. 3	1425–30	3,126	3,030	1.03
G.M. 4	1439–47	2,961	2,812	1.05
L.M. 244	1451–56	1,653	1,600	1.03

Note: G.M., *Grascia morti;* L.M., *Libri dei morti.*

Those individuals who were counted as children in this study usually were so listed in the Books of the Dead. In the early registers, *puer, puella* frequently appeared, occasionally *puera.* After 1400–5, some scribes prefer to identify a young child unambiguously as *fanciullo(a), fanciullino(a), bambolino(a),* or *figliuolo(a);* others preferred, it seems, the letter of the law, giving the full name of the deceased. Consequently, when specific notice of dependency is lacking, I counted "Chaterina d'Antonio" as a dependent child, since she lacks the standard identification as a wife, mother, nun, or widow, but "Giovanni di Ghabriello Buonamici" is known as a child only because the diagnosis accompanying his name is "born before the time." In the calculations made in this study, I did not count the latter example as a child, but did count the female dependent of Antonio as one. When three generations were named in a male entry, such as "Biondolino di Piero di Rossopieri," or "Lotto d'Antonio di Manno vinattiero," the individuals were counted as children. Even though this method undoubtedly counts some adults as children, far more children are uncounted even when their names appear, because the books give no record of age.

II: DEATHS BY QUARTER IN FLORENCE, PART I: JANUARY–15 MARCH (MODERN DATING)

Year	San Giovanni	Santa Croce	Santa Maria Novella	Santo Spirito	Not stated	"Fuori"	Total	% San Giovanni	% Santo Spirito
1441	62	22	19	36	—	—	139	44.6	25.9
1442	31	9	14	25	—	—	79	39.2	31.6
1443	59	14	42	35	9	—	159	37.1	22.0
1444	36	16	19	24	3	—	98	36.7	24.5
1445	44	12	16	28	—	—	100	44.0	28.0
1446	36	13	26	22	3	—	100	36.0	22.0
1447	54	23	24	41	1	—	143	37.8	28.7
1448	54	17	21	39	—	—	131	41.2	29.8
1449	56	18	28	48	3	—	153	36.6	31.4
1450	—	—	—	—	—	—	—	—	—
1451	54	25	23	45	1	3	151	35.8	29.8
1452	48	10	26	19	1	—	112	42.8	17.0
1453	35	13	19	11	—	—	78	44.9	14.1
1454	21	10	12	13	3	—	59	35.6	22.0
1455	49	18	18	23	2	—	110	41.5	20.9
1456	36	15	20	14	2	—	87	41.4	16.1
1457	75	25	26	47	2	—	175	42.9	26.9
1439	—	—	—	—	—	—	—	—	—
1440	64	20	30	35	—	—	149	42.9	23.5

II: DEATHS BY QUARTER IN FLORENCE, PART 2: 16 MARCH–30 APRIL

Year	San Giovanni	Santa Croce	Santa Maria Novella	Santo Spirito	Not stated	"Fuori"	Total	% San Giovanni	% Santo Spirito
1441	34	10	11	21	—	—	76	44.7	27.6
1442	24	4	7	12	—	—	49	49.0	24.5
1443	54	8	24	32	1	—	119	45.7	26.9
1444	34	8	10	22	—	—	74	45.9	29.7
1445	25	5	15	24	2	—	71	35.2	33.8
1446	56	14	21	29	1	—	121	46.3	24.0
1447	35	7	15	24	—	—	81	43.2	29.6
1448	30	8	8	21	1	—	68	44.1	30.9
1449	55	6	23	28	6	—	118	46.6	23.7
[1450]a	(27)	(7)	(14)	(9)	—	—	(57)	47.4	15.8
1451	50	27	28	18	1	1	125	40.0	14.4
1452	43	6	13	10	—	1	73	58.9	13.7
1453	31	5	11	10	—	—	57	54.4	17.5
1454	39	14	8	10	2	—	73	53.4	13.7
1455	23	9	21	14	—	—	67	34.3	20.9
1456	23	9	6	10	2	—	50	46.0	20.0
1457	47	12	11	17	2	4	93	50.5	18.3
[1439]a	23	7	11	17	—	—	58	39.7	29.3
[1440]	44	14	21	17	—	—	96	45.8	17.7

a 26 March–30 April.

II: DEATHS BY QUARTER IN FLORENCE, PART 3: 1 MAY–15 JUNE

Year	San Giovanni	Santa Croce	Santa Maria Novella	Santo Spirito	Not stated	"Fuori"	Total	% San Giovanni	% Santo Spirito
1441	18	9	7	11	1	—	45	40.0	24.4
1442	37	6	4	15	1	—	62	59.7	24.2
1443	36	7	10	22	—	—	75	48.0	29.3
1444	21	12	17	29	—	—	79	26.6	36.7
1445	32	10	4	25	—	—	71	45.1	35.2
1446[a]	(42)	(13)	(16)	(30)	2	—	103	40.8	29.1
1447	33	6	16	18	1	—	74	44.6	24.3
1448	27	8	13	16	1	—	65	41.5	24.6
1449	98	19	18	17	4	—	156	62.8	10.9
1450	61	11	19	19	—	—	110	55.4	17.3
1451	44	15	17	15	—	2	93	47.3	16.1
1452	41	10	9	8	—	—	68	60.3	11.8
1453	21	12	8	7	—	—	48	43.8	14.6
1454	17	3	4	10	—	—	34	50.0	29.4
1455	27	16	14	6	2	—	65	41.5	9.2
1456	20	13	17	9	3	—	62	32.2	14.5
1457	35	10	10	10	3	—	68	51.5	14.7
1439	34	7	9	26	2	—	78	43.6	33.3
1440	32	8	13	21	—	—	74	43.2	28.3

[a] Deaths from 1 May to 30 June.

II: DEATHS BY QUARTER IN FLORENCE, PART 4: 16 JUNE–31 AUGUST

Year	San Giovanni	Santa Croce	Santa Maria Novella	Santo Spirito	Not stated	"Fuori"	Total	% San Giovanni	% Santo Spirito
1441	59	13	17	35	1	—	125	47.2	28.0
1442	41	21	13	28	—	—	105	39.0	26.7
1443	28	16	7	27	1	—	79	35.4	34.2
1444	116	30	71	111	1	—	329	35.3	33.7
1445	77	35	28	42	2	—	184	41.8	22.8
1446[a]	(102)	(26)	(47)	(78)	(1)	—	(254)	40.1	30.7
1447	42	14	25	27	—	—	108	38.9	25.0
1448	69	23	37	71	3	—	203	34.0	35.0
1449[b]	(288)	(44)	(112)	(244)	(4)	—	(632)	36.1	38.6
1450	214	61	72	208	—	2	557	38.4	37.3
1451	67	27	34	44	—	2	174	38.5	25.3
1452	36	13	14	22	2	—	87	41.4	25.3
1453	36	16	34	17	—	—	103	35.0	16.5
1454	75	18	26	23	7	—	149	50.3	15.4
1455	67	19	24	15	1	—	126	53.2	11.9
1456	74	19	43	29	1	4	173	42.8	16.8
1457	152	34	52	35	2	11	286	53.1	12.2
1439	81	30	45	56	2	—	214	37.8	26.2
1440	53	13	16	40	—	—	122	43.4	32.8

[a] July and August only.
[b] 16 June to 3 July only.

II: DEATHS BY QUARTER IN FLORENCE, PART 5: SEPTEMBER–OCTOBER

Year	San Giovanni	Santa Croce	Santa Maria Novella	Santo Spirito	Not stated	"Fuori"	Total	% San Giovanni	% Santo Spirito
1441[a]	64	14	24	47	—	—	149	42.9	31.5
1442	25	11	8	26	—	—	70	35.7	37.1
1443	42	23	22	29	—	—	116	36.2	25.0
1444	46	15	28	50	1	—	140	30.0	35.7
1445	51	19	20	49	1	—	140	36.4	35.0
1446	61	20	22	51	1	—	155	39.3	32.9
1447	38	15	17	19	—	—	89	42.7	21.3
1448	64	22	36	76	—	—	198	32.3	38.4
1449	—	—	—	—	—	—	—	—	—
1450	199	57	83	163	4	6	512	38.9	31.8
1451	29	14	21	15	1	1	81	35.8	18.5
1452	45	22	12	14	1	—	94	47.9	14.9
1453	21	14	15	9	—	—	59	35.6	15.2
1454	33	15	26	4	1	—	79	41.8	5.1
1455	28	12	13	16	—	—	69	40.6	23.2
1456	54	18	41	24	2	—	139	38.8	17.3
1457	213	33	39	144	2	3	434	49.1	33.2
1439	86	10	20	39	1	—	156	55.1	25.0
1440	41	13	16	21	—	—	91	45.1	23.1

[a]Total September through December.

II: DEATHS BY QUARTER IN FLORENCE, PART 6: NOVEMBER–DECEMBER

Year	San Giovanni	Santa Croce	Santa Maria Novella	Santo Spirito	Not stated	"Fuori"	Total	% San Giovanni	% Santo Spirito
1441	—	—	—	—	—	—	—	—	—
1442	30	4	18	20	—	1	73	41.1	27.4
1443	32	9	22	20	—	—	83	38.6	24.1
1444	41	15	20	22	—	—	98	41.8	22.4
1445	38	12	18	23	8	—	99	38.3	23.2
1446	46	8	24	33	1	1	114	40.3	28.9
1447	42	12	21	18	—	—	93	45.2	19.4
1448	40	19	26	64	2	—	151	26.5	42.4
1449	—	—	—	—	—	—	—	—	—
1450	75	28	35	51	—	1	190	39.5	26.8
1451	47	16	18	17	3	—	101	46.5	16.8
1452	35	15	11	25	—	—	86	40.7	29.1
1453	23	16	16	6	—	1	62	37.1	9.7
1454	28	15	15	10	2	0	70	40.0	14.3
1455	18	13	10	4	—	—	45	40.0	8.9
1456	53	22	32	25	2	3	137	38.7	18.2
1457	112	26	44	38	3	—	223	50.2	17.0
1439	57	12	21	27	1	—	118	48.3	22.9
1440	35	10	8	28	3	—	84	41.7	33.3

Notes

INTRODUCTION

1. See especially Michael Flinn, *The European Demographic System* (Baltimore: Johns Hopkins University Press, 1981), citing the extensive literature on historical demography of early modern Europe. Some historical demographers have been concerned with the identities of infections in an epidemic crisis. See Paul Slack, "Mortality Crises and Epidemic Disease in England, 1485–1610," in Charles Webster, ed., *Health, Medicine, and Mortality in the Sixteenth Century* (Cambridge: Cambridge University Press, 1979), 9–60; and Lorenzo del Panta, *Le epidemie nella storia demografica italiana (secoli XIV-XIX)* (Turin: Loescher, 1980).
2. On differential mortality see Carlo M. Cipolla and Dante E. Zanetti, "Peste et mortalité differentielle," *Annales de démographie historique*, 1972: 197–202; Slack, "Mortality Crises"; Raymond Cazelles, "La peste de 1348–1349 en langue d'oil. Épidémie prolétarienne et infantile," *Actes du 87e congrès des sociétés savants, Poitiers, 1962*, Bulletin philologique et historique du comité des travaux historiques et scientifiques (Paris, 1965), 293–305.
3. On other books of the dead see Carlo Cipolla, ed., *Le fonti della demografia storica in Italia*, 2 vols. (Rome: CISP, 1972), 1: 851–952; del Panta, *Le epidemie*; and on their uses, Massimo Livi Bacci, *La société italienne devant les crises de mortalité* (Florence: Dipartimento statistico, 1978). On the general history of sanitary legislation in northern Italy see my "Plague Legislation in the Italian Renaissance," *Bulletin of the History of Medicine* 57 (1983): 508–25; Cipolla, *Public Health and the Medical Profession in the Renaissance* (Cambridge: Cambridge University Press, 1976); and Cipolla, "Origini e sviluppo degli uffici di sanità in Italia," *Annales cisalpines d'histoire sociale* 4 (1973): 83–101.
4. Jack D. Poland, "Plague," in Paul Hoeprich, ed., *Infectious Diseases*, 2d ed. (New York: Harper & Row, 1977), 1050–60; Robert Pollitzer, *Plague*, WHO Monograph No. 22 (Geneva: WHO, 1954); Lucian Fabian Hirst, *The Conquest of Plague* (London: Oxford University Press, 1953); (no author), "Plague Surveillance and Control," *WHO Chronicle* 34 (1980): 139–43.
5. Pollitzer, *Plague*, 251–78; D. H. S. Davis, "Ecology of Wild Rodent Plague," in Davis, ed., *Ecological Studies in Southern Africa* (The Hague: Junk, 1964), 301–14; M. Baltazard, "Déclin d'une maladie infectieuse: la peste," *Bulletin of the World Health Organization* 23 (1960): 247–62.
6. J. D. Poland and A. M. Barnes, "Plague," in J. H. Steele, ed., *CRC Handbook in Zoonoses* (Boca Raton, Fla.: CRC Press, 1979), sec. A, vol. 1: 515–22; and see Leo Kartman, "New Knowledge on the Ecology of Sylvatic Plague," *Annals of the New York Academy of Science* 70 (1958): 668–711.
7. John Norris tackles the thorny problems of plague ecology and the original appearance of plague in 1347; see "East or West? The Geographic Origin of the Black Death," *Bulletin of the History of Medicine* 51 (1977): 1–24. On the disappearance of plague see reviews by Andrew B. Appleby, "The Disappearance of

Plague: A Continuing Puzzle," *Economic History Review*, 2d ser., 33 (1980): 161–73; Paul Slack, "The Disappearance of Plague: An Alternative View," *Economic History Review*, 2d ser., 34 (1981): 469–76; Steven J. Kunitz, "Speculations on the European Mortality Decline," *Economic History Review*, 2d ser., 36 (1983): 349–64; Morris Silver, "Controlling Grain Prices and De-Controlling Bubonic Plague," *Journal of Social and Biological Structures* 5 (1982): 107–20; M. W. Flinn, "Plague in Europe and the Mediterranean Countries," *Journal of European Economic History* 8 (1979): 131–48; and recently Stephen R. Ell, "Immunity as a Factor in the Epidemiology of Medieval Plague," *Reviews in Infectious Diseases* 6 (1984): 866–79. I agree basically with Ell's position, one first stated by W. Glen Liston, "The Milroy Lectures, 1424, on 'The Plague,' " *British Medical Journal* 1 (1924): 900–3, 950–4; that Europe was never a permanent focus for enzootic plague. Kartman, "New Knowledge," over twenty-five years ago denied the possibility that quarantines drove plague from Europe: "The theoretical basis for [quarantine rules in plague] is rapidly become obsolete" (p. 673). One cannot prove that rats in infected port cities were not infected by wild rodent sources.

8. M. Baltazard, "Epidemiology of Plague," *WHO Chronicle* 14 (1960): 419–26, here p. 421.

9. Ibid., 423. Two issues of the *Bulletin of the World Health Organization* of 1960 are devoted to the supporting plague field studies. This feature of plague ecology is also emphasized by Leslie Bradley, "Some Medical Aspects of Plague," in *The Plague Reconsidered: A New Look at its Origins and Effects in 16th and 17th Century England*, Local Population Studies Supplement, 1977 (Derbyshire: LPS, 1977), 11–23, here p. 15.

10. N. Howard-Jones, "Kitasato, Yersin and the Plague Bacillus," *Clio Medica* 10 (1975): 23–7. Until 1975 plague was indexed under "Pasturella" in the Cumulated Index Medicus.

11. See Poland and Barnes, "Plague," and I. I. Cherchenko and A. I. Dyatlov, "Broader Investigation into the External Environment of the Specific Antigen of the Infectious Agent in Epizootiological Observation and Study of the Structure of Natural Foci of Plague," *Journal of Hygiene, Epidemiology, Microbiology and Immunology* 20 (1978): 221–8.

12. Emmanuel Le Roy Ladurie, "Un concept: l'unification microbienne du monde (XIVe–XVIIe siècles)," *Schweizerische Zeitschrift für Geschichte* 23 (1973): 627–96.

13. Harry Hoogstraal, "The Roles of Fleas and Ticks in the Epidemiology of Human Diseases," in R. Traub and H. Starcke, eds., *Fleas: Proceedings of the International Conference on Fleas* (Rotterdam: A. A. Belkema, 1980), 241–4; and Miriam Rothschild and Theresa Clay, *Fleas, Flukes and Cuckoos* (New York: Macmillian, 1957), 61–117 passim.

14. Vernon B. Link, *A History of Plague in the United States of America*, Public Health Monograph, No. 26 (Washington, D.C.: USPHS, 1955); and Kartman, "New Knowledge."

15. See above n. 11, and additionally Edward A. Eckert, "Boundary Formation and Diffusion of Plague: Swiss Epidemics from 1562 to 1669," *Annales de démographie historique*, 1978: 49–80; Eckert, "Seasonality of Plague in Early Modern Europe: Swiss Epidemic of 1628–30," *Reviews of Infectious Diseases* 2 (1980): 952–9; Ell, "Some Evidence for Interhuman Transmission of Medieval Plague," *Reviews of Infectious Diseases* 1 (1979): 563–6; and Robert S. Gottfried, *Epidemic Disease in Fifteenth-Century England* (New Brunswick, N.J.: Rutgers University Press, 1978).

CHAPTER 1. *Recurrent epidemic diseases: plague and other plagues*

1. A convenient survey of major published accounts of epidemic disease was made by Alfonso Corradi, *Annali delle epidemie occorse in Italia*, 5 vols. (1859–93: reprinted, Bologna: Forni, 1974), 1, 4, and 5, ad annum. Some archival sources that were brought to Corradi's attention are also included in the survey, but for

the most part the listings are restricted to chronicles, diaries, literary accounts, and notable medical descriptions. Lorenzo del Panta, *Le epidemie nella storia demografica italiana (secoli XIV-XIX)* (Turin: Loescher, 1980), has also relied heavily on Corradi.

2. Matteo Villani, *Cronica*, ed. F. Dragomanni, 2 vols. (Florence, 1846), 2: 300–1: "Non è da lasciare in obliazione la morìa mirabile dell'anguinaia in quest'anno [1363] ricominciata, simile a quella che principio ebbe nel 1348 infino nel 1350 . . . e fu di quella medesima infer[mi]tà d'enfiatura d'anguinaia e sotto il ditello come la prima generale, e si era passato dal tempo di quella e suo cominciamento a quello di questa per spazio di quattordici anni . . . ;" Giovanni Sercambi, *Cronica*, ed. Salvadore Bongi, Fonti per la storia d'Italia, nos. 19–21, 4 vols. in 3 (Rome, 1892), 1: 206 (1371): "la morìa a morire d'anguinaiae, sossitelli, bolle, e faoni"; Marchionne di Coppo Stefani, *Cronaca fiorentina*, ed. N. Rodolico, Rerum Italicarum Scriptores, new ed., vol. 30, pt. 1 (Città di Castello, 1927), 289–90 (1374): "una mortalità dell'usata pestilenza dello infiato dell' anguinaia, o sotto il ditello . . . ;" ibid., 426–7 (1383): ". . . pure al modo dell'altre mortalità, di quello segno dell grosso sotto il braccio e sopra la coscia all'anguinaia"; and Sercambi, *Cronica*, 1: 242–3 (1383): "una morìa d'anguinaia e altre pestilenze." Outside Florence, see Giovanni de Mussis, *Chronicon Placentinum*, Rerum Italicarum Scriptores, orig. ed., vol. 16 (Milan, 1730), 506–7; and Corradi, 4: 58.

3. Corradi, 1: 235: "et primo in pueris; primo namque turbabantur a pustulis, sive fersa cum vomitu et fastidio cibi, et post cum fluxu corporis. Deinde transivit ad majores et senes. Apparuerunt et glandulae, et febres cum pestiferis humoribus, et quasi sine numero perierunt. Sed tamen plus laesit rusticos qui propter guerram hic configuerant. . . . Huic quasi similis anno elapso fuerat hic, ex qua creditur mille pueros cecidisse. Tamen passio praesentis anni magis infecit [especially in June and July] quam illa." Some, but not all, accounts refer to the epidemics of 1388–90 as the fifth plague. See Corradi, 5: 216–17; and del Panta, *Le epidemie*, 117–23, 131; and the evidence from Arrezzo cited by Jean-Noël Biraben, *Les hommes et la peste*, 2 vols. (Paris: Mouton, 1975–6), 1: 193. However, reporting bubonic plague in these years is not uniform among chroniclers; most refer instead to pustules or nonspecific pestilences.

4. Corradi, 1: 236.

5. Ibid.

6. E. Bellondi, ed. *Cronica volgare di anonimo fiorentino dall'anno 1385 al 1409, giàattribuita à Piero di Giovanni Minerbetti*, Rerum Italicarum Scriptores, new ed., vol. 27, pt. 2 (Città di Castello, 1915), 27, pt. 2: 110: "E ancora in questo tempo cominciaro alcuni ad avere certe aposteme pestilenziose, e questi morivano in pochi dì; e duraro queste aposteme infino del mese di novembre, e molta gente uccise in questo tempo. Poi del detto mese di novembre mancò e quasi ristette. In questo tempo alcuna volta morivano molta gente, alcuna volta quando la luna era tonda, alcuna quando ell'era iscema, e così alcuna volta quando ella cresceva." Also see Pietro Buoninsegni, *Historia fiorentina* (Florence, 1581), 695–6 and 703.

7. *Cronache Sanese di Neri di Donato da Siena*, Rerum Italicarum Scriptores, orig. ed., vol. 15 (Milan, 1729), 241e [1363?]; Matteo Villani, *Cronica*, 2: 305 (IX, 112): "e l'Italia hebbe molti infermi di lunghe malattie, ed assai morti; e generale infermità di vaiuolo fu nelle state di fanciulli e ne' garzoni, ed eziandio negli uomini e femmine di maggiori etadi, ch'era cosa de stupore e fastidiosa a vedere [1360]." See also Corradi, 4: 61, attributing the high child mortality of the second plague outbreak to smallpox mixed with plague. Sercambi, *Cronica*, 1: 117–19, also describes the high child mortality in 1363: "molti ne morìnno & maximamente i più fanciulli da .xv. anni in giù," but he does not describe *bubonic* plague.

8. Corradi, 4: 61; and Arrigo Levasti, *My Servant, Catherine*, trans. Dorothy M. White (Westminster, Md.: Newman Press, 1954), p. 28, attributing her illness to chicken pox. I am grateful to Prof. Diane Owens Hughes, Amherst University, for the information about Saint Catherine.

9. Corradi, 4: 32; and Giovanni Villani, *Cronica*, ed. F. Dragomanni, 4 vols. (Florence, 1844–5), 3: 250 (II, 33), claiming all the children in Florence and its surrounding territory were "maculati diversamenti" and that over 2,000 died.

10. Corradi, 1: 234 (Venice, 1386); and 1: 239 (Bologna, 1393). Cases of smallpox may have occurred frequently in Lombardy in the later 1390s, for Giangaleazzo Visconti took them to presage the plague of 1400. See Aldo Bottero, "La peste in Milano nel 1399–1400 e l'opera di Gian Galeazzo Visconti," *Atti e memorie dell'accademia di storia dell'arte sanitaria*, ser. 2, 8 (1942): 19.

11. See the thorough discussion by Corradi, 1: 234–5.

12. Corradi, 1: 168–9 (1323); 1: 221 (1367); 4: 121 (1404); 5: 226 (1414); and Janet Shirley, ed. and trans., *A Parisian Journal* (Oxford: Oxford University Press, 1968), 85–6, 220–1. There was certainly a European-wide influenza in the summer of 1427; Corradi, 1: 266–7.

13. Bellondi, ed., *Cronica volgare*, 110. For a discussion of dysentery, see chap. 2, "Diseases of Little Children." Another major epidemic of dysentery occurred in Genoa in 1405; Corradi, 1: 247. Corradi, 4: 75, describes a bovine epizootic in 1387 in Romagna/Bologna: "Erat autem egritudo eorum suspiria, lacrimatio oculorum, et narium lippitudo, abstinentia a comestione, matie, et arefectione corporis subsequente, deinde moriebantur," a description best fitting anthrax. Other chroniclers describe an epizootic common to Bologna, Reggiano, Piacentino, with two thirds of the affected animals dying: "oportuit laborare cum equis, et asinis, et jumentis" (Corradi, 1: 236); another claims hens were also affected. The wider host range, and deaths within three to four days suggest anthrax. But a third description from Bologna is more clearly glanders: "grandissima infermità a i Buoi, e venne loro a i piedi, ma pochi ne morirono" (Corradi, 1: 234). Finally, see Giovanni de Mussis, *Chronicon*, p. 546, for an epizootic killing "the major part" of cattle in Lombardy in 1385.

14. On anthrax generally see A. B. Christie, *Infectious Diseases: Epidemiology and Clinical Practice*, 2d ed. (New York: Churchill Livingstone, 1974), pp. 787–815. One historically important sheep and cattle murrain was that in Britain and northern Europe in 1317–18. See Ian Kershaw, "The Great Famine and Agrarian Crisis in England, 1315–1322," *Past and Present*, no. 59 (1973): 3–50.

15. Table compiled from Corradi, passim.

16. Corradi, 1: 312–13.

17. Corradi, 1: 313.

18. Corradi, 1: 315.

19. Corradi, 1: 315: "Gli ammorbati condotti nel Lazzaretto miseramente perivano, perchè, tanta n'era la moltitudine, non potevano essere governati da' medici; i quali, oltre esser pochi, quasi tutti nell' ufficio loro soccombevano. Più timorosi che curanti della salute delle anime, Preti e Frati non soccorrevano i moribondi; ovvero per isconsigliata pietà il male accrescevano con le processioni. Gli accattoni ed i valligiani che la fame avea cacciato nella città, furono, once per loro maggiore corruzione non si spargesse, serrati in un postribolo; dal quale volendo pur uscire appiccarono tale incendio, che poco mancò loro stessi non consumasse. I *sotradori*, o beccamorti, commisero le solite ruberie e nefaudezze; alcuno ne fue che sin sui cadaveri sfogava la bestiale sua libidine. Ne' quattro mesi in cui maggiormente infuriò la pestilenza non meno di 200 erano i morti per dì."

20. Corradi, 5: 254.

21. Corradi, 5: 255.

22. Corradi, 1: 314.

23. Corradi, 1: 322, citing Brescian Jacopo Melga, March 1478: "incominciò a pullular a li humani corpi una certa pestifera infermitade chiamata dalli medici e dal volgo mal del zucho over del mazuch . . . . Vegnava uno terribilissimo smarrimento di testa, lo quale de bota se piliava."

24. See Corradi, 1: 314, 319–23, and 330–1; Corradi, 4: 195; and Corradi, 5: 251–5 for reports of much heavier mortality among older adults. See Corradi, 4: 195–201 for multiple instances of the combination of fever, delirium, and famine, including an epidemic in Florence in 1482.

25. Hans Zinsser, *Rats, Lice and History* (New York: Bantam Books, 1965 [1935]), 163; Major Greenwood, *Epidemics and Crowd Diseases* (London: Williams & Norgate, 1935), 173, stated: "It is not possible to isolate from the voluminous literature of fevers in pre-Renaissance medicine any clear cut description of what we now call typhus."
26. Letters used from this section come from the Mantuan State Archives, Archivio Gonzaga, *Lettere dalle paese agli Gonzaga*, F. II. 8, bustae 2398, 2401, 2422, and 2423 and refer predominantly to the plague year of 1478.
27. Mantuan State Archives, F. II. 8, busta 2398, letter no. 21 in the December bundle.
28. Mantuan State Archives, F. II. 8, busta 2423, by date of letter, Ostiglia bundle.
29. Ibid., "lei non havir macula alcuna et esser netta."
30. Ibid., "una Angonaglia et cussì uno brazo rosso et nizo, et per quello che dicono li suoi di casa, Questa donna soleva havere spese volte una sua certa doglia in una gamba. Et sentendose meglio del usato, dicono che la se mise ad andire a trovare de le granare et se la dovete andare là, andete per sina a Mullo, et vene poi quello dì a casa, caregata di granare, et gli s'alto è la febre adosso et finalmente è morta. . . . Non so che me debbe dire, ma secondo la relacione che ho havuto et ancho secondo la mia oppinione de quanti ne morti qui, non se trovato più vero signo di suspecto de peste como questo dì, e questei, benche li suoi dicono che'l sia proceduto per esser andato fare quella faticha."
31. On the clinical symptoms of human plague see the summary of J. D. Poland, "Plague," in Paul Hoeprich (ed.), *Infectious Diseases*, 2d ed. (New York, 1977), 1050–60.
32. Mantuan State Archives, F. II. 8, busta 2422, by day.
33. Ibid.
34. Mantuan State Archives, F. II. 8, busta 2020. "Lunedi matina venne lo vicario de Sancto Martino e non volse entrare sul ponte ma fece chiamare lo vicario qua e dissegli come la precedente notte erano morti doi putti in una notte et in una casa, fratelli, de' quali lo mazore era de etate de quatordeci anni, et perchè circa dece dì inanci era morto lo patre de essi, de morte assai presta, dubitando de quello che era fece portare essi putti su la via, e li fece vedere a doi medici quali habitano lì, e trovorono che uno de essi haveva parechi signi evidentissimi, l'altro era tutto petechiato, per la qual cosa era venuto qua; e pregeva lo vicario qua che ne desse aviso la S.V., dubitando esso che la prefata V.S. non havessi molesto le littere sue; et eo maxime perche molti havevano visitato lo patre de li putti cum li quali tutta la terra già haveva senza alcuno rispetto conversato; et de questo ne fece instantia grandissima, e cossi questo vicario li provvise de scrivere. Poi heri mattina mando a dire che una putta era morta in un altra casa, e questa mattina esso vicario è venuto qua presso al ponte e da ditto che un altra puta è morta in un altra casa et uno et infermo quale guarirà. De queste cose me parso darne notitia."
35. Mantuan State Archives, F. II. 8, busta 2422, July bundle.
36. For early descriptions of typhus see Ralph Major, ed., *Classic Descriptions of Disease*, 3d ed. (Springfield, Ill.: Thomas, 1947), 161–9.
37. For the true accounts of true meningococcemia, see *Classic Descriptions of Disease*, 188–91; and Elisha North, "Concerning the Epidemic of Spotted Fever in New England," reprinted in *Reviews of Infectious Diseases* 2 (1980): 811–16. The editors note that "the bibliography of cerebrospinal meningitis before the organism was isolated in Weichselbaum in 1887 is necessarily concerned with epidemics. Strangely, reasonable descriptions of the syndrome, with its characteristic rash, begin only in the first years of the nineteenth century, despite the attention paid earlier to descriptions of rashes."
38. J. McLeod Griffiss, "Epidemic Meningococcal Disease: Synthesis of a Hypothetical Immunoepidemiologic Model," *Reviews in Infectious Diseases* 4 (1982): 159–72.
39. Mary Matossian, *Ergots, Molds, and History*, unpublished ms.
40. See Frank J. Bové, *The Story of Ergot* (New York: Karger, 1970), 100, 169–87.

41. Mantuan State Archives, F. II. 8., busta 2423, Viadana bundle, by date; the podestà is writing to the Marchese.
42. Mantuan State Archives, F. II. 8., busta 2422, by date.
43. Ibid.
44. Mantuan State Archives, F. II. 8., busta 2398, letter no. 14.

CHAPTER 2. *Florentine deaths in the first plague century*

1. Lynn Thorndike, "Medicine Versus Law in Florence," in Thorndike, *Science and Thought in the Fifteenth Century* (New York: Columbia University Press, 1929), 24–58 and 261–4; Nancy Siriasi, *Taddeo Alderotti and His Pupils* (Princeton: Princeton University Press, 1981); and Dean Lockwood, *Ugo Benzi: Medieval Philosopher and Physician, 1376–1439* (Chicago: University of Chicago Press, 1951).
2. Alfonso Corradi, *Annali delle epidemie occorse in Italia*, 5 vols. (1859–93, reprinted in Bologna: Forni, 1974), passim.
3. Florentine State Archives, *Grascia morti*, and *Arte dei medici e speciali*, Libri dei morti, 244. Each death entry referred to will be located by date, and where there may be overlap, as in 1458, the date will be that of the *Grascia* series's entry:

   I. *Grascia morti*, 1 – 1385–97, and 1406
   II. *Grascia morti*, 2 – 1398–1412
   III. *Grascia morti*, 3 – 1424–1430
   IV. *Grascia morti*, 4 – 1439–49
   V. *Libri dei morti*,
         244 – 1450–8

   See also Guiseppe Parenti, "Fonti per lo studio della demografia fiorentina: i libri dei morti," *Genus* 5–6 (1943–9): 281–301; and David Herlihy and Christiane Klapisch-Zuber, *Les toscans et leurs familles* (Paris: SEVPEN, 1979). Parenti argues that the *Grascia* were not served well by their records, if they were kept in order to estimate grain needs; Herlihy and Klapisch-Zuber maintain that this was nevertheless the reason why the record was kept. Carlo Cipolla, "I libri dei morti," in Carlo Cipolla, ed., *Le fonti della demografia storica in Italia*, 1 vol. in 2 (Rome: CISP, 1972), 1, pt. 2: 851–952, reviews books of the dead in northern Italy and agrees with Herlihy and Klapisch-Zuber that grain provision motivated the keeping of these records. In contrast Andrea Schiaffino, "I registri dei morti della città di Mantua," *Le fonti*, 875–9, argues that the Mantuan registers were concerned with certifying deaths.
4. M. Cristina Pecchioli Vigni, ed., "Lo statuto in volgare della magistratura della grascia (a. 1379)," *Archivio storico italiano* 129 (1971): 3–70, esp. 68–70 for the clauses cited; and Gino Masi, ed., *Statutum Bladi Reipublicae Florentinae* (Milan: Società editrice 'Vita e pensiero,' 1934), 254. Also see Florentine State Archives, *Grascia morti*, 1, section 1, fol. 4–28.
5. Marchionni di Coppo Stefani, *Cronaca fiorentina*, ed. N. Rodolico, Rerum Italicarum Scriptores, new ed., v. 30, pt. 1 (Città di Castello, 1927), 426–7.
6. Paolo Emiliani-Guidici, "Ordinamenti intorno agli sponsali e ai moratorii [from the 1355 vernacular statutes]," in Emiliani-Guidici, *Storia politica dei municipi italiani*, 2 vols. (Florence, 1851), 2: 434–42. For the continuity of enforcement of sanitary legislation from the Executor of the Ordinances of Justice to the Guidici degli Appelagioni, see Gene Brucker, *The Civic World of Early Renaissance Florence* (Princeton: Princeton University Press, 1977), 37 and n. 107. Reform of sumptuary legislation was undertaken in 1388, and the *Grascia* soon thereafter abandoned records of banquets. See (Beato) Giovanni Dominici, *Regola del governo di cura familiare*, ed. D. Salvi (Florence, 1860), 235–6.
7. Aliberto Falsini, "Firenze dopo il 1348: le consequenze della pesta nera," *Archivio storico italiano* 129 (1971): 425–503. Florentines kept birth records dating from the same time (1380s); see Marco Lastri, *Richerche sull'antica e moderna populazioni della città di Firenze per mezzo dei registri del battistero di S. Giovanni dal 1451 al 1774* (Florence, 1775), 11; he suggests that documenting a person's age was the motive.

8. Raffaele Ciasca, ed., *Statuti dell' arte dei medici e speziale* (Florence: Vallechi, 1922), 46 and 80. See also Ciasca, *L'arte dei medici e speziali nella storia e nel commercio fiorentino dal secolo XII al XV* (Florence: Olschki, 1927), 118–22.

9. On funeral customs in Florence, see Robert Davidsohn, *Storia di Firenze*, 2 vols. (Florence, 1907–9), 2: 1171–4; Ciasca, *L'arte dei medici*, 20, n. 3; François Perrens, *Histoire de Florence*, 6 vols. (Paris, 1883), 3: 397–405; Francesco Puccinotti, *Storia della medicina*, 3 vols. (Leghorn, 1856–59), 2, pt. 2: 473; I. del Lungo, ed., *Dino Compagni e la sua cronica*, 3 vols. (Florence, 1879), 2: 88–9; and Sharon Strocchia, "In Hallowed Ground: The Social Meaning of Burial Revenues at S. Maria del Carmine, 1350–1380," *Michigan Academician* 14 (1982): 445–52.

10. Giovanni Boccaccio, *The Decameron*, ed. and trans. Mark Musa and Peter Bondanella (New York: Norton, 1977), 7–8.

11. Ibid., 11.

12. Stefani, *Cronaca fiorentina*, 231.

13. For this suggestion I am grateful to Prof. Richard Trexler, State University of New York at Binghamton.

14. Alberto Chiapelli, "Gli ordinamenti sanitari del comune di Pistoia," *Archivio storico italiano*, ser. 4, 20 (1887): 9–10.

15. On other early Tuscan books of the dead see Karl Belöch, *Bevölkerunsgeschichte Italiens*, 3 vols. (Berlin, 1939), 2: 170–1; Jean-Noël Biraben, *Les hommes et la peste*, 2 vols. (Paris: Mouton, 1975–6), 1: 193–5. Arezzo's *Libri mortuorum* begin in 1373, apparently the earliest surviving municipal registers. San Sepolcro had municipal death registers from 1378 (Prof. James Banker, North Carolina State University, personal communication, 1979). Burial registers for the Church of San Domenico in Siena were kept from 1336 to 1596; Lorenzo del Panta, *Le epidemie nella storia demografica italiana (secoli XIV-XIX)* (Turin: Loescher, 1980), 106, n. 13. See also n. 3 above, this chapter.

16. *Statuta Populi et Communis Florentinae*, 3 vols. (Freiburg: 1778–83), 2: 378.

17. A death could be simply announced, *banditur*, or the announcement could be accompanied by trumpets, *tubatur*. Each service had a fee (Prof. Sharon Stocchia, University of South Carolina, personal communication, 1981). The regulations of gravediggers recorded in the first *Grascia mòrti* cite the motive of controlling corruption by having the gravedigger report (fol. 4r.: "fraude et malitia remotis"), but it is not clear whether the abuses were excessive funeral display or the gravediggers' conduct. Nowhere in the Books of the Dead are the gravediggers' fees cited, nor the activities for which they could legitimately set a price.

18. Florentine State Archives, *Libri dei morti*, 244, f. 1. See also Parenti, "Fonti," 286–8; and Ciasca, *L'arte dei medici*, 737. There is no evidence that differentiation between burials and deaths led to the duplicate registrations in Florence, but this was clearly responsible for double series elsewhere in northern Italy. See Luigi Titarelli, "I libri dei morti: notizie per l'Umbria e in particolare per la diocesi di Perugia," in *Le fonti*, 1, pt. 2: 897–912; and Cipolla, "I libri dei morti," *Le fonti*, 852–5. On other registrations of cause of death see Dante E. Zanetti, "La morte a Milano," *Revista storica italiana* 88 (1976): 803–12.

19. See Creighton Gilbert, "When Did a Man in the Renaissance Grow Old?" *Studies in the Renaissance* 14 (1967): 7–32; Kenneth McKenzie, "Antonio Pucci on Old Age," *Speculum* 15 (1940): 164–85; and Herlihy, "Vieillir à Florence au Quattrocento," *Annales: Economies, Sociétés, Civilisations* 24 (1969): 1138–52. And in general see Joel T. Rosenthal, "Mediaeval Longevity and The Secular Peerage, 1350–1500," *Population Studies* 27 (1973): 287–93. On Renaissance medical ideas about ageing see Mirko D. Grmek, *On Ageing and Old Age: Basic Problems and Historic Aspects of Gerontology and Geriatrics*, Monographiae Biologicae, vol. 5, no. 2 (The Hague: Junk, 1958).

20. Florentine State Archives, *Libro dei morti*, 244, passim.

21. Herlihy and Klapisch-Zuber, *Les toscans*, 326–49, and 464.

22. Ibid., 199–204.

23. Alessandra Strozzi, *Lettere di una gentildonna fiorentina*, C. Guasti, ed. (Florence, 1877), 33.

24. Saint Antoninus, Archbishop of Florence, *Summa Theologica*, reprint of Verona, 1740 edition, 4 vols. (Graz: Akadademische Druk- und Verlagsanstalt, 1959), 1: 351–6.

25. Antonio di Giovanni, "Malati e malattie di altri tempi," *Scientia Veterum*, no. 58 (Pisa, 1964), lists those cited as "ill" in the Pisan catasto; Bruno Casini, *Il catasto di Pisa dal 1428–29* (Pisa: Giardini, 1964). I counted every eleventh household, finding 693 men to 704 women among those over sixty years old.

26. On "worm" lore of past cultures see R. Hoeppli, *Parasitic Infections in Early Medicine and Science* (Singapore: University of Malaya Press, 1959). From antiquity a diagnosis of worms or even "a pediculis consumatus" implied degradation when describing the death of an adult. See Thomas Africa, "Worms and the Death of Kings: A Cautionary Note on Disease and History," *Classical Antiquity* 1 (1982): 1–17. Antoninus mentions worms in this context, *Summa Theologica*, 1: 348. On the methods used to identify children in the *Grascia morti* see Appendix I.

27. Giovanni Michele Savonarola, *Practica de Febribus*, Tractatus III: De vermibus (Venice, 1517), fol. 132v.-137v.

28. *Il trattato ginecologico-pediatrico in volgare*, ed. Luigi Belloni (Milan: Società italiana di medicina interna, 1953), 186–9.

29. Savonarola, *Practica de Febribus*, fol. 134r.

30. Giovanni Morelli, *Ricordi*, ed. V. Branca (Florence, 1956), 76–8. For another example see Leon Battista Alberti, *Opera Omnia*, ed. Cecil Grayson, 3 vols. (Bari, 1960), 1: 35.

31. The asssociation of childhood diarrheas with this weanling diarrhea was first made by Herlihy and Klapisch-Zuber, *Les toscans*, 463–7. For the discussion that follows see also Nevin S. Scrimshaw, Carl E. Taylor, and John E. Gordon, *The Interactions of Nutrition and Infection* (Geneva: WHO, 1968), esp. 216–67; and Leonardo J. Mata, Richard Kronmal, Bertha Garcia, William Butler, Juan Urrutia, and Sandra Murillo, "Breast-feeding, Weaning, and the Diarrhoeal Syndrome in a Guatemalan Indian Village," *Ciba Foundation Symposia* 42 (1976): 311–38. Not all researchers accept the term weanling diarrhea, however, preferring to discuss diarrheal disease without reference to life events. See the recent review of Jon Eliot Rhode, "Selective Primary Health Care: Strategies for Control of Disease in the Developing World. XV. Acute Diarrhea," *Reviews of Infectious Diseases* 6 (1984): 840–54.

32. On the nutritional advantages of breast milk see A. M. Thomson and A. E. Black, "Nutritional Aspects of Human Lactation," *Bulletin of the World Health Organization* 52 (1965): 163–77.

33. Savonarola, *Il trattato ginecologico-pediatrico*, 146–9.

34. Derrick B. Jelliffe and E. F. Patrice Jelliffe, "Human Milk, Nutrition and the World Resource Crisis," *Science* 188 (1975): 557–61.

35. Robert Horvath, "The Scientific Study of Mortality in Hungary before the Modern Statistical Era," *Population Studies* 17 (1964): 189; and Patricia Herlihy, "Death in Odessa: A Study of Population Movements in a 19th Century City," *Journal of Urban History* 4 (1978): 432–6. Most historical demographers are more interested in the age structure of mortality than in the actual causes of death, and so there are few studies of preindustrial causes of death in infancy and childhood. Furthermore, demographers differentiate between deaths of infants under age one, and deaths of early childhood, ages one to five. In general see Michael Flinn, *The European Demographic System, 1500–1820* (Baltimore: Johns Hopkins University Press, 1981), 47–64; and Samuel H. Preston and Etienne Van de Walle, "Urban French Mortality in the Nineteenth Century," *Population Studies* 32 (1978): 281–4.

36. Salvatore Battaglia, ed., *Grande dizionario della lingua italiana*, 10 vols. (Turin: Unione Tipografico, 1961–78).

37. E. Bellondi, ed., *Cronica volgare d'anonimo fiorentino dall'anno 1385 al 1409, già attribuita à Piero di Giovanni Minerbetti*, Rerum Italicarum Scriptores, new ed., vol. 27, pt. 2 (Città di Castello, 1915), 110. As an example of the silence of other

chroniclers, Archbishop Antoninus was present in Florence at the time of this epidemic, but fails to mention it in his chronicle. Antoninus does record many of the plagues of the early fifteenth century. See Roaul Morçay, ed., *Chroniques di Saint Antonin: fragments originaux du titre XXII (1379–1459)* (Paris, 1913).

38. Strozzi, *Lettere di una gentildonna*, 55–6. She suffered during the 1449 plague, for which the death lists are not complete; thus we do not know if there were many pondi deaths that autumn. An epidemic of dysentery in Milan was simultaneous with that in Florence in 1425; see Corradi, 5: 228.

39. John Gordon, "Acute Diarrheal Disease," *American Journal of Medical Science* 246 (1964): 345–65; George F. Grady and Gerald T. Keusch, "Pathogenesis of Bacterial Diarrheas, Part 1," *New England Journal of Medicine* 285 (1971): 831–41; Rhode, "Acute Diarrhea"; and R. F. Bishop, "Spectrum of Infectious Agents in Acute Diarrhea," in V. S. Chadwick and F. S. Phillips, eds., *Gastroenterology*, vol. 2, *The Small Intestine* (London: Butterworth Scientific, 1982), 319–31.

40. Savonarola, *Il trattato ginecologico-pediatrico*, 191; and Zanetti, "La morte a Milano."

41. Ser Lapo Mazzei, *Lettere d'un notaro a un mercante*, ed. Cesare Guasti, 2 vols. (Florence, 1880), 1: 358, and 1: 433.

42. Iris Origo, "The Domestic Enemy," *Speculum* 30 (1955): 133.

43. Savonarola, *Il trattato ginecologico-pediatrico*, 135. See also the *Grande dizionario della lingua italiana*, s.v. *maestro* and *maestretto*. On neonatal tetanus see C. M. Smucher, G. B. Simmons, S. Bernstein, and B. D. Misra, "Neonatal Mortality in South Asia: The Special Role of Tetanus," *Population Studies* 34 (1980): 321–35.

44. Gregorio Dati, *Il libro segreto*, ed. Carlo Gargiolli (Bologna: Romagnoli, 1869), 74–5.

45. Walter A. Kukull and Donald R. Peterson, "Sudden Infant Death and Infanticide," *American Journal of Epidemiology* 106 (1977): 485–6; SIDS is a relatively rare phenomenon. Only 1 case in 10,000 live births, as a moderate estimate, occurs today, and almost all affected infants are between one and four months of age.

46. David Herlihy, "Medieval Children," in Bede K. Lackner and Kenneth R. Philip, eds., *The Walter Prescott Webb Memorial Lectures: Essays on Medieval Civilization* (Austin: University of Texas Press, 1978), 109–41.

47. Richard Trexler, "Infanticide in Florence: New Results and First Results," *History of Childhood Quarterly* 1 (1973): 99–116; and idem, "The Foundlings of Florence, 1395–1455," *History of Childhood Quarterly* 1: 159–84. On infanticide in the later middle ages see William Langer, "Infanticide: a Historical Survey," *History of Childhood Quarterly* 1: 353–65; Barbara Kellum, "Infanticide in England in the Later Middle Ages," *History of Childhood Quarterly* 1: 367–88; Y. B. Brissaud, "L'infanticide à la fin du Moyen Ages, ses motivations psychologiques et sa repression," *Révue historique de droit français et étranger* 50 (1972): 220–56; and Barbara A. Hanawalt, "Childrearing among the Lower Classes of Late Medieval England," *Journal of Interdisciplinary History* 8 (1977): 9–15.

48. A. Petrucci, ed., *Il libro di ricordanze dei Corsini (1362–1457)*, Fonti per la storia d'Italia, no. 100 (Rome: Istituto storico italiano, 1965), 147.

49. R. Major, ed., *Classic Descriptions of Disease*, 3d ed. (Springfield, Ill.: Thomas, 1947), 192–6.

50. Del Panta, *Le epidemie*, 115, illustrates the demographer's version of "normal" mortality, offering yearly estimates of thirty to forty deaths per thousand people as expected mortality. Mortality crises usually involve at least a doubling of this rate; see Michael Flinn, *European Demographic System*, 15–22 and 47–62.

51. The epidemic of dysentery in 1444 coincided with crop failures due to intense heat in late summer and no rain; Corradi, 4: 143. This almost ensures the facile transmission of enteric pathogens.

52. See chap. 1, n. 1.

CHAPTER 3. *Plague in Florence*

1. The literature discussing the plague of Athens in 430 B.C. is the most extensive example treating the problems of retrospective diagnosis. See J. C. F. Poole and A. J. Holladay, "Thucydides and the Plague at Athens," *Classical Quarterly* 73 (1979): 282–300; idem, "Thucydides and the Plague: A Footnote," *Classical Quarterly* 76 (1982): 235–6; James Longrigg, "The Great Plague of Athens," *History of Science* 18 (1980): 209–25; J. A. H. Wylie and H. W. Stubbs, "The Plague of Athens: 430–28 BC: Epidemic and Epizootic," *Classical Quarterly* 77 (1983): 6–11; and, of the older literature, Harry Keil, "The Louse in Greek Antiquity, with Comments on the Diagnosis of the Athenian Plague as Recorded by Thucydides," *Bulletin of the History of Medicine* 25 (1951): 305–23; and D. L. Page, "Thucydides' Description of the Great Plague at Athens," *Classical Quarterly* 47 (1953): 97–119.

2. On the demographic depression in north central Italy see Enrico Fiumi, *Demografia, movimento urbanistico e classi sociali in Prato dall' étà comunale ai tempi moderni* (Florence: Olschki, 1968), 84–137; David Herlihy, "Population, Plague, and Social Change in Rural Pistoia," *Economic History Review*, ser. 2, 18 (1965): 225–44; and Ruggiero Romano, "L'Italia nella crisi del XIV secolo," *Nuova Rivista Storica* 50 (1966): 660–739; Harry A. Miskimin, *The Economy of Early Renaissance Europe, 1300–1460* (Englewood Cliffs, N.J.: Prentice-Hall, 1969), 134ff.; Karl Heillinger, "The Population of Europe from the Black Death to the Eve of the Vital Revolution," in M. M. Postan and H. J. Habakkuk, eds., *The Cambridge Economic History of Europe*, 2d ed., 6 vols. in 8 (Cambridge: Cambridge University Press, 1966–78), 4: 1–95; and Lorenzo del Panta, *Le Epidemie nella storia demografica italiana (secoli XIV-XIX)* (Turin: Loescher, 1980), 102–37.

3. On population estimates for Florence see the monumental study by David Herlihy and Christiane Klapisch-Zuber, *Les toscans et leurs familles* (Paris: SEVPEN, 1979), 165–88. Also see A. Falsini, "Firenze dopo il 1348: le conseguenze della pesta nera," *Archivio storico italiano* 129 (1971): 425–503; E. Fiumi, "Fioritura e decadenza dell' economia fiorentina, pt. 2: Demografia e movimento urbanistico," *Archivio storico italiano* 116 (1958): 443–510; D. J. Osheim, "Rural Population and the Tuscan Economy in the Late Middle Ages," *Viator* 7 (1976): 329–46; K. Belöch, *Bevölkerungsgeschichte Italiens*, 3 vols. (Berlin, 1937), 2: 127–39; C. Klapisch, "Fiscalité et démographie en Toscane (1427–1430)," *Annales: Economies, Sociétés, Civilisations* 24 (1969): 1313–37; and the older accounts of G. Pardi, "Disegno della storia demografia di Firenze," *Archivio storico italiano* 74, pt. 1 (1916): 3–84; and Niccolò Rodolico, *La democrazia fiorentina nel suo tramonto (1375–1379)* (Bologna: Zanichelli, 1905), 7–45.

4. Herlihy and Klapisch-Zuber, *Les toscans*, 176.

5. Fiumi, "Fioritura e decadenza." On the depopulation of the contado see also Christine Meek, *Lucca, 1369–1400: Politics and Society in an Early Renaissance City-State* (Oxford: Oxford University Press, 1978), 91–2.

6. E.g., Robert Gottfried, *Epidemic Disease in Fifteenth-Century England* (New Brunswick, N.J.: Rutgers University Press, 1979), 225–30; Herlihy and Klapisch-Zuber, *Les toscans*, 189–95; E. Le Roy Ladurie, "Un concept: l'unification microbienne du monde (XIVe-XVIIe siècle)," *Schweizerische Zeitschrift für Geschichte* 23 (1973): 672; Edouard Baratier, *La démographie provençale du XIIIe au XVIe siècle* (Paris: SEVPEN, 1961), 121; and del Panta, *Le epidemie*, 136–7.

7. Romano, "L'Italia nella crisi del XIV secolo"; and Herlihy and Klapisch-Zuber, *Les toscans*, 425–6. See also, Zvi Razi, *Life, Marriage and Death in a Medieval Parish* (Cambridge: Cambridge University Press, 1980), for a comparative English example.

8. The major chronicles surveyed were Giovanni Villani, *Cronica*, ed. F. Dragomanni, 4 vols. (Florence, 1844–45); S. A. Barbi, ed., *Storie pistoresi*, Rerum Italicarum Scriptores, new ed., vol. 11, pt. 5 (Città di Castello, 1907–27); Matteo Villani, *Cronica*, ed. F. Dragomanni, 2 vols. (Florence, 1846); Donato Velluti,

La Cronica Domestica, ed. I. Del Lungo and G. Volpi (Florence, 1914); Marchionne Stefani, *Cronaca fiorentina*, ed. N. Rodolico, Rerum Italicarum Scriptores, new ed., vol. 30, pt. 1 (Città di Castello, 1927); Biblioteca Nationale Centrale, Florence, *Fondo panciatichiano*, 158; E. Bellondi, ed., *Cronica volgare di anonimo fiorentino dall'anno 1385 al 1409, già attribuita à Piero di Giovanni Minerbetti*, Rerum Italicarum Scriptores, new ed., vol. 27, pt. 2 (Città di Castello, 1915); Coluccio Salutati, *Epistolario*, ed. F. Novati, Fonti per la storia d'Italia, nos. 15–18 (Rome, 1891–1916); Filippo di Cino Rinuccini, *Ricordi storici*, ed. G. Aiazzi (Florence, 1840); Buonacorso Pitti, *Cronica*, ed. A. Bacchi della Lega (Bologna, 1869); Raoul Morçay, *Chroniques di Saint Antonin: fragments originaux du titre XXII (1379–1459)* (Paris, 1913); Armondo Petrucci, ed., *Il libro di ricordanze dei Corsini (1362–1457)*, Fonti per la storia d'Italia, no. 100 (Rome: Istituto storico italiano, 1965); Domenico Buoninsegni, *Storia della città di Firenze* (Florence, 1637); G. Zaccagnini, ed., *Sozomeni pistoriensis presbyteri Chronicon universale*, Rerum Italicarum Scriptores, new. ed., vol. 16, pt. 1 (Città di Castello, 1908); and Alessandra Strozzi, *Lettere di una gentildonna fiorentina*, ed. C. Guasti (Florence, 1877).

9. Compare with the totals from fifteenth-century mortality registers in Arezzo, provided by del Panta, *Le epidemie*, 25, 108–9.

10. For 1348 see M. Villani, *Cronica*, 1: 11; for 1363, Corradi, 4: 58; for 1374, Stefani, *Cronaca fiorentina*, 289–90; for 1383, ibid., 426–7.

11. "Nomi di uomini e di donne seppelliti in S. Maria Novella," in Idelfonso di San Luigi, *Delizie degli eruditi toscani* (Florence, 1777), 9: 123–203. Deaths registered by the confraternity of San Frediano, burying mostly poor persons, reflected the same spring increase in deaths in 1340, according to the data collected by Prof. James Banker, North Carolina State University (personal communication, 1976). On the coming of plague to Europe, see John Norris, "East or West? The Geographic Origin of the Black Death," *Bulletin of the History of Medicine* 51 (1977): 1–24. On the pestilences of 1339 to 1340 in Tuscany, see *Storie pistoresi*, 162, estimating 24,000 dead, or one quarter of those in the city and countryside of Pistoia. The chronicler says the pandemic extended to Pisa, Lucca, Prato, Venice, Lombardy, and Romagna. See also Giovanni Villani, 3: 342–4 (XI, 114), estimating 15,000 dead in Florence.

12. Ser Luca Dominici, *Cronica della venuta dei bianchi e della morìa, 1399–1400*, ed. G. Gigliotti, Rerum Pistoriensum Scriptores (Pistoia, 1933), 250–9 and 288. The only section of the Pistoia for which Dominici noted the day deaths were recorded was Porta Caldatica, which shows the same seasonal pattern as deaths in Florence:

1–15 May	6 deaths
16–31 May	19 deaths
1–15 June	23 deaths
16–30 June	47 deaths
1–15 July	126 deaths
16–31 July	114 deaths
1–15 August	32 deaths

Here the record ends. Dominici later noted, "E è vero che la moria di maggio cominciò forte, poi di giugno più, di luglio fracaciò, e d'agosto alleno e quasi ristetti . . . de certe furono i morti nella detta morìa più di 4000 bocche." See also Giovanni Sercambi, *Cronica*, ed. Salvadore Bongi, Fonti per la storia d'Italia, no. 21, 3 vols. in 4 (Rome, 1892), 3: 4–9, reporting plague in Lucca from May to September 1400.

13. Gene Brucker, *The Civic World of Early Renaissance Florence* (Princeton: Princeton University Press, 1977), 23.

14. Samuel Cohn, Jr., *The Laboring Classes in Renaissance Florence* (New York: Academic Press, 1980), 26.

15. The principal working-class districts in Florence were around the parishes of San Frediano, Santa Maria dei Camaldoli, Sant' Ambruogio, San Piero Gattolino, and San Lorenzo. See Brucker, *Civic World*, 44; idem, "The Florentine *Popolo*

Minuto and its Political Role, 1340–1450," in Lauro Martines, ed., *Violence and Civil Disorder in Italian Cities, 1200–1500* (Berkeley: University of California Press, 1972), 177–8; and Cohn, *Laboring Classes*, 115–28.

16. Giovanni Boccaccio, *The Decameron*, ed. Mark Musa and Peter Bondanella (New York: Norton, 1977), 4. Using the *Decameron* presents some historical problems, since Boccaccio almost certainly used Paul the Deacon's *Historia Langobardorum* in writing the introduction. See Vittorio Branca, *Boccaccio medievale* (Florence: Sansoni, 1956), 210–12. Others used Thucydides' account, or ones based on Thucydides' description of the plague of Athens, even though Thucydides could not have been describing bubonic plague. See Timothy S. Miller, "The Plague in John VI Cantacuzenus and Thucydides," *Greek, Roman and Byzantine Studies* 17 (1976): 385–95.

17. See chap. 5 for a brief discussion of plague treatises.

18. Giovanni Morelli, *Ricordi*, ed. V. Branca (Florence: Le Monnier, 1956), 76–8.

19. Dr. Robin Bernath, personal communication, 1982.

20. The only reference to "signs" of plague that I have found in Florentine literature is that of Alessandra Strozzi, *Lettere*, ed. C. Guasti, 37: [4 November 1448]: "La morìa ci fa pur danno, da quattro a cinque per dì, e a dì 29 del passato si disse che n'era morti undici di segno."

21. See Jean-Noël Biraben, *Les hommes et la peste*, 2 vols. (Paris: Mouton, 1975–6), 1: 13–15; R. Pollitzer, "A Review of Recent Literature on Plague," *Bulletin of the World Health Organization* 23 (1960): 360–1; Emmanuel Le Roy Ladurie, "Un concept"; and Stephen Ell, "Interhuman Transmission of Medieval Plague," *Bulletin of the History of Medicine* 54 (1980): 952–9. *Pulex irritans* will feed indifferently on rat or man, in contrast to *X. cheopis*, which strongly prefers the primary rat host. A wondrously preserved rat was found dating from late medieval Britain, and archaeologists were able to speciate the flea in its coat as *P. irritans*; see "Flea-bitten Rat Gives New Clues to Black Death," *New Scientist* 94 (1982): 492.

22. Lucian Fabian Hirst, *The Conquest of Plague* (Oxford: Oxford University Press, 1953), 236–46.

23. Gottfried, *Epidemic Disease*, 51–5, argues that the strong evidence for late fall, early winter epidemics in fifteenth-century England means that pneumonic plague must have been more prevalent then; Norris, "Review: Robert S. Gottfried, *Epidemic Disease in Fifteenth-Century England*," *Bulletin of the History of Medicine* 54 (1980): 593–6, finds the conclusion incompatible with the normal spread of *Y. pestis*. J. F. D. Shrewsbury, *A History of Plague in the British Isles* (Cambridge: Cambridge University Press, 1971), virtually denies that plague did much damage in England during that century; Christopher Morris, "Review: J. F. D. Shrewsbury, *A History of Plague in the British Isles*," *Historical Journal* 14 (1971): 205–15, disagrees with that conclusion. Whatever the case in Britain, there is no historical evidence for widespread pneumonic plague epidemics in fifteenth-century northern Italy.

24. On pneumonic plague see Pollitzer, *Plague* (Geneva: WHO, 1954), 504–18; idem, "Recent Literature," 367; Biraben, *Les hommes et la peste*, 1: 9–18; Hirst, *Conquest of Plague*, 34–5 and 220–53; Ell, "Interhuman Transmission"; and Wu Lien-Teh, *A Treatise on Pneumonic Plague*, League of Nations Health Organization, no. 13 (Geneva, 1926).

25. On the requirements of rat and flea for multiplication and transmission of plague to human populations, see Hirst, *Conquest of Plague*, 121–218; and D. C. Cavanaugh and J. E. Williams, "Plague: Some Ecological Interrelationships," in R. Traube and H. Starcke, eds., *Fleas* (Rotterdam, 1980), 245–56. For the latter reference I am indebted to Dr. Robin Bernath.

26. Biraben, *Les hommes et la peste*, 133–4, postulated a relationship between sunspots and movements of rodent populations to explain the cyclic return of plague to Europe. He found a periodicity of eleven to twelve years between major plague thrusts similar to the sunspot cycle. The theory is not verifiable with historical data, except that the well-known "Maunder Minimum" with no sunspot activ-

ity for most of the late seventeenth century does correspond with some of the disappearance of plague from Western Europe. Nevertheless, the seven-year intervals of the early fifteenth century might have compromised the ability of rodents to reproduce their numbers. On the seasonality of plague see also Edward Eckert, "Seasonality of Plague in Early Modern Europe: Swiss Epidemic of 1628–1630," *Reviews of Infectious Diseases* 2 (1980): 952–9.

27. See Pollitzer, *Plague*, 66 and 115–20; and J. E. Williams, "Atypical Plague Bacilli Isolated from Rodents, Fleas and Man," *American Journal of Public Health* 68 (1978): 262–4.

CHAPTER 4. *The social effects of plagues in Florence*

1. M. F. Hollingsworth and T. H. Hollingsworth, "Plague Mortality by Age and Sex in the Parish of St. Botolph's without Bishopsgate," *Population Studies* 25 (1971): 131–46, find an increased incidence of plague among older children, adolescents, and young adults during sixteenth-century plagues. See also Stephen Ell, "Immunity as a Factor in the Epidemiology of Medieval Plague," *Reviews of Infectious Diseases* 6 (1984): 866–79; Zvi Razi, *Life, Marriage and Death in a Medieval Parish* (Cambridge: Cambridge University Press, 1980); and Domenico Sella, "Premesse demografiche ai censimenti austriaci," in *Storia di Milano*, 16 vols. (Milan: Treccani, 1953–62), 12: 467–70. Most authorities claim that plague kills no age group preferentially, unless exposure to plague or the flea vector is increased; see the review of Leslie Bradley, "Some Medical Aspects of Plague," in *The Plague Reconsidered: A New Look at its Origins and Effects in 16th and 17th Century England*, Local Population Studies Supplement, 1977 (Derbyshire: LPS, 1977), 17. Bradley's own study of the 1665–6 Eyam (a rural village) plague showed a decreased percentage of burials among young children, but an increased percentage of burials among five to twenty year olds.

   Jack Poland, "Plague," in Paul Hoeprich, ed., *Infectious Diseases*, 2d ed. (New York: Harper & Row, 1977), 1050–60, reports the age incidence of plague cases in the United States from 1950 to 1975, showing highest morbidity and mortality among children under fifteen. The data on earlier plagues in the United States (compiled by Vernon B. Link, *A History of Plague in the United States of America*, Public Health Monograph no. 26 [Washington, D.C.: USPHS, 1955], 103), reveals that only 19 percent (101/523) of plague cases occurred among children under the age of fifteen years, and accounted for only 17 percent of fatal plague cases. Thus, before antibiotics were available to treat plague, the case fatality rate among those under fifteen years was 57 percent and 67 percent among those older than fifteen years.

2. Herlihy and Klapisch-Zuber, *Les toscans et leurs familles* (Paris: SEVPEN, 1978), 375. Also see R. Horvath, "The Scientific Study of Mortality in Hungary before the Modern Era," *Population Studies* 17 (1964): 187–91; C. Klapisch, "L'enfance in Toscane au début du XVe siècle," *Annales de démographie historique* 1973: 99–122; R. E. Jones, "Infant Mortality in Rural North Shropshire, 1561–1810," *Population Studies* 30 (1976): 305–17; George Rosen, "A Slaughter of Innocents: Aspects of Child Health in the 18th Century City," *Studies in Eighteenth Century Culture* 5 (1976): 293–316; and Alan Morrison, Julius Kirschner, and Anthony Molho, "Life Cycle Events in Fifteenth Century Florence: Records of the *Monte delle Doti*," *American Journal of Epidemiology* 106 (1977): 487–92.

3. Ell, "Immunity"; and Ell, "Plague Epidemics and Iron," *Journal of Interdisciplinary History* 15 (1985): 445–57.

4. J. M. Mann, L. Shandler, and A. H. Cushing, "Pediatric Plague," *Pediatrics* 69 (1982): 762–76. See also my "Infection, Hidden Hunger, and History," *Journal of Interdisciplinary History* 14 (1983): 249–64.

5. Ruggiero Romano, "L'Italia nella crisi del XIV secolo," *Nuova rivista storia* 50 (1966): 580–95; and Herlihy and Klapisch-Zuber, *Les toscans*, 425–6. Compare with Razi, *Life, Marriage and Death*; and John Hatcher, *Plague, Population and the English Economy* (London: Macmillan, 1977).

6. Bruni's *Laudatio Florentinae Urbis* is translated by Benjamin Kohl in Kohl and R. Witt, eds., *The Earthly Republic of the Italian Humanists* (Philadelphia: University of Pennsylvania Press, 1978), 138.

7. G. Villani, *Cronica*, ed. F. Dragomanni, 4 vols. (Florence, 1844–5), 1: 249; Gregorio Dati, *L'istoria*, ed. L. Pratesi (Norcia: Tondi, 1904), 111. For discussion see Francesco Carabellese, *La peste del 1348 e le condizione della sanitá pubblica in Toscana* (Rocca S. Casciano: Cappelli, 1897), ix-x, and 30; Lynn Thorndike, "Sanitation, Baths, and Street-Cleaning in the Middle Ages and Renaissance," *Speculum* 3 (1928): 192–203; A. G. Varron, "Hygiene in the Medieval City," *Ciba Symposia* 1 (1939): 205–14; A. Higounet-Nadal, "Hygiène, salubrité, pollutions au Moyen Age: l'exemple de Périgaux," *Annales de démographie historique* 1975: 81–92; George Rosen, *A History of Public Health* (New York: MD Publications, 1958), 67–80; and M. Poëte, *Une vie de cité: Paris de sa naissance a nos jours*, 2 vols. (Paris, 1924), 1: 613–19, and 2: 254–8.

8. Various editions of the statutes are referred to in the subsequent notes, and the following abbreviated references will be used: "1322" for Florentine State Archives, *Statuta Civitatis Florentinae*, 6 (1322–42); "1355" for Florentine State Archives, *Statuti, Comune di Firenze*, 16 (1355–70); "Caggese" for R. Caggese, ed., *Statuti della repubblica fiorentina*, 2 vols. (Florence, 1910–1912); "Puccinotti" for Francesco Puccinotti, *Storia della medicina*, 3 vols. in 4 (Leghorn, 1850–66), 2, pt. 1 (appendix); *Statuta Populi et Communis Florentinae*, 3 vols. (Freiburg, 1778–83); and "Statutum Bladi" for G. Masi, ed., *Statutum Bladi Reipublicae Florentinae* (Milan: Società editrice 'Vita e pensiero,' 1934). Here see 1322 (I, xvi), f. 13 and Caggese, 2: 49–51; on the sewers, 1322 (III, li), f. 99; Caggese, II: 324–5; *Statuta Populi*, 2: 461–62; and Puccinotti, ccvii.

9. See Thorndike, "Sanitation, Baths and Street-Cleaning."

10. 1322 (II, lxv), fol. 46v.; (V, xxix), fol. 135; (V, xlvii), fol. 139; (III, xxv), fol. 131; (III, cvi), fol. 165v.; (V, Lxxxiii), fol. 148–50. 1355 (III, xxiv), fol. 130v.-131; (III, cvii and cviii), fol. 165v.-166; (III, cxi), fol. 166–7 (also prohibits keeping goats); (IV, cx), fol. 245v.-6v. Caggese, 2: 133–4, 383, 394, 188–9, 216–18, 420–2. Puccinotti, cciii-cciv, ccvii, cxcviii, ccii, clxxxiii-clxxiv, clxxxiv-clxxxv. *Statuta Populi*, 2: 421, 455–6, 463–4, which adds that meat sellers may keep animals in their habitations, 244, 454, 456—8, 459–60. Also see Carabellese, *La peste del 1348*, 130–2; and *Statutum Bladi*, rub. 84, 124–5. Popular health treatises dating from the twelfth century cited the danger of living near drains and swamps; see "Flos Medicinae Scholae Salerni," in Salvatore De Renzi ed., *Collectio Salernitana ossia documenti inediti e trattati di medicina*, 5 vols. (Naples, 1852–9), 5: 2.

11. Florentine State Archives, *Provvisioni registri* (hereafter *Provv. reg.*) 18, fol. 27 (18 Nov. 1321); and reg. 34, fol. 4r. (17 Feb. 1346).

12. He is called "Medicus ossium" in Florentine State Archives, *Provv. reg.* 21, fol. 93r. and *Provv. reg.* 22, fol. 80v., his earliest appointments in 1325 and 1326. His sons took over after the plague; *Provv. reg.* 36, fol. 30r. (19 Nov. 1348). On municipal physicians generally see Vivian Nutton, "Continuity or Rediscovery? The City Physician in Classical Antiquity and Medieval Italy," in Andrew Russell, ed., *The Town and State Physician in Europe from the Middle Ages to the Enlightenment*, Wolfenbütteler Forschungen, 17 (Wolfenbütel: Herzog, August, 1981), pp. 9–46; Richard Palmer, "Physicians and the State in Post-Medieval Italy," in Russell, ed., 47–62; and Nancy Siraisi, *Taddeo Alderotti and His Pupils* (Princeton: Princeton University Press, 1982), passim.

    Florentine State Archives, *Provv. reg.* 28, fol. 93v. (9 Oct. 1336); *Provv. reg.* 32, fol. 115r. There were other specialists hired by the commune; see *Provv. reg.* 41, fol. 38; *Provv. reg.* 48, fol. 149v.-50 (1361). But Florentines were much less committed to the use of public physicians than were the Venetians. See B. Cecchetti, "La medicina in Venezia nel 1300," *Archivio veneto* 26 (1886): 77–111, and 251–70; and G. G. Alvisi, "Considerazioni documentali sull'arte medica e sul personale sanitario di Venezia dal X al XV secolo," *Giornale veneto di scienze mediche*, ser. 2, 11 (1858): 463–500.

13. A condemned doctor's hands were not removed because he could be of more use to ill prisoners with them: Florentine State Archives, *Provv. reg.* 31, fol. 13v. On the provision of other medical services by the commune see *Provv. reg.* 34, fol. 70r.; *Provv. reg.* 35, fol. 13r.; *Provv. reg.* 31, fol. 70r. In general see Puccinotti, 2, pt. 2: 475–8.

    1322 (I, xvii), fol. 19r., but officials for expelling lepers certainly existed before this time. See Florentine State Archives, *Provv. reg.* 16 (1319), fol. 2v., and *Signori missive*, Ia Cancelleria, reg. 9, fol. 8v.

    See examples during the famine and epidemic of 1347: Florentine State Archives, *Provv. reg.* 34, fol. 124v. and fol. 135. G. Villani (XI, 80–90) also alludes to evidences of communal charity everywhere during the difficult 1330s and 1340s.

14. The wording of the statute apparently comes from Florentine State Archives, *Provv. reg.* 16, fol. 9 (9 Jan. 1319). 1322 (III, cxv), fol. 72; Caggese, 2: 270–3; Puccinotti, cxcv–cxcvi; and *Statuta Populi*, 2: 415–18.

15. Carabellese, *La peste del 1348*, pp. 119–29. For another example, see Florentine State Archives, *Provv. reg.* 25, fol. 53v.-54r.

16. Carabellese, *La peste del 1348*, 41ff.

17. Carabellese, *La peste del 1348*, 44–5.

18. Carabellese, *La peste del 1348*, 45–6 n. 2, 55 and 58. Duties charged at the gates (*gabelles*) began again on 23 August 1348; see Florentine State Archives, *Provv. reg.* 36, fol. 1r.

19. Florentine State Archives, *Provv. reg.* 72, fol. 118v.-19r. (5 Aug. 1383). See also Biblioteca Comunale Ariostea, Ferrara, "Cose fiorentine," fol. 96r. "Apresso, perchè, per la mortalità molti cittadini si partivano et vedevasi che assai più s'adattavano a partire, et sentivasi delle minacie che facevano gli usciti di fare grande novità in Firenze nel tempo della mortalità, doppo molte praticho di rimedii si mandò per molti fanti fidati in casentino et altrove, che scripsono in Firenze per ghuardia."

20. Stefani, *Cronaca fiorentina*, ed. N. Rodolico, Rerum Italicarum Scriptores, new ed., vol. 16 (Città di Castello, 1927), 426–7.

21. Corradi, 1: 231, quoting from the chroniclers Ser Naddo and Sozemeno.

22. Biblioteca Comunale Ariostea, Ferrara, "Cose fiorentine" (Buoninsegni precursor), fol. 96. This chronicler reported that 60–100 deaths per day occurred in June, 200–300 in early July, rising to 400 a day by the end of the month. He claimed that 25,000 lire was imposed in taxes on the absentee citizens: "Essendo Adumque Rimasi si pochi cittadini in firenze una brighata di Ciompi Intendendosi con usciti di fuori levorono Romore la notte di Sca. Maria Magdalena. Et andarono per più parti della città Gridando vivano le venti quatto arti e I guelfi. Et rizarono arte bandiere. Ma mediante l'aiuto di dio e provedimenti de' signori e dell' gli otto, Et la fanchigia di Messere Cante da Ghobbio capitano I romoreggianti si fuggirono et spariromo. Et poi ne furono alquanti presi Et poi decapitati. Et poi con buona guardia I signori compierono honorevolemente el loro ufficio sanza altra novità alloro tempo." The ms. is undoubtedly a source used by Piero Buoninsegni, *Historia fiorentina* (Florence, 1581), 665–6.

23. On the Ciompi in general see Gene A. Brucker, "The Ciompi Revolution," in N. Rubenstein, ed., *Florentine Studies: Politics and Society in Renaissance Florence* (Evanston, Ill.: Northwestern University Press, 1968), 314–56; Michel Mollat and Philippe Wolff, *The Popular Revolutions of the Late Middle Ages* (London: Allen & Unwin, 1973), 142–61; Samuel Cohn, Jr., *The Laboring Classes in Renaissance Florence* (New York: Academic Press, 1980); Völker Hunecke, "The Conference on the *Tulmulto dei Ciompi* Held in Florence, 16–19 September, 1979," *Journal of Italian History* 2 (1979): 281–92, esp. 282: "The sense that the urban culture was threatened by an unpredictable enemy, and the feelings of fear and loathing that this evoked, found their epitome in the word *pestis*, plague, a metaphor which after 1348 acquired all too exact a meaning."

24. Francesco Novati, ed., *Epistolario di Coluccio Salutati*, 4 vols. (Rome, 1891–1911),

2: 81–98, 221–37. See also Ronald G. Witt, *Hercules at the Crossroads: The Life, Works and Thought of Coluccio Salutati* (Durham, N.C.: Duke University Press, 1983), 280–1.

25. E.g., Domenico Buoninsegni, *Storie della città di Firenze dall'anno 1410 al 1460* (Florence, 1637), 23. For a similar, non-Florentine example, see Philippe Wolff, "Vivre en temps de peste," *Provence historique* 23 (1973): 236–42.

26. Gregorio Dati, *Il libro segreto*, ed. C. Gargiolli (Bologna, 1869), 96.

27. I.e., Bologna and Rimini; see n. 24, this chapter.

28. See Saint Antoninus, *Chronicon*, ed. Raoul Morçay (Paris: Gabalda, 1913), 82–3 (tit. 22, cap. xii, no. 3) and Antoninus, *Summa Theologica*, 4 vols. (Graz, 1959), 4: I, tit. 5, cap. 1, no. 7. The major provision of 1448, one that Archbishop Antoninus introduced, is printed in A. Corsini, *La 'moria' del 1464 in Toscana e l'istituzione dei primi lazzaretti in Firenze ed in Pisa* (Florence: Libreria Claudiana, 1911), 31–3. Also see Luigi Passerini, *Storia della stabilmenti di beneficenza* (Florence, 1853), 295–9. And compare with similar measures taken this year in Perugia, A. Fabretti, ed., "Cronaca del Graziano," *Archivio storico italiano*, ser. 1, 16 (1850): 603. On Antoninus's association with the Buonuomini di San Martino, see Richard Trexler, "Charity and the Defense of Urban Elites," in F. Jaher, ed., *The Rich, the Well-born, and the Powerful* (Urbana, Ill.: University of Illinois Press, 1973), 81–94. Also see W. R. Gaugham, *Social Theories of Sant' Antoninus from his Summa Theologica* (Washington, D.C.: Catholic University Press, 1950), 45–58; and Bede Jarrett, *San Antonino and Medieval Economics* (London: Manaresa Press, 1914), 48–9. Antoninus was still arguing for charity during the plague of 1457–8; *Lettere di Sant' Antonino* (Florence, 1859), addressed to the Eight on Defense in Prato, 10 January 1457.

29. Antoninus was angry at the stingy provisions made for the starving; see the *Chronicon*, 97 (tit. 22, cap. xv, no. 3); and Passerini, *Stabilmenti di beneficenza*, 297. Antoninus urged and received communal aid during the hard times of 1456 and 1457; *Chronicon*, pp. 87–8 (tit. 22, cap xii, no. 5). Morçay cites supporting archival evidence: "Considerato che la moria si usi ampliando e che i cittadini si partano e che i poveri non guadagnono per che l'arti non fanno, è necessario fare gli otto a mano per la via de' consigli" (17 Aug. 1457). Another shows Antoninus's role: "Inteso al richordo che fa l'arcivescovo delle limosine, dicono essere necessario provedere; et per questo consiglano che la signoria use diligentia con l'arcivescovo, che si tragga da luoghi pii che anno superfluo quella quantità facesse di bisogno pro questo anno. Et se pur bisognasse per indurgli, che il comune inmettesse qualche cosa."

30. Florentine State Archives, *Provv. reg.* 155, fol. 58, printed in Corsini, *La 'moria,'* 33–40 (12 June 1464). In 1457 there was not yet an isolation facility; see Passerini, *Stabilmenti di benificenza*, 296–7, and 693. The foundling hospital of Santa Maria della Scala was apparently used for many plague cases. See Luca Landucci, *Diario*, ed. I. del Badia (Florence, 1883), 27–8.

31. Corsini, *La 'moria,'* 48–53. The new hospital, outside the porta della Giustitia was to be called the Spedale di San Bastiano, for Saint Sebastian. I am especially grateful to Prof. Richard Trexler, State University of New York at Binghamton (personal communication, 1976), who made me aware of this legislation and added the following references to the *provvisioni* provided by Corsini: Florentine State Archives, *Provv. reg.* 156, fol. 211v.-212; *Provv. reg.* 158, fol. 99 and 212–213; *Provv. reg.* 163, fol. 126v.-127v.; and *Provv. reg.* 170, fol. 16, all representing fund-raising attempts for the new plague hospital.

32. "Habentes notitiam . . . quod aliqui nuper obierunt Pisis ex contagione pestis, et dubitantes quod talis contagio ulterius non procedat"; Corsini, *La 'moria,'* 5; also see 28–31; and Passerini, *Storia di benificenza*, 297–8.

33. In 1476 charity was still a principal motive for building a lazaretto, but the Signoria acknowledged that the poor were the chief recipients of a lazaretto: "Desiderosi . . . che nella città si mantegna la sanità, et che quella si conservi maxime da ogni contagione di peste, et per questo effecto ogni opportuno rimedio ordi-

nare quanto far si può col consdiglio [*sic*] humano, et considerato non potersi sempre tanta diligentia usare che per varii modi qualche volta tale peste per contagione non offenda la città, et però essere necessario ordinarsi qualche luogo separato dove siano racceptati et governati quegli che da tale morbo fussino oppressi, et dove siano ritenuti quando recuperassino la sanità, acciò che la contagione degl' altri infermi di nuovo nella medesima infermità non gli riducessi; stimando questa opera di carità perchè e tutta favore di poveri, dovere essere potissim cagione a placare l'omnipotentia di Dio et farlo condiscendere a usare misericordia verso questo popolo et preservarlo da talle pestifero morbo." Corsini, *La 'moria,'* 44.

34. See Giovanni Antonelli, "La magistratura degli Otto di Guardia a Firenze," *Archivio storico italiano* 112 (1954): 3–39; and Nicolai Rubenstein, *The Government of Florence under the Medici (1434–1494)* (Oxford: Oxford University Press, 1966), 199–200.

35. Florentine State Archives, *Otto di guardia e balia*, 94, fol. 45r.

36. Ibid., fol. 32r.

37. The *Otto di Pratica* is discussed by Rubenstein, *Government of Florence*, 199–200 and 232–4. The office was abolished in the 1490s, after the downfall of Piero de' Medici. For the legislation see Florentine State Archives, *Provv. reg.* 184, fol. 44v.-45v.

38. Florentine State Archives, *Provv. reg.* 184, fol. 85v.-86v.

39. The law creating the balìa does not survive in the *Provv. reg.* of this year, but the first edict of the body, 18 March 1494, reports they are "newly created."

40. Florentine State Archives, *Balìe* 41, fol. 14v., 10 April: ". . . no lasciate entrare in Fireenze, nesuno birbone o ciuromentore, o poveri o altre genti ad pie che vanno accattando, et maximamente forestiere." Associating the poor with the spread of disease increased dramatically in the sixteenth century; see Natalie Z. Davis, "Poor Relief, Humanism and Heresy: the Case of Lyon," *Studies in Medieval and Renaissance History* 5 (1968), 215–75; Brian Pullan, *Rich and Poor in Renaissance Venice* (Cambridge, Mass.: Harvard University Press, 1971), 197–430; and Pullan, "The Famine in Venice and the New Poor Law: 1527–29," *Bollettino dell' istituto di storia dello stato veneziano* 5–6 (1963–4): 141–202.

41. Exceptions to the plague policies included orators from Charles VIII and a large party of Florentine merchants traveling from Rome, including a "Niccolò di Bernardo Machiavelli." See Florentine State Archives, *Balìe* 41, fol. 28, 112v.-13r., 123v.-6r. Citizen Luca Landucci reports the comings and goings of the French orators with no worry that they might carry plague, see his *Diario*, 68–9.

42. Florentine State Archives, *Balìe* 41, fol. 78 (17 March 1494).

43. Ibid., fol. 115r.

44. Ibid., fol. 191v., 24 July 1494: "Perche i cani sogliono essere instrumento di portar quà e là la contagione della peste, voliano facci subito ammazare tucti i cani." The Eight were killing dogs in the 1460s. See Florentine State Archives, *Otto di guardia e balìa*, 17, fol. 4r. (3 March 1466).

45. Ibid., fol. 172–3r. On early theories of contagion see Vivian Nutton, "The Seeds of Disease: An Explanation of Contagion and Infection from the Greeks to the Renaissance," *Medical History* 27, supp. 1 (1983): 1–34.

46. The agent in Rome had gone to the trouble of securing lay and medical opinion on the remaining cases and, as he described the condition of the air in the city, remained undecided whether there was a risk of contagion.

47. The letter to Andrea de' Medici relaxing guard is dated 5 September 1494 (fol. 210r.), though final news from Rome was not sent until 9 September.

48. Florentine State Archives, *Provv. reg.* 186, fol. 209v. (3 March 1496).

49. *A Florentine Diary*, trans. Alice Jarvis, ed. Del Badia (New York, 1927), 103–14. The early history of syphilis is still unsettled. In contrast to many reports Landucci denies that the new disease killed many. On this early epidemic see 'Hesnaut,' *Le mal français à l'époque de l'éxpedition de Charles VIII en Italie, d'après les*

documents originaux (Paris, 1886); Karl Sudhoff, *Graphische und typographische Erstlings der Syphilisliteratur aus den Jahren 1495 und 1496* (Munich, 1912); and Antonio Benivieni, *On the Hidden Causes of Disease*, trans. Charles Singer (Springfield, Ill.: Thomas, 1954), 8–21.

50. Landucci, *Diario*, 141.
51. *A Florentine Diary*, 116.
52. Roberto Ridolfi, *The Life of Girolamo Savonarola*, trans. Cecil Grayson (New York, 1951), 66–171, and 203–16; Pasquale Villari, *La storia di Girolamo Savonarola*, new ed., 2 vols. (Florence, 1930), 2: xxxv–xxxvi.
53. *A Florentine Diary*, 120–2. Savonarola wrote to Brother Alberto that cases of plague were few beside the "febroni pestilenziali"; see *Lettere*, ed. Ridolfi (Florence: Olschki, 1933), 154–5.
54. *Lettere*, 152–3; Landucci, *Diario*, 152, reports 100 deaths per day, "ch'era nella quintadecima la luna."
55. *A Florentine Diary*, 141. The Italian version is more specific: *poveri* is the antecedent of "them," not "unfortunate sufferers." A surviving document in the Archivio del Monte records the financial activities of the Ufficiali del Morbo from 1 December 1497 through the following May, noting especially the funds disbursed for food, mattresses, and alms to the spedale del morbo. For this reference, *Monte* 1510, I am very grateful to Prof. Anthony Molho of Brown University.
56. Carlo M. Cipolla cites the *Signoria* action in June 1527, as "decisive," in his *Public Health and the Medical Profession in the Renaissance* (Cambridge: Cambridge University Press, 1976), 13–14. The permanent magistracy had five officials, as did the Balìa of 1494, and the early hospital commission of 1464.

CHAPTER 5. *Plague controls become social controls*

1. Alberto Chiappelli, "Gli ordinamenti sanitari del comune di Pistoia," *Archivio storico italiano*, ser. 4, 20 (1887): 3–24. This is in part reviewed also by Anna Campbell, *The Black Death and Men of Learning* (New York: Columbia University Press, 1931), 115–18.
2. Chiappelli, "Gli ordinamenti sanitari," 9–10. The record of deaths has not survived. Chiappelli reprints the 2 May 1348 legislation that includes more traditional sanitary efforts without the special attention to plague in the legislation here cited. A marginal gloss in the manuscript of 2 May, however, describes these ordinances to "correctio ordinamentorum factorum tempore mortalitatis" (p. 17), and deals chiefly with foodstuffs.
3. Chiappelli, "Gli ordinamenti sanitari," 4–5. The records end 27 June, and do not resume until October, after the elders agree that government cannot depend upon a legal quorum of legislators. For the funeral measures discussed, see 20–4. Also see Campbell, *Black Death*, 111–21.
4. Francesco Carabellese, *La peste del 1348 e le condizioni della sanità pubblica in Toscana* (Rocca S. Casciano: Cappelli, 1897), 36–7, n. 3.
5. Ariodante Fabretti, ed., "Cronica della città di Perugia dal 1309 al 1491," *Archivio storico italiano*, ser. 1, 16 (1853): 148–9; Giulio Giani, "Le pestilenze del 1348, del 1526 e del 1631–32 in Prato," *Archivio storico pratese* (1930): 49–63, and 97–108. The latter does not discuss the sanitary measures taken in Prato during 1348, but he does give details about the special balia created that year to ensure the orderly transmission of governmental authority during the crisis.
6. Wealthy Venetians preferred not to bury their dead as quickly as plague provisions dictated. See Bruno Cecchetti, "Funerali e sepolture dei veneziani antichi," *Archivio veneto* 34 (1887): 265–70.
7. Mario Brunetti, "Venezia durante la peste del 1348," *Ateneo veneto* 32 (1909): vol. 1, fasc. 3, 289–311, and vol. 2, fasc. 1, 5–42. Venetians actually had the first board of health since their three officials assumed duties 3 April, eight days before the Florentine commission. Corradi had cited much of this legislation de-

cades before Brunetti published; see Alfonso Corradi, *Annali delle epidemie occorse in Italia*, 5 vols. (repr. Bologna: Forni, 1974) 4: 36–38. George Sarton, *Introduction to the History of Science*, 3 vols. in 5 (Baltimore: Johns Hopkins University Press, 1927–48), 3, pt. 2: 1658–9, misdates the re-creation of the health boards by 100 years (1385 instead of 1485).

8. Brunetti, "Venezia durante la peste," 294. On the plague provisions see also Bruno Checchetti, "La medicina in Venezia nel 1300," *Archivio veneto* 25 (1883): 377–80; Carlo Cipolla, "Origine e sviluppo degli uffici di sanitá in Italia," *Annales cisalpines d'histoire sociale*, ser. 1, 4 (1973): 83–101; and Richard Palmer, "L'azione della Repubblica di Venezia nel controllo della peste," in *Venezia e la peste, 1348/1797* (Venice: Marsilio, 1979), 103–11.

9. For the general timetable of these sanitary events see Carlo Cipolla, *Public Health and the Medical Profession in the Renaissance* (Cambridge: Cambridge University Press, 1976), 9–10; and C. Ravasini, *Documenti sanitari: bolli e suggelli di disinfezione nel passato* (Trieste: 1958), 10–12. Ragusa was undoubtedly an exception in the development of communal plague controls. See Susan M. Stuard, "A Communal Program of Medical Care: Medieval Ragusa/Dubrovnik," *Journal of the History of Medicine and Allied Sciences* 28 (1973): 126–42. Biraben, *Les hommes et la peste*, 2 vols. (Paris: Mouton, 1975–76), 2: 103ff. Mirko Grmek, "Le concept d'infection dans l'antiquité et au Moyen Age, les anciennes mésures sociales contre les maladies contagieuses et la fondation de la première quarantine à Dubrovnik," *RAD Jugoslavenske Akademije Znanosti i Umjetnosti*, no. 384 (Zagreb: 1980), 28–32. Grmek contends that quarantine was a rational response to plague, and that it would not have served the epidemics of the thirteenth century, among which he finds smallpox, dysenteries, and epidemic typhus. He also speculates that quarantine served plague uniquely, because the procedure was not effective against genuinely contagious diseases. Thus the quarantine is best understood in the "contagion of the air" context, defining infection or tainting of the air in the immediate vicinity of the person or commodity coming from an infected region. See also Campbell, *The Black Death*; and Owsei Temkin, "An Historical Analysis of the Concept of Infection," in Temkin, *The Double Face of Janus and Other Essays* (Baltimore: Johns Hopkins University Press, 1977), 456–71.

10. *Chronicon Regiense*, Rerum Italicarum Scriptores, orig. ed., vol. 18 (Milan, 1730), 82, reprinted in Grmek, "Le concept d'infection," p. 41, n. 108; and Biraben, *Les hommes et la peste*, 2: 108.

11. On the traditional treatment of lepers in the Middle Ages see Charles Creighton, *A History of Epidemics in Britain*, 2 vols. (Cambridge, 1891), 1: 100–13; Saul N. Brody, *The Disease of the Soul: A Study of Moral Associations of Leprosy in Medieval Literature* (Ithaca, N.Y.: Cornell University Press, 1974), 60–106; and Stuart Jenks, *The Black Death and Würzburg: Michael de Leone's Reaction in Context*, Yale University dissertation, 1976 (Ann Arbor, Mich.: University Microfilms, 1976), 139.

12. Mantuan State Archives, *Cride*, busta 2038, fasc. 1, fol. 5; and Corradi, 5: 213–15.

13. Grmek, "Le concept d'infection," 50, concludes that Ragusa's absolute dependence on outside trade motivated the halfway solution of temporary isolation, a measure the Milanese and Mantuan states may not have been forced to take.

14. Mantuan State Archives, *Cride*, busta 2038, fasc. 2, fol. 2r.

15. Ravasini, *Documenti sanitari*, 10.

16. Corradi, 4: 81.

17. A. Bottero, "La peste in Milano nel 1399–1400 e l'opera di Gian Galeazzo Visconti," *Atti e memorie dell'accademia di storia dell'arte sanitaria*, ser. 2, 8 (1942): 17–28; and Antonia Pasi Testa, "Alle origini dell'ufficio di sanità del Ducato di Milano e principato di Pavia," *Archivio storico lombardo* 102 (1977): 376–80.

18. Giovanni de Mussis, *Chronicon Placentinum*, Rerum Italicarum Scriptores, orig. ed., vol. 16 (Milan, 1730), 560; and Corradi, 4: 87–8.

19. Bottero, "La peste in Milano."

20. See A. Bascapé, *Storia di Milano*, 16 vols. (Milan, 1953–61), 8: 396.

21. Pasi Testa, "Alle origini dell' ufficio di sanità," 379–80.
22. Pasi Testa, "Alle origini dell'ufficio di sanità," 382–3.
23. Corradi, 1: 260.
24. Corradi, 1: 261.
25. Corradi, 4: 132–4; and again in 1432, Corradi, 4: 136–7.
26. E.g., Venetian State Archives, *Senato miste*, reg. 54, fol. 147r. (4 Sept. 1423); reg. 56, fol. 12r. (14 May 1426), and reg. 59, fol. 139r. (27 December 1435).
27. Mantuan State Archives, *Cride*, busta 2038, fasc. 4, fol. 9–11; fasc. 5, fol. 1–6. This kind of legislation was probably widespread. For brief examples see Corradi, 1: 287.
28. Mantuan State Archives, *Cride*, busta 2038, fasc. 5, fol. 6v.
29. Ibid., fol. 7.
30. Ibid., fol. 14r.: "Havendo sentito . . . che a fiorenza qualunche non gli sia grande infectione di peste gli ne sono pur manchati alcuni et prencipue nel hospitale grande et in du' altra contrata, come desyderoso de preservare mediante la divina gratia questa sua terra de ogni contagione."
31. Compare with Henri Dubled, "Les épidémies de peste à Carpentras et dans le Comtat Venaissin," *Provence historique* 19 (1969): 17–48. Dubled finds isolation and quarantine first applied in Carpentras during the plague of 1468.
32. Lorenzo Leonii, "La peste e la compagnia del cappelletto a Todi al 1363," *Archivio storico italiano*, ser. 4, 2 (1878): 3–11. Venetians closed off entrances to the city in 1348; Brunetti, "Venezia durante la peste," 297, n. 1.
33. The earliest use of guards in Venice, specifically for guarding the properties of the absentee, was in 1420, before a lazaretto was used. See Venetian State Archives, *Consiglio dei dieci*, Miste, reg. 10, fol. 31r. (28 Sept. 1420) and fol. 32r. (6 Nov. 1420). Their reasoning may be demonstrated with an example from 1423, ibid., fol. 60v. (11 Aug. 1423): "Cum sicut est omnibus manifestum propter Intemperium aerem multi nobiles et alii cives nostri exiverunt et quotidie exeant de venet. dimettendo domos suos cum massariciis et bonis suis propter quod est bonum providere et obviare malis que possent committi sunt." Thus they assigned bargemen, supervised by the *officiales de nocte*.
    Guards were not uniformly used to protect properties in the 1420s. For example the Perugians posted guards fearing Milanese invasion in 1424. At the same time they issued travel bans. But by 1435, they used guards to protect properties of the wealthy. See "Cronaca del Graziani," *Archivio storico italiano*, ser. 1, 16, pt. 1 (1850), 287–8 and 401; and again in 1448, ibid., 603–4. Guards (*policia portalium*) were not used in Provence until 1468; Dubled, "Les épidémies de peste," 28.
34. Brunetti, "Venezia durante la peste," 292–3, n. 2.
35. Venetian State Archives, *Consiglio dei dieci*, Miste, reg. 15, fol. 104v., 121r., 126r., 132r., 135v.
36. Venetian State Archives, *Senato, Terra*, reg. 4, fol. 10v. [26 June 1456]: ". . . h[a]ec civitas plena innumerabilibus personis preservari possit a contagione morbi pestiferi que propter inobedientiam multorum qui non timent penas, que imposite sunt, non sufficiunt ad evitanda discrimina que undique imminent huic civitate iam in diversis locis infecte. Et hoc principaliter procedat ex copiosa conductione sclavorum et albanensis." Also see Corradi, 1: 272; 4: 182; and 5: 243. Although Marin Sanudo claimed that the Albanians were plague carriers as early as the 1430 plague, there is no contemporary support for this. His ancestor, another Marin Sanudo, was involved in legislation concerning Istria, particularly ousting Jewish moneylenders. Anti-Slavic concerns in the 1430s included the fear of insurrection and the fear of Venetian sailors marrying Albanian women.
37. Venetian State Archives, *Notatorio del Collegio*, reg. 9, fol. 41r. (8 Jan. 1455). Both contemporaries and historians disputed whether plague was actually transported from Istrian colonies to the mainland; see Corradi, 1: 292–3; and 5: 236; and Bernardo Schiavuzzi, "Le epidemie di peste bubbonica in Istria," *Atti e memorie della società istriana d'archeologia* 4 (1889): 423–47.
38. On preplague concern with Albanian immigrants see Venetian State Archives,

Senato, Terra, reg. 8, fol. 33r. Concern with sodomy was also increasing at the same time; see *Consiglio dei dieci*, Miste, reg. 15, fol. 50v. (2 May 1455), as was the fear of thefts and other social disruptions, because of the famine (ibid., fol. 76r.).

39. Corradi, 4: 169.
40. Corradi, 1: 299; and 4: 243.
41. Corradi, 4: 169.
42. Venetian State Archives, *Senato*, Miste, reg. 54, fol. 140v.(28 Aug. 1423). It was not an overwhelmingly popular decision, with 53 in favor, 31 against, and 12 abstentions.
43. Ibid., reg. 57, fol. 220r. (2 June 1430). On other charitable efforts during plagues see Corradi, 5: 226–7 (Siena, 1417).
44. Corradi, 1: 276. See also Luigi N. Cittadella, *Notizie relative a Ferrara* (Ferrara, 1864), 391–7.
45. Carlo Decio, *La peste in Milano nell' anno 1451 e il primo lazzaretto a Cusago: appunti storici e note inedite tratte degli archive milanese* (Milan: Cogliati, 1900), 9–13, and appendix.
46. Decio, *La peste in Milano*, 16–21. See also Pietro Canetta, *Il lazzaretto di Milano* (Milan, 1881); and Luca Beltrami, "Il lazzaretto di Milano," *Archivio storico lombardo* 9 (1882): 403–41. On the plague this year in Milan, see Corradi, 1: 283; 4: 162; and 5: 234–5.
47. Beltrami, "Il lazzaretto di Milano," 405–7; Canetta, *Il lazzaretto di Milano*, 5–7.
48. Corradi, 1: 302.
49. Corradi, 1: 301, 305–6; 4: 170, 175; 5: 253–4. Corradi, 4: 125, refers to a very early lazaretto in Gemona, 1407, apparently the temporary use of an older leprosarium outside the city walls. Also see Palmer, "L'azione della repubblica di Venezia nel controllo della peste," in *Venezia e la peste*, 109; Decio, *La peste*, 21; Beltrami, "Il lazzaretto di Milano," 407; Carlo d'Arco, ed., "Cronaca di Mantova dal MCCCCXLV al MCCCCLXXXIV," in G. Müller, ed., *Raccolta di cronisti e documenti storici lombardi*, 2 vols, (Milan, 1857), 125. By 1508 little Pistoia had an "ospedale della morte" designated for the poor only: Ser Luca Dominici, *Cronaca della venuta dei Bianchi e della morìa, 1399–1400*, ed. G. Gigliotti, Rerum Pistoriensium Scriptores, no. 1 (Pistoia, 1933), 293–4. In 1474 legislators in Carpentras (in Provence) first decided to build a hospice for plague victims, outside the city walls. The project was not begun until 1533; Dubled, "Les épidémies de peste," 41–2.
50. Luciano Banchi, "Provvisioni della Repubblica di Siena contro la peste degli anni 1411 e 1463," *Archivio storico italiano*, ser. 4, 14 (1884): 325–32.
51. Ibid.
52. Corradi, 5: 264.
53. Cipolla, *Public Health and the Medical Profession*, 14–17.
54. Ibid., 1–31; and Cipolla, "Origine e sviluppo degli uffici di sanità in Italia." Similar measures were taken in Provence; e.g., Carpentras first created temporary health deputies in 1474, but the board of health was established in the sixteenth century; see Dubled, "Les épidémies de peste," 26.
55. See Corradi, 1: 297; and 4: 169; and Domenico Malipiero, "Annali veneti, dall'anno 1457 al 1500," ed. F. Longo, *Archivio storico italiano*, ser. 1, 7, pt. 2 (1843), 653, on the establishment of a temporary board of health in 1459–60, Venice.
56. Venetian State Archives, *Senato, Terra*, reg. 10, fol. 4 (17 March 1486). See also *Provveditori alla sanità*, Decreti e ordini, reg. 725, 8v-9r (7 May 1490); and see Brian Pullan, *Rich and Poor in Renaissance Venice* (Cambridge, Mass.: Harvard University Press, 1971), 219–20.
57. Guido Ruggiero, "Sexual Criminality in the Early Renaissance: Venice, 1338–1358," *Journal of Social History* 8 (1974–5): 18–37.
58. Corradi, 5: 259 (Spoleto, 1484), and 4: 207: No one may shelter "venales mulieres, vel meretrices, et lenones."
59. Mantuan State Archives, *Cride*, busta 2038, fasc. 8, fol. 15r.: ". . . che questa sua

inclita Citade non patisca tanta ignominia che sia novamente uno postribulo et receptaculo de' Ruffiani, fa Far publica Crida . . . che non sia personal alchuna da che Condicione . . . dar a Femine Meretrice ne de Cativa fama ad affecto casa alchuna in la citade sua excepto circa le Mura de la Citade da Redevalle."

60. Corradi, 1: 332: "Tutte e singule meretrice et loro homini ruffiani et zarlotti." Also in Bologna, 1486: "Ad placandum Dominum, ne pestis ulterius grassaretur, ordinatum est per patritios, ut omnes pueri Mendicantes vestimento albo ex aere publico vestirentur, cum cruce rubea in pectore." Also see Corradi, 5: 265.

61. Corradi, 1: 332–3; 5: 264–5. In 1486 Perugians banned poor mendicants and gypsies as well, "ad obviare ad omne contagione"; Corradi, 4: 209.

62. E.g., Venetian State Archives, *Maggior Consilio*, Leona, fol. 187v. (1409).

63. Prof. Guido Ruggiero, University of Cincinnati, personal communication, 1980.

64. Venetian State Archives, *Provveditori alla sanità*, Decreti e Ordini, reg. 725, fol. 2v.(20 March 1486), and fol. 7r. (24 March 1490). Venice also had health regulations against the prostitutes as early as 1486. See Corradi, 5: 263.

65. Venetian State Archives, *Provveditori alla sanità*, Decreti e Ordini, reg. 725, fol. 8v.-9r. (7 May 1490).

CONCLUSION

1. See Emmanuel Le Roy Ladurie, *The Peasants of Languedoc*, trans. John Day (Urbana: University of Illinois Press, 1974), 1–79. On the general social and economic history of early modern Europe see Fernand Braudel, *The Structures of Everyday Life* (New York: Harper & Row, 1979), 31–103; and Brian Pullan, *Rich and Poor in Renaissance Venice* (Cambridge, Mass.: Harvard University Press, 1971), 189–240.

2. Lucian F. Hirst, *The Conquest of Plague* (London: Oxford University Press, 1953), 14–49; George Sarton, *Introduction to the History of Science*, 3 vols. in 4 (Baltimore: Johns Hopkins University Press, 1927–48), 3, pt. 2: 1658; Karl Sudhoff, "The Hygienic Idea in World History," in Fielding H. Garrison, ed., *Essays in the History of Medicine*, (New York: Medical Life Press, 1926), 134–35; George Rosen, *A History of Public Health* (New York: MD Publications, 1958), 69.

3. Jacques Revel, "Autour d'une épidémie ancienne: la peste de 1666–70," *Revue d'histoire moderne et contemporaine* 17 (1970): 953–83.

4. Vivian Nutton, "The Seeds of Disease: An Explanation of Contagion and Infection from the Greeks to the Renaissance," *Medical History* 27 (1983): 1–34.

5. Nutton, "Seeds of Disease," 19.

6. Nutton, "Seeds of Disease," 14.

7. Nutton, "Seeds of Disease," 23. See also Charles and Dorothea Singer, "The Scientific Position of Girolamo Fracastoro [1478?-1553], with Especial Reference to the Source, Character and Influence of His Theory of Infection," *Annals of Medical History* 1 (1917): 1–34; and N. Howard-Jones, "Fracastoro and Henle: A Reappraisal of Their Contribution to the Concept of Communicable Diseases," *Medical History* 21 (1977): 61–8. In general see C. E.-A. Winslow, *The Conquest of Epidemic Disease* (1943; reprint, Madison: University of Wisconsin Press, 1980), 117–43; Owsei Temkin, "The Scientific Approach to Disease: Specific Entity and Individual Sickness," in Temkin, *The Double Face of Janus* (Baltimore: Johns Hopkins University Press, 1977), 442–48; Saul Jarcho, "Medical and Nonmedical Comments on Cato and Varro, with Historical Observations on the Concept of Infection," *Transactions and Studies of the College of Physicians of Philadelphia* 43 (1975–6): 372–8; and Joanne H. Phillips, "On Varro's *animalia quaedam minuta* and the Etiology of Disease," ibid. 4 (1982).

8. Girolamo Fracastoro, *De Contagione et Contagiosis Morbis et Eorum Curatione, Libri III*, ed. and trans. Wilmer C. Wright (New York: Putnam's Sons, 1930), 84–93, and 109–13. See also my "Plague Legislation in the Italian Renaissance," *Bulletin of the History of Medicine* 47 (1983): 523–5.

APPENDIXES

1. David Herlihy and Christiane Klapisch-Zuber, *Les toscans et leur familles* (Paris: SEVPEN, 1979), 446–68; and Ser Lapo Mazzei, *Lettere d'un notaro a un mercante*, ed. C. Guaste, 2 vols. (Florence, 1880), 1: 243–50.

2. For example, Florentine State Archives, *Grascia morti*, 2: 21 June, 16 July, and 18 July 1400, contain entries of "quedam monialis in Sancto Nicolay . . . "; 17 November 1399, "Frater Giari ordinis fratrum predicatorum, sepelitur in Santa Maria Novella per fratres"; 29 November 1399, 26 January (1400), and 13 February 1400 record deaths of hospitalized paupers.

3. Guiseppe Pardi, "Disegno della storia demografica di Firenze," *Archivio storico italiano* 74, pt. 1 (1916): 3–84, esp. 69. Pardi also believed mendicants were not included in communal surveys.

4. Florentine State Archives, *Santa Maria Nuova*, registers 730 and 731. In general see Luigi Passerini, *Storia degli stabilmenti di benificenza e d'istruzione elementare gratuita della città di Firenze* (Florence, 1853); and Giuseppe Parenti, "Fonti per lo studio della demografia fiorentina: i libri dei morti," *Genus* 5–6 (1943–9): 294–5. For analysis of admissions and deaths at the hospital of San Paolo in the sixteenth century, see Bernice J. Trexler, "Hospital Patients in Florence: San Paolo, 1567–8," *Bulletin of the History of Medicine* 48 (1974): 41–59.

5. Richard C. Trexler, "The Foundlings of Florence, 1395–1455," *History of Childhood Quarterly* 1 (1973): 259–83.

6. B. Trexler, "Hospital Patients," 41 and 54–5.

7. Mazzei, *Lettere d'un notaro*, 1: 243–4, 6 July 1400: "iere morirono quì [Florence] 201 sanza gli spedali, preti, frati e monasteri, e gente che fanno sanza beccamorti: che solo allo Spidale nostro [Santa Maria Nuova] va, il dì, otto sei e dieci; e non manca: e infermi circa 250 abbiamo oggi."

8. R. Trexler, "Foundlings of Florence." San Gallo became an orphanage/refuge for older children by the mid-fifteenth century, but only accepted 261 charges between 1430 and 1439.

9. R. Trexler, "Foundlings of Florence," 265–75. Gregorio Dati, *L'istoria di Firenze dal 1380 al 1405*, ed. L. Pratesi (Norcia, 1904), 118–19, mentions that the spedale nuova in the Piazza de' Servi cared for abandoned children before 1405.

10. R. Trexler, "Foundlings of Florence," 266–7; Passerini, *Beneficenza*, 703–5; Brian Pullan, *Rich and Poor in Renaissance Venice* (Cambridge, Mass.: Harvard University Press, 1971), 197–216; Claudine Billot, "Les enfants abandonnés à Chartres à la fin des Moyen Ages," *Annales de démographie historique*, 1975: 167–79.

Bibliographical essay

Interdisciplinary histories must manage such a wide range and diversity of materials that, however comprehensive the notes testifying to the sources consulted, some general reflection on the developments in contributing fields of scholarly endeavor is necessary for those who wish to explore the topic further. There is no attempt here to reproduce notes to the text, which offer references to the literature specifically used in this study. For example, Florentine studies and works on the general social history of early modern Europe are not reviewed here. Neither are primary sources discussed. The following essay offers some guidance to the literature of the history of medicine, the history of human infections, and the specialized literature on plague, for the early modern European period.

I

Within the past twenty years the social history of medicine has been a much discussed alternative to traditional histories of medicine examining the ideas and activities of physicians in the past. Unfortunately there are far more programmatic statements that call for research into the "history of patients" than there are examples of a desirable end product. Henry E. Sigerist, George Rosen, and Erwin Ackerknecht a generation ago urged medical historians to turn away from "iatrocentric" studies of medical activity, particularly those that were seen to result in "progress" leading to twentieth-century medical successes. Instead we must understand the behavior of physicians and other healers in the past, and the social and ecological conditions for health and disease in past populations. Sigerist achieved an overview of the social history of medicine in his popular *Civilization and Disease* (1943; reprint, Chicago: University of Chicago Press, 1962), but he did not reach his ambition to produce a comprehensive social history of medicine. The first volume, *A History of Medicine: Primitive and Archaic Medicine* (New York: Oxford University Press, 1951), was the only one he lived to complete; a second, posthumously published volume on Indian and early Greek medicine, did not even fully encompass Hippocratic medicine. Erwin H. Ackerknecht's "A Plea for a Behaviorist Approach in the History of Medicine," *Journal of the History of Medicine and Allied Sciences* 22 (1967): 211–14; and George Rosen's "People, Disease and Emotions," *Bulletin of the History of Medicine* 41 (1967): 5–23, clarified goals that Sigerist had employed. Rosen's publications subsequently remained circumscript, article-length studies.

Many historiographical surveys, for the most part recommendations for future study in the social history of medicine, have followed lines similar to Rosen's suggestions. A collection of essays edited by Edwin Clarke, *Modern Methods in the History of Medicine* (London: Athlone Press, 1971), helped to refine and separate the topics and methods within the social history of medicine. Other collections of essays offering exemplars of the social history of medicine as well as the protocol include Patricia Branca, ed., *The Medicine Show: Patients, Physicians and the Perplexities of the Health Revolution in Modern Society* (New York: Science History Publications, 1977), and Charles E. Rosenberg, ed., *Healing and History* (New York: Neale Watson, 1979). Useful review articles are J. Woodward and D. Richards, "Towards a Social History of Medicine," in Woodward and Richards, eds., *Health Care and Popular Medicine in Nineteenth-Century England* (London: Holmes & Meier, 1977), 15–55; Gerald Grob, "The Social History of Medicine and Disease in America," *Journal of Social History* 10 (1977): 391–409; Jacques Revel and Jean-Pierre Peter, "Le corps: l'homme malade et son histoire," in Le Goff and P. Nora, eds., *Faire de l'histoire*, 3 vols. (Paris, 1975), 3: 169–91; and most recently Charles Webster, "Medicine as Social History: Changing Ideas on Doctors and Patients in the Age of Shakespeare," in L. Stevenson, ed., *A Celebration of Medical History* (Baltimore: Johns Hopkins University Press, 1982), 103–26. All find hopeful, if limited, evidence of a growing interest in the history of patients. Rosenberg, whose *The Cholera Years* (Chicago: University of Chicago Press, 1962) remains one of the classic exemplars of a social history of medicine, recently reviewed "The History of Disease: Now and in the Future," in *A Celebration of Medical History*, 32–36. Rosenberg finds that both the "new social history" examining ordinary people in the past and the history of disease have encouraged development in the social history of medicine perhaps more than reform within the ranks of historians of medicine. Although the current study cannot be described as a history of patients *as* patients, the extent to which it attempts a social history of medicine has depended on just these two areas of historical development that Rosenberg describes, rather than on the literature of the history of medicine.

Medical historians have paid much more attention to the history of medicine as part of the history of science, and a number of these studies have some bearing on topics in late medieval, early modern Italian medicine. Northern Italian medical treatises are conveniently reviewed by Nancy Siraisi, "Reflections on Italian Medical Writing of the Fourteenth and Fifteenth Centuries," *Annals of the New York Academy of Sciences* 412 (1983): 155–67. Illustrious individual practitioners and their works have commanded many efforts, including Siraisi's careful and thorough study, *Taddeo Alderotti and His Pupils* (Princeton: Princeton University Press, 1981); Luke DeMaitre, *Bernard of Gordon: Professor and Practitioner* (Toronto: Pontifical Institute of Medieval Studies, 1980); Dean Lockwood, *Ugo Benzi: Medieval Philosopher and Physician, 1376–1439* (Chicago: University of Chicago Press, 1951), and a host of less comprehensive biographies. A few of the more famous practitioners are subjects of individual entries in the *Dictionary of Scientific Biography*. For comparable studies of French physicians see Danielle Jacquart, *Le milieu medical en France du XXIIe au XVe siècle* (Geneva: Droz, 1981).

Useful discussions of late medieval scholastic medicine include, in addition to those already listed, Owsei Temkin, *Galenism: The Rise and Decline of a Medical Philosophy* (Ithaca: Cornell University Press, 1973); Paul Oskar Kristeller, "Philosophy and Medicine in Medieval and Renaissance Italy," in S. F. Spicker, ed., *Organism, Medicine and Metaphysics* (Dordrecht: Reidel, 1978), 29–40; John M. Riddle, "Theory and Practice in Medieval Medicine," *Viator* 5 (1974): 157–83; Michael M. McVaugh, "Medicine," in Edward Grant, ed., *A Sourcebook of Medieval Science* (Cambridge, Mass.: Harvard University Press, 1974), 700–808; Vern L. Bullough, *The Development of Medicine as a Profession: The Contribution of the Medieval University to Modern Medicine* (New York: Karger, 1966); Luke DeMaitre, "Scholasticism in Compendia of Practical Medicine, 1250–1450," in Siraisi and DeMaitre, eds., *Science, Medicine, and the University, 1200–1550: Essays in Honor of Pearl Kibre, Manuscripta* 20 (1976): 81–95; Charles H. Talbot, "Medicine," in David Lindberg (ed.), *Science in the Middle Ages* (Chicago: University of Chicago Press, 1978); and Siraisi, "Some Recent Work on Western European Medical Learning, ca. 1200–ca. 1500," *History of Universities* 2 (1982): 225–38. A good recent bibliographic guide to the history of science and medicine is Pietro Corsi and Paul Weindling, eds., *Information Sources in the History of Science and Medicine* (London: Butterworth Scientific, 1983).

In the late nineteenth and early twentieth centuries local and regional histories of medicine combined biobibliographical studies of Italian physicians and of the practice of medicine with careful archival research. Many of these are quite valuable since they publish documents useful to both historians of medical science and to social historians. Medical practice in Florence is reviewed by Raffaello Ciasca, *L'arte dei medici e speziali nella storia nel commercio fiorentino dal secolo XII al XV* (Florence: Olschki, 1927); Arturo Castiglioni, "La medicina ai tempi e nell'opera di Dante," *Archivio della storia della scienza* 3 (1922): 211–36; Francesco Puccinotti, *Storia della medicina*, 3 vols. in 4 (Leghorn: Wagner, 1850–66); Salvatore de Renzi, "La medicina in Italia ai tempi di Dante," in M. Cellini and G. Ghivizzani, eds., *Dante e il suo secolo* (Florence: Cellini, 1865–6), 533–44. Venetian medicine attracted other early researchers, for example Bruno Cecchetti, "La medicina in Venezia nel 1300," *Archivio veneto* 25 (1883): 361–81, and 26 (1884): 77–111, 251–70.

More recent studies in Italian medicine that examine the institutional and local history of the practice of medicine focus on public health. The works of Carlo M. Cipolla certainly dominate here, especially his *Public Health and the Medical Profession in the Renaissance* (Cambridge: Cambridge University Press, 1976). See also Cipolla, "Origine e sviluppo degli uffici di sanitá in Italia," *Annales cisalpines d'histoire sociale*, ser. 1, 4 (1973): 83–101; Richard Palmer, "L'azione della repubblica di Venezia nel controllo della peste," in *Venezia e la peste, 1348–1797* (Venice: Marsilio, 1979), 103–111; idem, "Physicians and the State in Post-Medieval Italy," in Andrew Russell, ed., *The Town and State Physician in Europe from the Middle Ages to the Enlightenment*, Wolfenbütteler Forschungen, 17 (Wolfenbüttel: Herzog August Bibliothek, 1981), 47–62; Vivian Nutton, "Continuity or Rediscovery? The City Physician in Classical Antiquity and Mediaeval Italy," ibid., 9–46; Susan M. Stuard, "A Communal Program of Medical Care: Medieval Ragusa/Dubrovnik," *Journal of the History of Medicine and Allied Science* 28 (1973): 126–42; and Carlo Ravasini, *Documenti sanitari: bolli e suggelli di disinfezione nel passato* (Trieste: Minerva medica, 1958), all emphasize Italian public medicine.

French comparisons include Sylvette Guilbert, "A Châlons-sur-Marne au XVe siècle: un consiel municipal face aux épidémies," *Annales: Economies, Sociétés, Civilisations* 23 (1968): 1283–1300; and Arlette Higounet-Nadal, "Hygiene, slaubrité, pollutions au Moyen Age: l'exemple de Perigueux," *Annales de démographie historique* 1975: 81–92. Many other specialized studies are referred to in the notes to the text. I was unable to see Katherine Park, *Doctors and Medicine in Early Renaissance Florence* (Princeton: Princeton University Press, 1985), before this book went to press.

There is no recent general history of public health to replace the older, useful work of George Rosen, *A History of Public Health* (New York: MD Publications, 1958). Still older surveys of the history of medicine and public health especially relevant to early modern Italy include Adalberto Pazzini, *La medicina: bibliografie di storia della medicina italiana*. Enciclopedia biografica e bibliografie di storia della medicina italiana, ser. 31 (Milan: EBBI, 1939), and idem, *Storia dell'arte sanitaria dalle origini a oggi*, 2 vols. (Rome: Minerva medica, 1973); Arturo Castiglioni, *A History of Medicine*, 2d ed., trans. E. B. Krumbhaur (New York: Knopf, 1947); Francesco Puccinotti, *Storia della medicina;* and F. Cirenei and C. A. Ferretti, "L'igiene scolastica in Italia," *Scientia Veterum*, no. 84 (1965): 7–40.

One further subtopic in the history of medicine, in addition to the literature on the history of infectious diseases and on the plague that will be discussed later, requires mention. There are several valuable scholarly articles on the history of medical concepts of disease. Three general articles by Owsei Temkin are still the most valuable overviews: "Health and Disease," "The Scientific Approach to Disease: Specific Entity and Individual Sickness," and "An Historical Analysis of the Concept of Infection," all of which are reprinted in *The Double Face of Janus* (Baltimore: Johns Hopkins University Press, 1977). Other general works include Charles Edward A. Winslow, *The Conquest of Epidemic Disease. A Chapter in the History of Ideas* (Princeton: Princeton University Press, 1944); F. K. Taylor, *The Concepts of Illness, Disease and Morbus* (Cambridge: Cambridge University Press, 1979); Lester King, *Medical Thinking* (Princeton: Princeton University Press, 1982); Mirko Grmek, "Le concept d'infection dans l'antiquité et au Moyen Age, les anciennes mésures sociales contre les maladies contagieuses et la fondation de la première quarantine à Dubrovnik," *RAD Jugoslavenske Akademije Znanosti i Umjetnosti*, no. 384 (Zagreb, 1980): 9–54; and most recently Robert P. Hudson, *Disease and Its Control: The Shaping of Modern Thought* (Westport, Conn.: Greenwood Press, 1983). Discussion of ontological theories of disease in the Renaissance is best handled by Vivian Nutton, "The Seeds of Disease: An Explanation of Contagion and Infection from the Greeks to the Renaissance," *Medical History* 27 (1983): 1–34. Dorothea Waley Singer, "The Scientific Position of Girolamo Fracastoro, with Especial Reference to the Source, Character and Influence of His Theory of Infection," *Annals of Medical History* 1 (1917): 1–34, is quite useful as well.

II

William H. McNeill's *Plagues and Peoples* (New York: Anchor, 1976) has become an enormously popular volume, renewing the interest of physicians and scientists in the history of infectious diseases, but McNeill's research was in part based on a vast, interdisciplinary literature that has grown over the past three decades. An earlier survey that is still quite serviceable is that by Erwin Ackerknecht, *The History and Geography of the Most Important Diseases* (New York: Hafner, 1965). *The Biology of Man in History,* a collection of essays originally published in the *Annales: Economies, Sociétés, Civilisations* (ed. and trans. Robert Forster and Orest Ranum [Baltimore: Johns Hopkins University Press, 1975]), offers readers yet another approach to the broad topic of history and human infections. Additionally, the *Journal of Interdisciplinary History* 14 (Autumn 1983) issue was devoted to "Hunger and History," with many articles related to the history of human infections. Notes to the present text include many individual, specialized studies that have been useful to understanding the Florentine mortality registers and will not be systematically repeated here.

Sir Macfarlane Burnet and David O. White, *Natural History of Infectious Diseases,* 4th ed. (Cambridge: Cambridge University Press, 1972), is still the best introduction to the medical and scientific principles underlying a study of human infections. Three others are also valuable: Richard Fiennes, *Zoonoses and the Origins and Ecology of Human Disease* (New York: Academic Press, 1978); Ronald Hare, *Pomp and Pestilence* (London: Victor Gollanez, 1954); and T. Aidan Cockburn, *The Evolution and Eradication of Infectious Diseases* (Baltimore: Johns Hopkins University Press, 1963). Biologists and physicians who have offered briefer overviews of infectious diseases and human history include Frank Fenner, "Infectious Diseases and Social Change," *Medical Journal of Australia* 58 (1971); 1043–7, 1099–1102; and Edward H. Kass, "Infectious Diseases and Social Change," *Journal of Infectious Diseases* 123 (1971): 110–14.

Much of the book-length literature on epidemic disease in early modern Europe, an area more fully researched in the 1500–1800 period, has been presented by historical demographers. The most extensive and intensive survey is by Edward A. Wrigley and Roger S. Schofield, *The Population History of England* (London: Edward Arnold, 1981). For the earlier, Italian period David Herlihy and Christiane Klapisch-Zuber, *Les toscans et leurs familles: un étude du catasto florentin de 1427* (Paris: SEVPEN, 1978), is indispensable. Several French regional histories, both social and demographic, have no parallel in Italian studies of the period before 1800: Pierre Goubert, *Beauvais et le Beauvaisis de 1600 à 1730* (Paris: SEVPEN, 1960); Edouard Baratier, *La démographie provençale du XIIIe au XVIe siècle* (Paris: SEVPEN, 1961); and Francois Lebrun, *Les hommes et la mort en Anjou* (Paris: Mouton, 1971). Yet there are a few good surveys of mortality crises, epidemic diseases, and historical demography for Mediterranean countries, including Vicente Pérez Moreda, *Las crisis de mortalidad en la España interior. Siglos XVI-XIX* (Madrid: Siglo vientiuno, 1980); Lorenzo del Panta, *Le epidemie nella storia demografia italiana (secoli XIV-XIX)* (Turin: Loescher, 1980); Massimo Livi Bacci, *La société italienne devant les crises de mortalité* (Florence: Dipartimento statistico, 1978); and Bartolomé Bennassar, *Recherches sur les grandes épidémies dans le nord de l'Espagne à la fin du XVIe siècle* (Paris: SEVPEN, 1969).

General socioeconomic histories occasionally undertake substantial discussion of medical and demographic problems. Keith Thomas, *Religion and the Decline of Magic,* rev. ed. (New York: Penguin, 1980); and Emmanuel Le Roy Ladurie, *The Peasants of Languedoc,* trans. John Day (Urbana: University of Illinois Press, 1974), are two of the best. I found very few models for mapping the progress and social influence of epidemic mortality. The only two that gave me the courage to attempt it were Louis Chevalier, *Laboring Classes and Dangerous Classes in Paris during the First Half of the Nineteenth Century*, trans. Frank Jellinek (New York: Fertig, 1973); and Ernst Woelkens, *Pest und Ruhr im 16. und 17. Jahrhundert* (Hannover: Niedersächsisches Heimatbund, 1954). Class conflicts have not often been linked to epidemics with documentary evidence; among those relevant to this study were René Baehrel, "La haine de classe en temps d'épidémie," *Annales: Economies, Sociétés, Civilisations* 7 (1952): 351–60; and Brian Pullan, "The Famine in Venice and the New Poor Law: 1527–9," *Bolletino dell'istituto di storia della società dello stato veneziano* 5–6 (1963–4): 141–202. Carlo Cipolla and Dante E. Zanetti, "Peste et mortalité différentielle," *Annales de démographie historique* (1972): 197–202; and Jean-Noël Biraben, "Les pauvres et la peste," in Michel Mollat, ed., *Etudes sur l'histoire de la pauvrété* (Paris: Sorbonne, 1974), 505–18, both suggest that there were strong class differences in plague mortality.

Studies of English demographic history, with emphasis on the history of epidemic diseases, are more numerous than those of continental countries or regions, for any time period. The best single study of the sources and methods for studying epidemic mortality is that of Paul Slack, "Mortality Crises and Epidemics, 1485–1610," in Charles Webster, ed., *Health, Medicine and Mortality in the Sixteenth Century* (Cambridge: Cambridge University Press, 1979). Other good recent surveys include Leslie Clarkson, *Death, Disease and Famine in Pre-Industrial England* (Dublin: Gill & Macmillan, 1975); Jonathan D. Chambers, *Population, Economy and Society in Pre-Industrial England* (Oxford: Oxford University Press, 1972); John Hatcher, *Plague, Population and the English Economy, 1348–1530* (London: Macmillan, 1977); Andrew B. Appleby, *Famine in Tudor and Stuart England* (Stanford, Calif.: Stanford University Press, 1978); Robert S. Gottfried, *Epidemic Disease in Fifteenth-Century England* (New Brunswick, N.J.: Rutgers University Press, 1979); and Thomas R. Forbes, *Chronicle from Aldgate. Life in Shakespeare's London* (New Haven: Yale University Press, 1971). Shorter studies include Ursula M. Cowgill, "Life and Death in the Sixteenth Century in the City of York," *Population Studies* 21 (1962): 53–62; R. E. Jones, "Infant Mortality in Rural North Shropshire, 1561–1653," *Annales de démographie historique*, 1978: 105–34.

The best general introduction to historical demography of early modern Europe is Michael Flinn, *The European Demographic System, 1500–1820* (Baltimore: Johns Hopkins University Press, 1981), especially because Flinn provides an extensive bibliography. Guides to the demographic sources of Italy may be found in Carlo Cipolla, ed., *Le fonti della demografia storica in Italia*, 1 vol. in 2 (Rome: CISP, 1972). Publications of the proceedings of several international meetings supply many valuable smaller studies as well: Paul Harsin and Etienne Hélin, eds., *Colloque international de démographie historique, Liege, 1963* (Paris: M. Th. Génin, 1965); Hubert Charbonneau and André Larose, eds., *Les grandes mortalités: étude méthodologique des crises démographiques du passé* (Liège: Ordina, 1979). Karl Helleiner, "The Population of Europe from the Black Death to the Eve of the Vital Revolution," in Rich and Wilson, eds., *Cambridge Economic History*, 2nd ed., 6 vols. in 8 (Cambridge: Cambridge University Press, 1966–78), is still a good survey of the history of European population in the period before 1600, as are Cipolla, *Before the Industrial Revolution* (New York: Norton, 1976); and Harry Miskimin, *The Economy of Early Renaissance Europe, 1300–1460* (Englewood Cliffs, N.J.: Prentice-Hall, 1969).

Several articles reviewing the problems of writing an interdisciplinary history of human infections merit additional attention. Mirko Grmek, "Préliminaires d'une étude historique des maladies," *Annales: Economies, Sociétés, Civilisations* 24 (1969): 1476–80; Jean-Pierre Peter, "Les mots et les objects de la maladie," *Revue historique* 49 (1971): 14–37; R. S. Roberts, "Epidemics and Social History: An Essay Review," *Medical History* 12 (1968): 305–16; Emmanuel Le Roy Ladurie, "Un concept: l'unification microbienne du monde (XIVe-XVIIe siècle)," *Schweizerische Zeitschrift für Geschichte* 23 (1973): 627–96; E. Ackerknecht, "Causes and Pseudocauses in the History of Disease," in *A Celebration of Medical History*, 19–31; Guenter Risse, "Epidemics and Medicine: The Influence of Disease on Medical Thought and Practice," *Bulletin of the History of Medicine* 53 (1979): 505–19; Lorenzo del Panta, "Chronologia e diffusione delle crisis de mortalità in Toscana dalla fine del XIV agli inizi del XIX secolo," *Richerche storiche* 7 (1977): 293–343; Evan Stark, "The Epidemic as a Social Event," *International Journal of the Health Services* 7 (1977): 681–705; and Abdel R. Omran, "The Epidemiologic Transition. A Theory of Epidemiology of Population Change," *Milbank Memorial Fund Quarterly* 49 (1971): 509–38. Although far removed in time from this period, Samuel H. Preston and Etienne Van de Walle, "Urban French Mortality in the Nineteenth Century," *Population Studies* 32 (1978): 281–4, contains a nice discussion of the ordinary causes of death in cities before modern sanitary intervention.

III

The literature on plague is so extensive that it needs a separate section for discussion. Modern literature on the biology of plague was reviewed in the Introduction, which together with the notes should serve to review this material. Here I will note general historical studies of plague in Europe, the specialized literature on the Black Death of 1348, and work of particular interest in studying the epidemics of Florence and northern Italy.

Jean-Noël Biraben, *Les hommes et la peste*, 2 vols. (Paris: Mouton, 1975–6), is now the standard work on plague in Europe, the first volume reviewing the biology and the incidence of plague, the second, social effects of and responses to plague outbreaks. Biraben's voluminous bibliography is particularly useful as a guide to French regional studies of plague. J. F. D. Shrewsbury, *A History of Bubonic Plague in the British Isles* (Cambridge: Cambridge University Press, 1970), discusses the impact of plague in England, but it should be read in connnection with the review of Christopher Morris, republished in the valuable collection *The Plague Reconsidered: A New Look at its Origins and Effects in 16th and 17th Century England*, Local Population Studies Supplement (Derbyshire: LPS, 1977).

Three nineteenth century surveys are noteworthy sources for the history of pestilences. By far the best is Alfonso Corradi, *Annali delle epidemie occorse in Italia dalle prime memorie al 1850*, 5 vols. (Repr. Bologna: Forni, 1974), indispensable to the current study. Corradi did offer evaluation and opinion about the nature and significance of many Italian epidemics, but devoted his life to recording the evidence for disease and weather disasters, in a year-by-year chronology. Twice adding to his original survey, Corradi included numerous archival citations, frequently printing unpublished accounts, and thereby surpassed similar, earlier surveys of diseases elsewhere in Europe: Joaquin de Villalba, *Epidemiologia española* (Madrid: Vilalpando, 1803); and J. A. F. Ozanam, *Histoire médicale générale et particulière des maladies épidémiques, contagieuses et épizootiques, qui on réné en Europe depuis les temps les plus reculés jusqu'à nos jours,* 2nd ed., 4 vols. (Lyons: Boursy, 1835). At the end of the century Charles Creighton published his still popular *A History of Epidemics in Britain,* 2 vols. (Cambridge: Cambridge University Press, 1891), but his stance against the germ theory of disease and his strong antivaccinationist views tinted the work considerably.

Most twentieth-century scholars have been content to undertake less comprehensive studies of plague, and the outbreak in 1348–50 has drawn the greatest historical attention. Most recently the survey of Robert S. Gottfried, *The Black Death: Natural and Human Disaster in Medieval Europe* (New York: Free Press, 1983), replaces G. G. Coulton, *The Black Death* (New York: Macmillan, 1930) for general historical audiences. Philip Ziegler's *The Black Death* (New York: Harper & Row, 1969) will still be widely read because it is written engagingly, as is Barbara Tuchman's *A Distant Mirror: The Calamitous Fourteenth Century* (New York: Knopf, 1978). However, Gottfried's book is more sensitive to current historical work on the 1200–1500 period than are either of the latter works.

Regional and topical studies of the Black Death include some superb books. Anna M. Campbell, *The Black Death and Men of Learning* (New York: Columbia University Press, 1931), details medical reactions to the plague. Dominick Palazzotto's dissertation, *The Black Death and Medicine: A Report and Analysis of the Tractates Written Between 1348 and 1350,* Ph.D. diss., University of Kansas, 1977 (Ann Arbor, Mich.: University Microfilms, 1978), provides extensive translations of plague treatises. Stuart Jenks, *The Black Death and Würzburg: Michael de Leone's Reaction in Context,* Ph.D. diss., Yale University, 1976 (Ann Arbor, Mich.: University Microfilms, 1976), provides a fascinating account of psychological reactions to plague in a city that escaped infection. Zvi Razi, *Life, Marriage, and Death in a Medieval Parish,* uniquely traces the longer term demographic effects of plague in a small English manor. Elizabeth Carpentier's "Autour de la Peste Noire: famines et épidémies dans l'histoire du 14e siècle," *Annales: Economies, Sociétés, Civilisations* 17 (1962): 1062–92, and her *Une ville devant la peste: Orvieto et la peste noire en 1348* (Paris: SEVPEN, 1963), have rightly become classic studies of an Italian city faced with the Black Death. William M. Bowsky, "The Impact of the Black Death upon Sienese Government and Society," *Speculum* 39 (1964): 1–34, offers a similar case study. Michael Dols, *The Black Death in the Middle East* (Princeton: Princeton University Press, 1977), surveys the effects of plague in Islamic society. Daniel Williman, ed., *The Black Death: The Impact of the Fourteenth-Century Plague,* Medieval and Renaissance Texts and Studies, vol. 13 (Binghamton, N.Y.: SUNY Press, 1982), presents recent work on plague in literature and art. In particular it reprints the important article of Robert E. Lerner, "The Black Death and Western European Eschatological Mentalities," *American Historical Review* 86 (1981): 533–52. Millard Meiss, *Painting in Florence and Siena after the Black Death* (New York: Harper & Row, 1964), saw great changes in art following the plague, a thesis in large part refuted by Bruce Cole, *Giotto and Florentine Painting, 1280–1375* (New York: Harper & Row, 1976), and Henk Van Os, "The Black Death and Sienese Painting: A Problem of Interpretation," *Art History* 4 (1981): 237–49. William Bowsky, ed., *The Black Death: A Turning Point in World History?* (New York: Holt, Rinehart and Winston, 1971), contains an older, but still useful, selection of articles on the Black Death.

To emphasize the effects of the Black Death in southern Europe, the following works are cited: Raymond Cazelles, "La peste de 1348 en langue d'oïl, épidémie proléterienne et infantile," *Comités des travaux historiques et scientifiques: Bulletin philologique et historique,* 1962: 293–305; Francesco Carabellese, *La peste del 1348 e le condizioni della sanità pubblica in Toscana* (Rocca S. Casciano: Cappeli, 1897); Alberto Chiappelli, "Gli ordinamenti sanitari del comune di Pistoia," *Archivio storico italiano,* ser. 4, 20 (1887): 3–24; Mario Brunetti, "Venezia durante la peste del 1348," *Ateneo veneto* 32 (1909): 1, fasc. 3: 289–311, and 2, fasc. 1: 5–42. Aliberto B. Falsini, "Firenze dopo il 1349: le consequenze della Pesta Nera," *Archivio storico italiano* 130 (1971): 425–503; Yves Renouard, "Conséquences et intérets démographiques de la peste noire de 1348," *Population* 3 (1948): 459–66; Genève Prat, "Albi et la Peste Noire," *Annales du Midi* 64 (1952): 15–25; Stephen d'Irsay, "Defense Reactions During the Black Death, 1348–49," *Annals of Medical History* 9 (1927): 169–79; P. Gras, "Le régistre paroissial de Givry (1334–1357) et la Peste Noire en Bourgogne," *Bibliothèque de l'école des chartes* 100 (1939): 295–308; and René Neu Watkins, "Petrarch and the Black Death: From Fear to Monuments," *Studies in the Renaissance* 19 (1972): 196–223.

Valuable studies of plague mortality over the course of several generations include David Herlihy, "Population, Plague, and Social Change in Rural Pistoia," *Economic History Review,* ser. 2, 18 (1965): 225–44; Henri Dubled, "Les épidémies de peste à Carpentras et dans le comtat Venaissin," *Provence historique* 19 (1969): 17–48, and idem, "Consequences économiques et sociales des 'mortalités' du XIVe siècle, essentiellement en Alsace," *Revue d'histoire économiques et sociale* 37 (1959): 273–94; L. Aubert, "De quelques mésures sanitaires édictées à l'occasion des épidémies de peste," *Annales d'hygiene publique et de médecine legale,* ser. 4, 15 (1911): 247–65; Dante E. Zanetti, "La morte a Milano nei secoli XVI-XVII. Appunti per una ricerca," *Rivista storica italiana* 87 (1976): 803–51: Josiah C. Russell, "Effects of Pestilence and Plague, 1315–1385," *Comparative Studies in History and Society* 8 (1965–6): 464–73; and Sylvia Thrupp, "Plague Effects in Medieval Europe," ibid., 476–83; William J. Cortenay, "The Effect of the Black Death on English Higher Education," *Speculum* 55 (1980): 696–714; Bernardo Schiavuzzi, "Le epidemie di peste bubbonica in Istria," *Atti e memorie della società istriana d'archeologica* 4 (1889): 423–47; M. J. Larenaude, "Les famines en Languedoc aux XIVe et XVe siècle," *Annales du Midi* (1952): 27–39; Hugues Neveaux, "La mortalité des pauvres à Cambrai, 1377–1473," *Annales de démographie historique* 1968: 73–97; Hubert Cleu, "Les maladies épidémiques et contagieuses en Lorraine du IXe au XIXe siècle," *Bulletin de la société francaise d'histoire de la médecine* 13 (1914): 236–49; and Robert Favreau, "Epidémies à Poitiers et dans le centre ouest à la fin du Moyen Age," *Bibliothèque de l'école des chartes* 125 (1967): 349–98.

Specialized literature on Italian plague defense includes Carlo M. Cipolla, *Faith, Reason and the Plague in Seventeenth-Century Tuscany* (New York: Norton: 1979); idem, *Fighting the Plague in Seventeenth-Century Italy* (Madison: University of Wisconsin Press, 1981); idem, *Christofano and the Plague* (London: Berkeley, 1973); Aldo Bottero, "La peste in Milano nel 1399–1400 e l'opera di Giangaleazzo Visconti," *Atti e memorie dell'accademia di storia del arte sanitaria*, ser. 2, no. 8 (1942): 17–28; Carlo Decio, *La peste in Milano nell'anno 1451 e il primo lazzaretto a Cusago: appunti storici e note inedite tratte degli archive milanese* (Milan: Cogliati, 1900); Pietro Canetta, *Il lazzaretto di Milano* (Milan: Cogliati, 1881); Luca Beltrami, "Il lazzaretto di Milano," *Archivio storico lombardo* 9 (1882): 403–41; Manlio Brusatin, *Il muro della peste. Spazio della pietà e governo del lazzaretto* (Venice: Cluva Libreria, 1981); Andrea Corsini, *La "moria" del 1464 in Toscana e l'instituzione dei primi lazzaretti in Firenze et in Pisa* (Florence: Libreria Claudiana, 1911); Piero Giacosa, "Documents sur deux épidémies de peste in Italia en 1387 et en 1448," *Janus* 6 (1889): 130–3; Gulio Giani, "Le pestilenze del 1348, del 1526, et del 1631–32 in Prato," *Archivio storico pratese* 9 (1930): 49–63, 97–108; Paolo Preto, *Peste e società a Venezia nel 1576* (Venice: Neri Pozza, 1978); Antonio del Fiumi, "Medici, medicine, e peste nel veneto durante il secolo XVI," *Archivio veneto*, ser. 5, 116 (1981): 33–58; Emilio Motta, "Morti in Milano dal 1452 al 1552," *Archivio storico lombardo* 18 (1891): 241–86; Luciano Banchi, "Provvisioni della Repubblica sanese contro la peste degli anni 1411 e 1463," *Archivio storico italiano*, ser. 4, 14 (1884): 325–32; and Marisa Brogi Ciofi, "La peste del 1630 a Firenze con particolare riferimento ai provvedimenti igienico-sanitari e sociali," *Archivio storico italiano* 142 (1984): 47–75.

Finally, a few references on plague treatises. Karl Sudhoff published close to three hundred of the medical treatises on plague early in this century, with an index and summary appearing in his "Pestschriften aus dem ersten 150 Jahren nach der Epidemie des schwarzen Tod 1348," *Sudhoffs Archiv* 17 (1925): 264–91. Works studying the plague treatises written between 1348 and 1500 include, in addition to Anna Campbell, *The Black Death and Men of Learning,* and Dominick Palazzotto's dissertation, already mentioned, the following: Arturo Castiglioni, "I libri italiani della pestilenza," in *Il volto di Ippocrate: istorie di medici e medicine d'altri tempi* (Milan: Unitas, 1925), 147–69; Dorothea Waley Singer, "Some Plague Tractates (Fourteenth and Fifteenth Centuries)," *Proceedings of the Royal Society of Medicine* 9, pt. 2 (1916): 159–212; Ian M. Lonie, "Fever Pathology in the Sixteenth Century: Tradition and Innovation," *Medical History,* supp. 1 (1981): 19–44; Lawrence I. Conrad, "Arabic Plague Chronologies and Treatises: Social and Historical Factors in the Formation of a Literary Genre," *Studia Islamica* 54 (1981): 51–93; and idem, "*Taun* and *Waba*: Conceptions of Plague and Pestilence in Early Islam," *Journal of the Economic and Social History of the Orient* 25 (1982): 268–307. Melissa P. Chase's study of changes in plague treatises between 1350 and 1450, "Fevers, Poisons, and Apostemes: Authority and Experience in Montpellier Plague Treatises," in Pamela O. Long, ed., *Science and Technology in Medieval Society,* Annals of the New York Academy of Sciences, n. 441 (New York: NYAS, 1985), appeared too late for me to incorporate her findings into this study.

Index

Abbondanza, Ufficiali dell', 28; *see also* Grain
  Office (Florence)
Albanian and Slavic immigrants, *see* car-
  riers of plague
Anquinaia, see bubo
anthrax, 14; *see also* epizootics, nonplague
Antoninus, Saint, Archbishop of Florence,
  39, 62, 102, 151 n37, 158

bachi, see diarrheal disease; worms
beccamorti, see gravediggers
becchini, see gravediggers
beggars, 104; *see also* poor; ruffians
  as carriers of plague, 107, 124–6
  treatment of, during epidemics, 17
Black Death (1348), 3, 10, 60, 79, 108–10,
  173–4
  in Florence, 29–30
  legislation during, 98–9, 108–10, 160
  n2–3
black rat, *see Rattus rattus*
Boccaccio, Giovanni *(The Decameron)*, 29,
  79–80, 154 n16
Boletino, see travel and trade restrictions
Books of the Dead (Florence), 4, 27
  description, 31–2, 70, 133–5
  reporting causes of death, 32–4
Books of the Dead (outside Florence), 30,
  148 n3, 149 n15 and 18
breast feeding, 44–5; *see also* diarrheal disease
Brescia, epidemic in, 16–17
bubo, 79–80
  mentioned in historical sources, 10–11,
  19–21, 145 n2
  as symptom of *Y. pestis*, 10–11, 23
bubonic plague, 19, 87–8
  clinical diagnosis, 12
  differentiated from other epidemics, 17–
  18
  presence of bubo in, 20–1

burial, 16–17, 29, 70, 133–5, 149 n17
  in epidemics: 29–30, 109–10, 161 n6

carriers of plague, 2, 90, 103–5, 149 n18
  Albanian and slavic immigrants, 117–18,
  162 n36–8
catasto, 37–8, 71, 91
cause-of-death diagnoses, 4, 19, 35–58
charity (as motive for plague relief), 102,
  113–15, 119–21, 158 n28
chicken pox, 54
children, 134–5
  attitude toward, 52–3
  deaths in plague, 90–4, 157 n23
Ciompi revolt, 99–100, 117, 157 n23
Cipolla, Carlo, 123
contagion
  evidence of, in Renaissance plagues, 77–
  8, 80–4, 127
  as explanation for plague, 1–2, 104–7,
  112–14, 124–6
  medical theories of, 2–3, 18, 102–3,
  111–15, 127–31, 161 n9
  popular notions of, 22
Corradi, Alfonso, 17–18
corruption of the air theory, 97, 100–1,
  161 n9
crises, mortality, *see* mortality, crisis

Decameron, see Boccaccio
dehydration, 45, 47, 50
diagnosis; *see also* cause-of-death diagnoses
  in Books of the Dead, 33, 78–9
  postmortem, 19–20
  process of, 3–4, 19, 22, 34, 39
  retrospective, 9, 13–14, 18–26, 54, 58–
  9, 152 n1
  retrospective, of plague, 20
diaries, 37
diarrheal disease, 41–5, 95, 150 n31
diseases of children, 49–50
dogs, as carriers of plague, 105

dysentery, epidemic, 10, 14, 33, 35, 46–8, 63, 151 n38, 152 n51

England, plagues in, 90–1
epidemics, 11, 16–17; *see also* mortality
  augmented by famine, 17–18
  charity during, 17
  demographic effects of, 3
  recurrent, 10, 13–14
epidemiology, historical (methods), 3–5, 8–9, 18, 54–8, 69–60, 63–4, 88–9
enzootic plague, 5–6, 8
epilepsy, 49–50
epizootic plague, 5, 8, 85, 87–9
epizootics, nonplague, 14, 146 n13–14

famine, 11, 60, 65, 118, 127–8
  associated with epidemics, 17, 24
  in Florence, 105–6, 157 n13
  provisions for, 28
fever, 40, 50, 95, 106
  and plague, 21, 83–4
fleas, 17, 85, 88
  bites, 22–3
  "blocked," 7–8
  human, 85–6, 154 n21
  as plague vector, 7, 154 n21
flight, from plague, 100–1
Florence
  demography, 60–1, 133–5, 153 n11
  ecology, 57–8
  geography, 67, 70–1, 154 n15
  foundling homes, 52–3, 158 n30, 165 n8–9
Fracastoro, Girolamo, 128

gatekeepers, 109
Grain Office (Florence), 27–8, 30, 133–5
Grascia, see Grain Office (Florence)
Grascia morti, see Books of the Dead (Florence)
gravediggers
  behavior during epidemics, 17, 29–30
  communal legislation regarding, 28–9
  reporting burials, 32
  reporting cause of death, 19
guards in plague, 99, 113, 116–17, 162 n33

health, general urban, fifteenth-century, 8, 127–8
health boards, 3, 105–6, 114, 116, 120, 123–7, 160 n56, 163 n54
  in 1348, 99, 108–10, 160 n5, 161 n7
Herlihy and Klapisch-Zuber, 37–8, 61, 90–1
historical epidemiology, *see* epidemiology, historical (methods)

hospitals, 52, 102, 113, 116, 118–21, 133–4; *see also* lazaretto
humoral medicine, 41–2

illness, 39–49; *see also* individual diseases
immunity, 95
  in plague, 90, 91–3
infancy, diseases in, 42–3
infanticide, 51–3
influenza, epidemic, 10–11, 13, 56
isolation; *see also* quarantine
  effect on mortality patterns, 107, 126–7, 130
  of plague sufferers, 2, 18, 110–13, 121
  of villages, 22, 161 n13, 162 n32

Jews, 124, 128

lazaretto, 3, 16–18, 25, 102, 108, 118–21, 127, 163 n49
  of Florence, 102–4, 158 n31, 159 n33, 160 n55
legislation
  crisis, 98–100, 108–11
  plague, 90, 108–19, 127–9, 161 n9
  sanitary, 90, 95–8, 108–11, 125, 156 n10
  sumptuary, 28, 109
  and wet nurses, 44
leprosy and lepers, 98, 124, 157 n13
Libri dei morti, see Books of the Dead (Florence)
lice, 17, 23
life expectancy, 35, 45

Mantua
  epidemics, 16–26
  plague legislation, 112–15, 124
mal maestro, 49–50
mal mazzuco, see typhus, epidemic
malnutrition, 45–6, 58
measles, 53–4
medical theory
  of plague, 100–1
  of public health, 96, 156 n10
meningococcemia (meningitis), 23–4, 50, 147 n37
Milan
  epidemics, 16, 90, 120–1, 151 n38
  plague legislation, 112–15, 119–21, 162 n33
mortality
  child, 90–1, 134–5, 150 n35, 155 n1
  crisis, 8–9, 11–12, 95, 151 n50
  differential, 4, 17–18, 90–1, 143, 155 n1
  estimates and rates, 16–17, 61–2, 67
  female, 37–8, 90–1, 135
  male, 37, 39, 90–1, 135

neonatal, 49–51, 95
ordinary, nonepidemic, 27, 33, 55–8
records, 27, 148 n3
urban, 4, 13, 172
mycotoxicoses, 24

natural plague foci, 6; *see also* plague, ecology
neonatal infection, 49–51
nonplague epidemics, 10–11, 15, 26, 60, 65, 105–6
significance of, 2–3, 10
nutrition and illness, 44

old age, 35–6, 150 n25

Pasturella pestis, see Yersinia pestis
periodic epidemicity, *see* epidemics, recurrent
pest houses, *see* lazaretto
pestilence, as nonspecific epidemic, 2–3, 15, 145 n3
pestilential pustules, 11–12, 14, 145 n3; *see also* anthrax; plague, pustules
petecchiae, 17–18, 22–3
phthisis (tuberculosis), 53–4
physicians
  municipal, 97–8, 115, 119–21, 156 n12–13
  reporting causes of death, 78–9
  roles during plague, 16–17, 110
  theories of plague, 80, 114
physicians' guild (Florence), 27, 32
Pistoia, 109–10, 153 n12, 160 n2–3
plague
  community provisions in, 25
  compared to nonplague epidemics, 65–6
  contagion and, 24–6
  diagnosis of, in Books of the Dead, 32–3, 35
  diagnosis of, in clinical cases, 18–26
  disappearance of, 143–4 n7
  ecology, 87–8, 154 n21, 155 n26
  fifteenth-century, 1, 10–26, 61–2, 65–70, 73, 87–9, 95, 101
  fourteenth-century, 11, 63–4, 72–3
  fourteenth- and fifteenth-century, compared, 1, 59, 71–2, 93–4
  general social effects, 3
  historical descriptions, 62
  immunity, 12, 88, 90, 95
  legislation in Florence, 101–3
  legislation (Florentine *balìa*), 103–6
  mortality, differential, 155 n1
  mortality rates, 157 n22
  names for, 13, 33, 79
  nonbubonic, 16

and poverty, 77–8, 90
pustules, 22
recurrent, 10, 13
rural, 1
season, 87–8
treatises, 80
undifferentiated pestilence, 15
virulence, 89
Plague of Athens (fifth century B.C.), 152 n1
pneumonic plague, 86–7, 154 n23
pondi, see dysentery, epidemic
poor, 38
  carriers of plague, 103–4, 107, 123–6, 131, 159 n40, 164 n61
  deaths of, 30, 77–8, 126–8, 153 n11
  treatment during epidemics, 17–18, 101–2, 109, 113, 123–6, 163 n49
population changes in, 127, 143, 152 n2; *see also* Florence, demography
prematurity, 50–1, 95; *see also* mortality, neonatal
priests, role during epidemics, 16–17, 109
prostitutes, 98–9, 123–5, 128
Pulex irritans, see fleas, human

quarantine, 3, 110–12, 144 n7, 161 n9 and 13, 162 n31; *see also* isolation

Ragusa, 111–12, 161 n9 and 13
Rattus rattus, 5–6
rodents, 5–7, 87–8
Rome, epidemics, 16, 160 n46–7
rubella, 54
ruffians, 103, 107, 124–6; *see also* beggars; poor, prostitutes

Salutati, Coluccio, chancellor of Florence, 100–1
sanitation, *see* legislation, sanitary; street cleaning
Savonarola, Fra Girolamo, 106
Savonarola, Giovanni Maria, 41
scarlet fever, 54
season, of epidemics, 56–8, 62–3
segregation, of households, 19–20, 25
septicemic plague, 7, 21
SIDS (sudden infant death syndrome), 51–2, 151 n45
Siena, plague legislation, 122–3
"signs," of plague, 20, 79–80, 88, 101, 154 n20
smallpox, 10–13, 53–4, 95, 146 n9–10
social unrest, related to plague, 99–100
street cleaning, 96–7
sylvatic plague, *see* enzootic plague
syphilis, 105, 160 n49

temporary plague foci, 6; *see also* plague,
    ecology
tetanus, neonatal, 49
trade and travel restrictions during plague,
    111–16
typhus, epidemic, 16–18, 23, 146 n24, 161
    n9

vaiuolo, see smallpox
Venice
    epidemics, 90
    plague legislation, 114–15, 123–4, 161
        n7, 162 n33
Visconti, Giangaleazzo, 112–14

weanling diarrhea, *see* diarrheal disease
wet nurses, 52–3
"wild plague," *see* enzootic plague
wills and testaments, in plague, 28–9

women, deaths of, 37–8
worms, 15, 41, 46, 150 n26
    and plague, 83–4
    and fleas, 85

Yersinia pestis, 61, 95
    clinical symptoms, 18, 20–1
    contagion in, 85–6, 154 n21
    defined as "true" plague, 2, 4–5, 10
    ecology, 5–9
    immunity in humans, 7
    immunity in rodents, 6
    microbiology, 5, 7
    mortality rates, 20–1
    pneumonia, 86–7
    virulence, 7

Zinsser, Hans, 18